S0-FQV-575

INVENTION IN THE REAL

INVENTION IN THE REAL

Papers of the Freudian
School of Melbourne
Volume 24

Edited by
Linda Clifton

KARNAC

First published in 2012 by
Karnac Books Ltd
118 Finchley Road
London NW3 5HT

Copyright © 2012 to Linda Clifton for the edited collection, and to the individual authors for their contributions.

The rights of the contributors to be identified as the authors of this work have been asserted in accordance with §§ 77 and 78 of the Copyright Design and Patents Act 1988.

All rights reserved. No part of this publication may be reproduced, stored in a retrieval system, or transmitted, in any form or by any means, electronic, mechanical, photocopying, recording, or otherwise, without the prior written permission of the publisher.

British Library Cataloguing in Publication Data

A C.I.P. for this book is available from the British Library

ISBN-13: 978-1-85575-889-6

Typeset by V Publishing Solutions Pvt Ltd., Chennai, India

www.karnacbooks.com

CONTENTS

ACKNOWLEDGEMENTS

Chapter Eight: The child and seduction (Michael Plastow)

Excerpt from "This Be The Verse" by Philip Larkin reproduced by kind permission of the publisher Faber and Faber Ltd. Taken from *Collected Poems* by Philip Larkin.

Chapter Twelve: The treatment setting: demand, transference and the contract with the parents and for their child (Jean Bergés and Gabriel Balbo)

The translation of the first half of Chapter 5 (*"Le cadre de la cure: demande, transfert et contrat avec les parents et pour L'Enfant"*) of the book *L'Enfant et la Psychanalyse: Nouvelles Perpectives* (*The Child and Psychoanalysis: New perspectives*), 2nd edition, by (Jean Bergés and Gabriel Balbo), published by Masson, Paris, 1996, reproduced by kind permission of the author Gabriel Balbo.

Chapter Twenty One: The *Invention of Solitude*—the invention of a style (Tine Norregaard Arroyo)

Excerpts from *The Invention of Solitude* by Paul Auster reproduced by kind permission of the publisher Faber and Faber Ltd.

Chapter Twenty Three: The art of interpretation—drawing a line (David Pereira)

Excerpts from *Looking Back at Francis Bacon* by David Sylvester, © 2000 David Sylvester. Reprinted by kind permission of Thames & Hudson Ltd., London.

Excerpts from *The Enduring Rip: A History of Queenscliffe* published by Melbourne University Press, Melbourne, 2004, reprinted with kind permission of the author Barry Hill.

Images reproduced by kind permission of the artist David Beaumont.

Chapter Twenty Five: Erotics of mourning in a time of dry death (Jean Allouch)

Translation and publication of excerpts from *Erotique du Deuil au Temps de la Mort Sèche* carried out with the kind permission of the author Jean Allouch.

ABOUT THE EDITOR AND CONTRIBUTORS

Jean Allouch is a psychoanalyst practising in Paris. He was a member of the *Ecole Freudienne de Paris* until it was dissolved and is currently a member of the *Ecole Lacanienne de Psychanalyse*. He states: "Lacan, ni Freud ne furent un 'systeme de pensee'" (www.JeanAllouch.com). He has published extensively in French, Spanish, Portuguese, German and English, including papers in *The Papers of the Freudian School of Melbourne* and *Lacan Love. Melbourne Seminars and other Works* (Bookbound Publishers, 2007). At the Editions Epel, he supervises the publishing of *Les grands classiques de l'erotologie moderne* which endeavors to introduce feminist and queer theory and gay and lesbian studies from North America into France.

Madeline Andrews is a member of the *Freudian School of Melbourne, School of Lacanian Psychoanalysis*. She works as a senior clinician and secondary consultant to mental health services in Victoria, and in private psychoanalytic practice in Melbourne. Madeline has regularly presented papers at psychoanalytic seminars and conferences. She has published in *Écritique: Letters of the Freudian School of Melbourne, School of Lacanian Psychoanalysis* and in the *Papers of the Freudian School of Melbourne*. She is a co-editor of *Écritique*.

Gabriel Balbo is a psychoanalyst and was previously a member of the *Association Lacanienne Internationale*. He subsequently founded, in 2005, *Libre Association Freudienne*. He is co-author with Jean Bergès of *L'enfant et la psychoanalyse* (*The child and psychoanalysis*), *Jeu des places de la mère et l'enfant: essai sur le transitivisme* (Game of the place of the mother and the child: essay on transitivism) and *Psychose, autisme et défaillance cognitive chez l'enfant* (Psychosis, autism and cognitive deficit in the child).

Jean Bergès, deceased in 2004, was a psychoanalyst, member of the *Association Lacanienne Internationale*, and child neuropsychiatrist at the Sainte-Anne hospital in Paris. He founded the *École de la psychanalyse de l'enfant à Paris* under the auspices of the *Association Lacanienne Internationale*.

Linda Clifton is a psychoanalyst. She is an Analyst of the School, a former Director of the Freudian School of Melbourne and current Editor of its Papers. Her psychoanalytic papers are published in the *Papers of the Freudian School of Melbourne* and in *Ecritique, the Newsletter of the School*.

Gustavo Etkin is originally from Argentina but has lived and practised as a psychoanalyst for many years in Salvador, in the state of Bahia in Brazil. There he was a founding member of the *Escola Lacaniana da Bahia*. Gustavo Etkin has published many papers in the field of psychoanalysis. He is the author of *Uma introdução a Lacan: o real e a metáfora paterna* (*An introduction to Lacan: the real and the paternal metaphor*). He has visited Melbourne on three occasions as a guest speaker at the Freudian School of Melbourne's annual conference *Homage to Lacan*, each time presenting several public lectures. Many of these papers have been published in the *Papers of the Freudian School of Melbourne*. He is also an editor of the psychoanalytic journal *Bord(a)s da psicanálise*, based in Brazil.

Dr. Peter Gunn is a psychoanalyst who practises in both private and public settings. He is an Analyst Member of The Freudian School of Melbourne and also occupies the position of Secretary. He has published numerous psychoanalytic papers in the *Papers of The Freudian School of Melbourne* and elsewhere, and presents regularly in the various forums of the School. He has a background in mathematics and his initial professional training was as a social worker. As a psychoanalyst he currently acts as clinical consultant to an innovative program which works intensively with those who are chronically homeless. He has a particular interest in perversion as well as the various littorals of psycho-analysis. He recently facilitated a seminar, *Literature for Psychoanalysis*.

Rodney Kleiman is a psychoanalyst. He is an Analyst of the School and Co-Director of the Freudian School of Melbourne. Originally trained as a psychiatrist, he now works predominantly in private analytic practice with an ongoing appointment as consultant with mental health services. He has published numerous articles in the *Papers of the School* and is a regular presenter at seminars and analytic conferences. He has a particular interest in the questions posed by psychosis and its poten-tial treatment.

Tine Norregaard Arroyo is a psychoanalyst working in private and public practice, and she is an Analyst Member of The Freudian School of Melbourne. She has trained with the Freudian School of Melbourne, Psykoanalytisk Kreds in Copenhagen and Centre for Freudian Analysis and Research, as well as with the Tavistock Clinic and the Group Ana-lytic Society in London. She is a regular presenter at the Seminar of the Freudian School of Melbourne, and has been an associate lecturer at the University of Copenhagen. In 1993 she was part of the initiative to found La Fondation Françoise Dolto in Bruxelles.

From 2000 to 2003 she was co-editor of Ecritique, the Newsletter of the Freudian School of Melbourne. Since 2007 she has been co-convenor of the monthly seminar *Psychoanalysis and the Child* together with Michael Plastow. She has published several psychoanalytic arti-cles in English, Danish and French, as well as a number of translations from French to English.

David Pereira is a psychoanalyst in private practice in Melbourne, Australia, where he is an Analyst of the School and is currently a Direc-tor of the Freudian School of Melbourne. He has written numerous articles on theoretical and clinical psychoanalysis published in both the *Papers of the Freudian School of Melbourne* and elsewhere and was formerly Consultant Psychoanalyst with the Alfred Hospital Child and Adolescent Mental Health Service, and Senior Clinician with the Department of Child Psychotherapy, Royal Childrens Hospital, Melbourne.

Michael Plastow is a psychoanalyst (Analyst of the School, the Freudian School of Melbourne) in private practice in Melbourne and is also a child psychiatrist at the Alfred Hospital. He has published numerous papers in the field of psychoanalysis in Australia and abroad. He has co-convened the seminar *Psychoanalysis and the Child* with Tine Norregaard Arroyo since 2007.

Michael Plastow has an interest in translation and has translated papers from French, Spanish and Portuguese into English. He has recently completed a revision of his translation of the seminar *The Knowledge of the Psychoanalyst of Jacques Lacan.*

Erik Porge is a psychoanalyst practising in Paris and a member of *la lettre lacanienne, une école de la psychanalyse.* He is editor of the journal *Essaim* and author of various works, including his most recent book *Des fondements de la clinique psychanalytique (Foundations of the Psychoanalytic Clinic),* published by Érès, Paris.

Dr. Christiane Weller, Senior Lecturer in German Studies, Monash University, Melbourne. She is a member of the *Freudian School of Melbourne. School of Lacanian Psychoanalysis.* She has published widely in the area of literature and psychoanalysis, particularly with regard to trauma, melancholia and psychosis. She is a co-editor of *Limbus: Australisches Jahrbuch für germanistische Literatur—und Kulturwissenschaft/Australian Yearbook of German Literary and Cultural Studies, and a co-editor of Ecritique. Letters of the Freudian School of Melbourne. School of Lacanian Psychoanalysis.*

Oscar Zentner is a practising Lacanian Psychoanalyst trained in Argentina. He introduced Lacan's psychoanalytic ideas in Australia in 1977, when he co-founded the first School of Lacanian Psychoanalysis in the English speaking world. For several years he was co-founder and Editor of *Papers of The Freudian School of Melbourne,* the first psychoanalytic publication in Australia. He held his Lacanian Psychoanalytic Seminar for many years at Prince Henry's Hospital, Department of Psychological Medicine, Monash University. He is co-editor of the book *Lacan Love—Melbourne seminars and other works* by Jean Allouch, published by *Lituraterre,* Melbourne, 2007. He is co-author of the book *El problema económico Freud,* Buenos Aires Argentina, 1980; and author of the book *A Escuta Psicanalitica—Efeitos de uma Etica,* Recife, Brazil, 1995; and has also published numerous psychoanalytic articles in English, French, Portuguese and Spanish.

LOGOS

If as much seriousness was put into analysis as I put in to the preparation of my seminar, well then, it would be so much the better. ... For that ... one would have to have in analysis, as I have ... the sentiment of an absolute risk.[1]

In contrast to this seriousness, this sentiment of absolute risk with which Lacan approaches his seminar in Paris, we have his account of a class, a type of psychiatrist encountered on his trip to America.

Good god, why ask oneself questions, and especially if they are any bit metaphysical when, god knows, after all everything is going so well, that you finish work at half past five, you have a whisky, you read a novel, usually a spy novel and you settle down in front of television.

Lacan continues:

I do not see why one should reproach what constitutes a social class for having its comforts, simply that it is for us to see what this involves, of course, in terms of inertia and of being too settled.[2]

This contrast between a sentiment of absolute risk and an inertia, a comfort, a "being too settled" is reminiscent of a contrast drawn by Freud:

> Life is impoverished, it loses its interest when the highest stakes in the game of living, life itself may not be risked. It becomes as shallow and empty as let us say, an American flirtation, in which it is understood from the first that nothing is to happen, as contrasted with a continental love affair in which both partners must constantly bear its serious consequences in mind .... the tendency to exclude death from our calculations in life brings in its train many other renunciations and exclusions.[3]

Lacan spoke of his sentiment of absolute risk in the seminar in which he addressed his longstanding transference to the writings of James Joyce, that monumental writer whose extraordinary relationship with language incited Lacan to question the function of this very creativity for Joyce as a subject. In the throes of his perplexity about Joyce were the ever multiplying creative possibilities of the Borromean knot but this controversial Joycean project was certainly not without risk for Lacan. As highlighted in the Dublin Papers in Volume 23 of the Papers of the Freudian School of Melbourne to take an artist as a case is in apparent contradiction to Lacan's own teaching.

If, as Freud suggests, life loses its interest when the highest stake in living is not risked is it not also the case that, without the sentiment of absolute risk, without the seriousness spoken of by Lacan, psychoanalysis is likewise impoverished?

Jean Allouch in explicating what he designates as the Freudian method, points to a paradoxical risk in applying this method, a risk relating to its "quasi suicidal aspect". The paradox of this method arises from the requirement that, as Lacan writes ...

> psychoanalysis is a practice subordinated to that which is most particular in the subject and when Freud emphasizes this to the point of saying that psychoanalytic science must be called into question with the analysis of each case ... he shows the analysand the way of his formation.[4]

Allouch continues:

> ... for those who put the Freudian method into practice this methodological trait sets apart something like two different

"furnaces" [Ferenczi's term for the transference] which can produce new statements and formulate the problems raised by the analysis in their actuality. There is Freud's text ... above all a teaching; but there is also what can be gleaned from the application [unique in every case] of the method, which one calls analytical practice ...

Every practitioner is put [by Freud] in a position of having to stop short when it comes to knowing whether he welcomes what comes out of one or other of the these two furnaces as truths that are comparable or not in a way which is not only internal to each of them but in the encountering with their respective statements. The radical Freudian principle is to maintain them apart. Freud inscribes in his method a trait, which, when applied is likely to refute the results at any moment. Described in this way there is in the Freudian method a point which is quasi - suicidal.[5]

The Papers of the Freudian School of Melbourne, Volume 24 give testament to that quasi - suicidal risk taken by analysts and members of the School, in applying, not a technique, but the Freudian method to their clinical practice, to their seminars, to their writing and to the functioning of the School itself. In pursuing a practice that seeks to avoid the inertia spoken of by Lacan, the contributors to this volume take the risk of encountering the impasses of the clinic today and the incompleteness of Lacanian theory with invention. Being marked by the residue of the psychoanalytic clinic they continue to work their transference to that clinic and to the texts of Freud and Lacan. In doing so they attempt to "declare their reasons" as demanded by Lacan.[6] More than a flirtation, this affair of love with psychoanalysis, this love affair, being of necessity neither "continental" nor "American" must take its own risks in the reading and writing of psychoanalysis in Melbourne, Australia. Melbourne, named after a British prime minister in the time of Queen Victoria, is a city in which we are thus subjected to, spoken by the "Queen's English", with the attendant effects -risks- produced by that tongue in relation to our formation or deformation as psychoanalysts. Psychoanalysis, of course was originally a continental affair.

Included in this volume is a paper by Oscar Zentner, founder of the School as well as translations of papers and extracts from books by analysts from overseas–Jean Allouch, Erik Porge, Jean Bergès, Gabriel Balbo and Gustavo Etkin.

To conclude with just a few indications about the diverse content and style of these papers, the title of this volume, Invention in the Real, marks both a time in the history of the Freudian School of Melbourne and a direction with regard to its orientation to theory and practice. Central to this volume are papers written to mark the thirtieth anniversary of the foundation of the School. Now three decades since the death of Lacan, this series of papers addresses The Lacanian Clinic Today and examine questions of Time and History in relation to psychoanalysis.

Controversies in the history of the analysis of children and the complexities of that clinic today are examined in Psychoanalysis and the Child and included in these papers are translations of extracts from books by Bergès and Balbo and Erik Porge on the psychoanalytic clinic of the child.

The relation between the arts and psychoanalysis is worked anew in papers on Analysis, the Arts and the Well Spoken and on Psychoanalysis and Death as homage is paid to literature, painting and other visual arts. Goethe, Dostoevsky, Mishima, Tanizaki, Bacon, Duchamp— these artists show the way for psychoanalysis in relation to desire, *jouissance*, sexuality and death. In this regard Oscar Zentner writes in *An Architecture of Death from Tanizaki to Mishima* in this volume that, "Literature has taught me in my work as an analyst that psychoanalytic practice is akin a practice of fiction." With a rare inventiveness, David Pereira in *The Art of Interpretation—Drawing a Line* renews the question of psychoanalytic interpretation through the interrogation of a series of paintings by one artist, creating thereby what is ultimately a fiction in which it is possible to hear something new about the art of psychoanalytic interpretation.

I believe that it can be read in this latest volume of writings of the Freudian School of Melbourne that psychoanalysis is a practice which, like Bacon's painting attempts to "keep the vitality of the accident and yet preserve a continuity".[7] In order to do so it demands seriousness and the sentiment of absolute risk in the pursuit of the possibility of invention in the real.

Linda Clifton

Notes

1. Lacan, J. The Seminar of Jacques Lacan Book XXIII *Joyce and the Sinthome* 1975–1976 Trans. Cormac Gallagher Lesson of December 16 1975.
2. Lacan, J. The Seminar of Jacques Lacan Book X111 *The Object of Psychoanalysis* 1965–1966 Trans. Cormac Gallagher Lesson of March 23 1966.
3. Freud, S. *Thoughts for the Times on War and Death II Our Attitude towards Death* St. ed. Vol. XIV p. 290.
4. Lacan, J. in Allouch, J. *The Secretarial Function, Element of the Freudian Method* Papers of the Freudian School of Melbourne 15 Ed. Pereira, D. p. 195.
5. Allouch, J. *ibid.,* p. 196.
6. Lacan, J. The Seminar of Jacques Lacan Book XXIV 1976–1977 Appendix 1 *The Opening of the Clinical Section* Talk delivered on 5 January 1977 Trans. Collins, D.
7. Cited in this volume by Pereira, D. *Must Every Analyst Recapitulate the History of Psychoanalysis in His Own Way?* no. 14.

PART I

TIME AND HISTORY

CHAPTER ONE

Must every psychoanalyst recapitulate the history of psychoanalysis in his own way?

David Pereira

N ot long ago, I was listening to a man in the context of those interviews preliminary to the possibility of any analysis sometimes referred to as a history taking. If indeed I was *taking* a history, he was certainly in the position of being able to *give* a history. As the interviews progressed it became clear that there may have been a trifle too much give and take, such that, despite a narrative coherence, I was left wondering where *he* was in this history. There was a distinct lack of markers of enjoyment and presence. This manner of proceeding eventually produced the following observation in him: that he was anguished by the fact that, in some way, he had failed to translate his history.

He elaborated that whilst he felt he represented his family, and the family name, a matter he had no choice in, that there was something which he was unable to procure for himself in that. His attempts to translate and transmit the essence of his family preserved as a "closed unity shielded from all accident, change, deformation and corruption", as I read recently in another 'interview',[1] left him devoid of an element which allowed him to situate his presence in it. It was clear in these interviews that he suffered from the need to preserve and perpetuate a history and that he had clearly succeeded in this regard. The statement, therefore, that he had failed to *translate* his history, stood in some contrast to the success with which he had preserved and perpetuated it.

What this opens for us is the question of a relation to history into which is introduced a distinction between a preservation and perpetuation on the one hand, and a translation on the other. Such a distinction also causes us to question the psychoanalyst's relation to the history of psychoanalysis; how it may be possible, in any way, to transcend the weight of history as a tendency to preservation and reproduction.

In this paper, therefore, I want to take up the question of what psychoanalysis does when it is not "doing history"—in the sense of giving meaning to a past in a narratively coherent way? In his quest for originality how does the psychoanalyst inscribe his debt to a history in a way which yet maintains the transmission of an original creativity, a vitality marked by a certain *jouissance*, rather than via the preservation of a corpus of work through a joyless repetition which eventually spells the death of psychoanalysis?

Such a question, referenced however to the way in which the practice of the painter keeps a relation with the history of art, is very much the concern of the painter Francis Bacon, and it is from a book by Deleuze about Bacon's work that I have made a paraphrased appropriation for the title of this paper.[2] If I appropriate it, it is in order to indicate that such a question is one which the psychoanalyst cannot ignore in considering his relation to the history of psychoanalysis.

On the question of history and the relation we keep with it, consider now the following from an interview Bacon gave to David Sylvester.

> Well we're so saturated with the arts, through all the means of reproducing them and everything, that the saturation point has come so strongly that one just longs for new images and new ways by which reality can be created. After all, man wants invention, he doesn't want to go on and on just reproducing the past. I mean, it was the end of Greek art, it was the end of Egyptian art, because they went on and on reproducing themselves. We can't go on reproducing the Renaissance or 19th Century art or anything else. You want something new. Not an illustrative realism but a realism that comes about through a real invention of a new way to lock reality into something completely arbitrary … completely artificial.[3]

At first glance Bacon takes an almost Nietzschean view of the historical subject.

The "true" subject of history, the sovereign subject, is the one unburdened from his past. It is a subject capable of forgetting, and in this it wills for itself a future and guarantees that future. It is a subject capable of forgetting in his foundation of a present unburdened by the past.[4]

Contrasted with this, my patient, in his failure, found himself to be Nietzsche's subject of *resentiment* in which he passively suffers what he is unable to translate or appropriate; remaining affected by its excess. He remains chained to a narrative to be preserved and represented.

Looking at this more closely, whilst man may long for the new, he is a curious beast inasmuch as this longing for the new is not without a reproduction of the old. Psychoanalysis casts some doubt on the Nietzschean solution, upon which Bacon apparently leans, insofar as it recognizes the strong drive to repetition as a consequence of the torsion and stricture of what the subject is ensnared by.

The extent of this constraint is clearly indicated by Lacan in the Seminar of 19th January 1955.

> … the unconscious is the discourse of the Other. This discourse of the Other is not the discourse of the abstract other, of the other in the dyad, of my correspondent, nor even my slave, it is the discourse of the circuit in which I am integrated. I am one of its links. It is the discourse of my father for instance in so far as my father made mistakes which I am absolutely condemned to reproduce—that's what we call the *super-ego*. I am condemned to reproduce them because I am obliged to pick up again the discourse he bequeathed to me, not simply because I am his son, but because one can't stop the chain of discourse, and it is precisely my duty to transmit it in its aberrant form to someone else.[5]

If the notion of recapitulation acquires a certain imperative tone in my title, it is insofar as I ascribe a dominance to history and the function of repetition it is witness to which we cannot afford to be naïve to. What my patient gave eloquent expression to is, after all, the struggle which every analysand who belongs to that monstrous species snared in the net of language is subject to. So, whilst the invitations to transcend one's history are everywhere, psychoanalysis reminds us constantly of the relentless sway of history in the realization of the truth the subject.

Such a reminder tempers somewhat Bacon's apparent project in relation to history as it leans on Nietzsche's proposition concerning the historical subject. I say apparent, because, as we will come to see, perhaps Bacon was not so naïve.

The question of history is already posed for us; we are included in it in a way which is not reducible to a narrative. Not, "the physical past whose existence is abolished, nor the epic past as it has become perfected in the work of memory, nor the historical past in which man finds the guarantee of his future, but rather the past which manifests itself in an inverted form in repetition."[6] Such repetition begins to deviate from a reproduction conceived of as an attempt to preserve. In its stead repetition assumes the weight of a signifying determination.

History, therefore, is not given by the narrative but by the weight of signifying determination; a weight carried by the insistence of the signifying chain as a repetition automatism. Such an insistence, such a weight, ensnares Bacon, as anybody.

As we first encounter this dimension of repetition, it is as Freud described it in *The Interpretation of Dreams* as a kind of crossing back and forth over the signifying network; a crosschecking which excludes chance. For Freud, there was nothing arbitrary or accidental in this field. We might note here that very radical determinism which Lacan gave voice to in his statement concerning the subject being ensnared within the signifying chain. The capture of the subject within the operation of the signifying chain, as it supports a function of repetition automatism, radically excludes the element of chance.

And yet, in this crosschecking of the network of signifiers, in our immersion in the field of signifying determinism, do we not find the possibility of an encounter with something at the limit of this determinism? Indeed, this crosschecking produces a relation with causality in as much as the subject encounters a "causal gap."[7] Such a gap functions as a limit to repetition automatism and the weight of history experienced purely as the determinism of the signifier. In the crosschecking we encounter something of the enigmatic *Widerholen*. "The subject in himself, the recalling of his biography, all this goes only to a certain limit, which is known as the real ...."[8] Beyond a tendency to reproduce as repetition automatism, we encounter something that occurs "as if by chance". "This is something that we analysts", Lacan contends, "never allow ourselves to be taken in by, on principle."[9]

On which principle? The pleasure principle as support of signifying determinism.

The encounter with the real is beyond repetition automatism, beyond the return of the signifying structure by which we see ourselves governed by the pleasure principle.[10] The real, therefore, is something to be found outside of a repetition of an original. In this, originality, in participating in something "more real"—to borrow an imperative of Bacon's—is to be separated from the joyless repetition of the original.

In the work of Francis Bacon, or more to the point, the account he gives of the way he works, the way he paints, we find a well theorized articulation between the function of an insistent repetition as testament to the circuit of history within which he is integrated, and the element of chance. Bacon's work may be read as a testament to the intersection of the force of recapitulation within which a debt is inscribed and the chance which this produces to write the debt in "one's own way."

The exemplary instance of Bacon's struggle with history in his work is given in his relation to Velasquez and in particular to the portrait of *Pope Innocent X*.

Wieland Schmied has noted that:

> Bacon's fascination with Velasquez's portrait of *Innocent X* must surely be without parallel in the history of art: as an instance of obsession with a specific picture by another major artist ... Yet Bacon never saw the original portrait. Although he spent three months in Rome in 1954, he carefully avoided visiting the Galleria Doria Pamphilj. He seemed afraid of encountering the original, as if he were insufficiently prepared for the experience of seeing it with his own eyes, or as if he felt unworthy of the privilege .... Over the years he had acquired a large collection of books, catalogues and postcards with reproductions of the portrait, which he had studied over and over again, to the point where he knew every last detail of it like the back of his hand. In his mind Velasquez's portrait had taken on a life of its own ...[11]

What we find in Bacon's relation to *Innocent X* is certainly not an exercise in the faithful reproduction of an original. It is rather, we could say, a repetition, a cross-checking, through which the signifying field is exhaustively worked to the point of a gap appearing in the field of signifying determinism - in the field of causality as a radical determinism. This repetition is not, however, one which guarantees the preservation and homage to the original as ideal. Rather, it is a matter of making an original present beyond a reference to a past as narrative history. To this extent, the encounter with *Innocent X* is a missed encounter. Now Lacan was no innocent, but perhaps as for Lacan in Caracas, Bacon wanted to see what was possible to transmit when the original was not there to act as a screen; to produce resemblance through non-resembling means, to cite another of Bacon's maxims.

Bacon does start with the historical subject which gradually, if the work goes well, if he encounters an element of "chance", "withers away and leaves this residue" which he calls "more real" than reality, and which "perhaps has something tenuously to do with what one started with but very often has very little to do with it."[12]

Do we not discover here something which the patient I began speaking of referred to as a "translation"? At that point where the insistence of repetition opens onto the possibility of a translation, Bacon situates that moment of "chance" which becomes central to his theorizing and practice. It is constantly referred to and is assigned a major role in the painting process.

The significance of chance is also often referenced against Bacon's passion for gambling. It should be argued, however, that this reference fails to take account of a vital distinction to be made between the gambler's passion and that of the function of chance which Bacon works with in his art. Indeed, this division helps us to make clear the distinction between the chance of the Aristotelian *tyche*, of an encounter with the real, and the chance of repetition automatism.

To give something a chance, is therefore fundamentally different than to place our bet on the fatalism of taking our chances. To be clear, the gambler's passion remains trapped within the determinism of the signifier whilst chance as *tyche*, is an encounter with what is more present, more real—in Bacon's terms—a real which is encountered at the limit point of the determinism of the signifier.

For Bacon, the question of chance referred itself to the problem of how what he painted might not become a cliché; how to make the original present in a "more real" way, beyond the past as representational.

Deleuze notes, concerning Bacon's technique, that:

> Free marks will have to be made rather quickly on the image being painted so as to destroy the nascent figuration in it and to give the

Figure a chance, which is the improbable itself. These marks are accidental, "by chance", but clearly the same word, "chance", no longer designates probabilities, but now designates a type of choice or action without probability.[13]

It is a case here of "manipulated chance" as opposed to "conceived or seen probabilities." With this, as Bacon noted himself, he was "attempting … to keep the vitality of the accident and yet preserve a continuity."[14]

Bacon makes this distinction even clearer in an interview with David Sylvester when discussing the work of Duchamp. Duchamp allowing three threads to fall upon a painted canvas and fixing them exactly where they fell, was not the operation of chance but a working within the set of probabilities. As we noted earlier this was Bacon's passion in regard to gambling but was not his penchant with regard to painting. In the latter domain he *worked with chance, rather than remaining passive in relation to it.*

Once again, Bacon gives a very clear account of this relation between the function of chance and the attempt to produce something "more real", in his struggle with the weight of history. Working with chance involved a certain knowledge of artifice—of producing resemblance through non-resembling means. "The more artificial you can make it, the greater chance you've got of its looking real."[15] If not recreated through artifice, through the openness to chance at the limit of the crosschecking of sig-nifying determinism, art remained for Bacon something illustratively second hand; joylessly passed from hand to hand.[16]

As distinct from a joylessly repeated history or legacy, there is a func-tion of repetition which "commemorates" Lacan says, "an irruption of *jouissance.*"[17] *Jouissance* marks the point of insertion of a causal gap in the chain, the deterministic chain which ensnares the subject of history. It is, therefore, this irruption of *jouissance* which indicates a limit of the subject's relation to history as given by the determinism of the chain, to what one finds oneself constrained by, and opens the possibility that the recapitulation of history has the chance of being taken in one's own way.

In this, the translation of a history requires a submission to the point of an encounter with a real, wherein resides the necessity, not the possibility nor the probability, of a recapitulation which might bare the stamp of "one's own way". Through this, each analyst will encounter what is capable of sustaining his practice—the recognition of a necessity in the density and destiny of history.

Notes

1. Sylvester, David. *Interviews with Francis Bacon*. Thames and Hudson, New York, 1981, p. 85.
2. Deleuze, Gilles. "Every Painter Recapitulates the History of Painting in His or Her Own Way ...", in *Francis Bacon: The Logic of Sensation*. Translated by Daniel W. Smith. Continuum, London, 2003.
3. Sylvester David. Ibid.
4. Nietzsche, Friedrich. 'First Essay' in, *On the Genealogy of Morals*. Translated by Douglas Smith. Oxford University Press, Oxford, 1996.
5. Lacan, Jacques. *The Seminar of Jacques Lacan. Book II. The Ego in Freud's Theory and in the Technique of Psychoanalysis 1954–1955*. Translated by Sylvana Tomaselli. Jacques-Alain Miller (Ed.).Cambridge University Press, Cambridge, 1988, Lesson of 19th January 1955, p. 89.
6. Lacan, Jacques. "The Function and Field of Speech and Language in Psychoanalysis", in *Écrits*. Translated by Bruce Fink. Norton, New York, 2006, p. 261–262.
7. Lacan, Jacques. *The Four Fundamental Concepts of Psycho-Analysis*. Translated by Alan Sheridan. Jacques-Alain Miller (Ed.). Norton, New York, 1981, p. 46.
8. Lacan, Jacques. Op. cit., p. 49. "Nothing has been more enigmatic than this *Widerholen*".
9. Lacan, Jacques. Op. cit., p. 54.
10. Lacan, Jacques. Op. cit., p. 53.
11. Schmied, Wieland. *Francis Bacon*. Prestel, Munich, 2006, p. 13.
12. Sylvester, David. *Interviews with Francis Bacon*. Thames and Hudson, New York, 1981, pp. 180–181.
13. Deleuze, Gilles. Op. cit., p. 66.
14. Sylvester, David. Op. cit., p. 17.
15. Sylvester, David. Op. cit., p. 148.
16. In art's confrontation with the real, Bacon hoped for an immediate response—a presence—which impacted upon the viewer's nervous system directly. In these terms he designates a limit of representation as something which touches on a *jouissance* of the body. This "more real" for Bacon meant less narratively illustrative, and more "despairingly exhilarating".
17. Lacan, Jacques. *The Reverse of Psychoanalysis*. 1969–1970. Translated by Cormac Gallagher from uneditedsw French manuscripts. Lesson of 11th February 1970.

CHAPTER TWO

Once upon a time

Michael Plastow

In his seminar *The Object Relation*, Lacan sets out to provide a critique of the prevalence in psychoanalysis of the object relations approach or theory which re-centred the analytic endeavour on the object. He puts forward that through this movement the object had become the prime theoretical element in analysis at the expense of sustaining the focus in psychoanalysis on the drive, desire and so on. He notes though that in regard to this object relation it is difficult to set out from the Freudian texts themselves because it is not in them and that this direction thus constituted a deviation of analytic theory.

Nonetheless, Lacan refers us to the last section of Freud's *Three Essays on the Theory of Sexuality* entitled "The Finding of an Object". Here we might consider the relevant passage from this text. Freud puts forward that:

> At a time at which the first beginnings of sexual satisfaction are still linked with the taking of nourishment, the sexual drive has a sexual object outside the infant's body in the shape of the mother's breast. It is only later that the *drive loses that object*, just at the time, perhaps, when the child is able to form a total idea of the person to whom the organ that is giving him satisfaction belongs. As a rule the sexual

11

drive then becomes auto-erotic, and not until the period of latency has been passed through is the *original relation* restored. There are thus good reasons why a child sucking at his mother's breast has become the prototype of every relation of love. *The finding of an object is in fact a refinding of it.*[1] [My italics]

Here in Freud's formulation, there once *was* an object, an object that was able to give satisfaction to the subject, an object that comes to be forever lost. That is, in this account, the subject, once upon a time, found an object, a "finding of an object" subsequent to which any other search for an object becomes an attempt to *refind* it. Let us take up the question of such a finding of an object and the time in which this finding is said to have taken place. To do so we might need to go beyond this sentimentality and nostalgia evoked by the mother's breast.

Immediately after the passage just cited, Freud goes on to say the following:

But even after sexual activity has become detached from the taking of nourishment, an important part of this first and most significant of all sexual relations is left over, which helps to prepare for the *choice of an object* and thus *to restore the happiness that has been lost.*[2]

It is here that with Lacan we can speak of the object in Freud as being a *lost object*. It is through this notion that Lacan is able to put forward that consequently in Freud we can no longer take the object as:

… a fully satisfying object, the type object, the object par excellence, the harmonious object, the object which founds man in an adequate reality—in the reality which proves maturity—the infamous genital object.[3]

Nonetheless, a doubt persists in Freud's formulation and perhaps in Lacan's reformulation at the time of the *Object Relation* seminar, as to the mode, the place and the time of this object, since it was necessarily posited in Freud as having once existed in order to now be lost, rather than, say, inexistent. After all, if the first object for the infant is "a sexual object outside the infant's body in the shape of the mother's breast" and the "mother's breast has become the prototype of every relation of love" then we have a very concrete object and an actual encounter put forward.

But to which encounter with the breast is Freud referring exactly? Is it the very first encounter with the breast? The first few encounters? Is it love at first sight? Or is it all of the encounters synthesised into one, in which case such an encounter might perhaps still be occurring, even as an adult?

In *The Object Relation* seminar Lacan makes reference to Freud's *Project for a Scientific Psychology* in relation to this question of the lost object in Freud that he takes up. Let us follow this reference then to endeavour to determine how Freud conceives of this encounter with the primary object.

Here in the section entitled "Cognition and Reproductive Thought" Freud proposes the following:

> Let us suppose, for instance, that the mnemic image wished for is the image of the mother's breast and a front view of its nipple, and that the first perception is a side view of the same object, without the nipple. In the child's memory there is an experience, made by chance in the course of sucking, that with a particular head movement the front image turns into the side image. The side image which is now seen leads to the head movement; an experiment shows that its counterpart must be carried out, and the perception of the front view is achieved.[4]

We see in this passage, in Freud's account, an effort by the infant, even at this early stage, to re-establish a *prior* situation, one associated with a satisfaction in relation to the mother's breast. That is, the satisfaction is here posited as being prior, and we might propose here that perhaps satisfaction is posited as being prior *per se*.

Freud continues this line of thought into the *Interpretation of Dreams*. Here he notes that:

> An essential component of this experience of satisfaction is a particular perception [...] the mnemic image of which remains associated thenceforward with the memory trace of the excitation produced by the need. As a result of the link that has been thus established, next time the need arises a psychical impulse will at

once emerge which will seek to re-cathect the mnemic image of the perception and to re-evoke the perception itself, that is to say, to *re-establish the situation of the original satisfaction*.[5] [My italics]

Here Freud has introduced the notion of the *"original satisfaction"*, one proposed here as having existed prior, and which the infant subject attempts by all means to repeat. Well might we ask when this original satisfaction existed and indeed if it did exist. Can we accept that there was once a satisfaction? Or might we begin to see this as a sort of mythical encounter? After all there is something quite fantastical about this account of the infant first looking from one direction and then another, comparing these views and reversing its head movements, attempting to get a view of the promised land of milk and honey, or milk at least. All of this occurs, moreover, when the poor infant, newly emerged from the womb, can hardly see at all so far as we can tell.

What is consistent though about this first encounter is that it is one that Freud never attempts to describe as such in that it functions only as a retrospective proposition. That is, it is a type of prehistory, outside of the subsequent chronological sequencing of events. In this way it is a sort of anchoring point of reference for all subsequent encounters with an object, be it the breast itself or any of the later objects for a particular subject. That is, the supposed "finding" of an object functions as a logical exception to all attempts to "refind" an object in the quest for the Holy Grail of satisfaction.

In any case this notion that the infant gains satisfaction at the breast is criticised by Lacan. As Jean Allouch notes:

> ... far from in this seeing a bliss or even more simply a pleasure, [Lacan] interprets it as a reaction of defence against that which includes the dissatisfaction in itself of having been fed. Much more is earned by falling asleep that having to deal with the persistent distance between the sought after satisfaction and the obtained one, with the deception that this distance carries![6]

We have noted, moreover, that Freud says that "a child sucking at his mother's breast has become the prototype of every relation of love". What is this to be a *proto*-type? *Proto*-type is derived from a Greek word πρωτότυπος, the *"first* type", that is, again something that is defined as being first, primary or original which we might again suggest functions as a mythical first experience.

We might also note that it evokes for us what Freud also puts forward in the *Project* as the πρωτον ψευδος[7], that is, the first lie. Freud develops this here in reference to his working of the *nachträglichkeit* or retroactivity. But we could take this up in a different way in order to propose this encounter of satisfaction with the breast as mythical invention, a necessary invention that Freud produces in order to theorise the fundamentally unsatisfactory and unsatisfying attempt to "refind" the object.

A footnote in the *Project* alerts us to the fact that the term πρωτον ψευδος is drawn from Aristotle in his work of logic *Prior Analytics*. Aristotle proposed here that:

> A false argument come about by reason of the first falsity (πρωτον ψευδος) in it.[8]

Here we have a first lie, or, we could say, Freud's original invention of a mythical fully satisfying first encounter, which is necessary to found the means of structuring the inherently unsatisfying relation to the object. We can say that Freud produces a type of temporal logic, or rather makes use of this "first time" to produce a structural or logical necessity.

If we refer to Freud's working of his initial model of the psyche in the *Interpretation of Dreams* we can discern more of how he structures this. In this model he notes that:

> ... excitation passes through the systems in a particular *temporal* sequence.

However,

> ... the psychical systems are actually arranged in a *spatial* order.[9]

Hence a *spatial* or *structural* arrangement is made of perceptions occurring, or proposed as occurring, *temporally*, and we note the previous references to "perceptions" of the infant associated with the notional primordial satisfaction.

Freud proposes that the "basis of association lies in the mnemic systems" but that there is:

> ... not one but several such *Mnem.* elements, in which one and the same [perceptual] excitation ... leaves a variety of different permanent records.[10]

He proposes then that "the first of these *Mnem.* systems will naturally contain the record of association in respect to *simultaneity in time*", again the latter being italicised by Freud himself. The *first* of these *Mnem.* systems then differentiates itself from all the others by this aspect, the others pertaining to the unconscious and the pre-conscious in Freud's schema, being arranged "in respect to other kinds of coincidence", "for instance … relations of similarity, and so on with the others".[11]

Here we make an association between the *first satisfaction* as an exception and the first system that Freud puts forward as exception in structuring the psychical apparatus as he elaborates it here. The same modality of temporal logic which we have noted above also operates here. This is, it is what is designated as *first*, in this instance a system, that differentiates itself from all the others, providing an exception to the rule, an exception to the usual diachrony.

The *first satisfaction*, as we have noted, is also an exception by being the only one not to be described *per se*, therefore outside the chronological sequencing of events. In other words it is based on a synchronicity as a structural element as opposed to the usual diachronicity. It is also distinguished by being the *finding* on which the series of attempts to *refind* is founded. The *first system* is distinguished primarily by being arranged in respect of "simultaneity in time", in other words by a synchronicity.

So here we find a type of temporal logic in Freud's work where there is a "first" that is marked by a synchronous logic and a series of other "secondary" experiences, perceptions and so on marked by a diachronicity. We can see a similar type of logic operating in other parts of Freud's theory, always where there is a "primary" or exceptional event that sets the scene for a "secondary". As instances of this we have the primal scene, the father of the primal horde, primary and secondary repression and so on. In these parts of Freud's theory, the "primary" is always a later postulate even if it is posited as occurring *prior*, although we might say that it is logically prior rather than chronologically.

Let us enquire further into the first system of the model of the psyche that Freud proposes in the place in which he first elaborates this, that is in the correspondence with Wilhelm Fleiss. Here in the well-known letter of 6th December 1896, known as *Letter 52*, the first system or inscription is given a name, that of Wahrnehmungszeichen, *Wz*, or signs of perception. Freud states here that the *Wz* "is quite incapable of consciousness".[12] These *Wz* have a curious status, neither being available to consciousness nor pertaining to the unconscious like the later registrations. What may we ask then are these *Wz*? Lacan in the seminar *The Four Fundamental Concepts of Psychoanalysis*, gives a precise answer to this. He refers to these *Wahrnehmungszeichen*:

> ... to which there is a place to immediately give them, according to what I have taught you, their true name, in other words, signifiers ...[13]

This reading is disputed by some, for instance by Guy Le Gaufey in his work *The Incompleteness of the Symbolic* where he stresses Freud's nomination of these as "signs". He puts forward that, ordered as signs according to the pleasure principle, they "must be put in relation to an external reality". Thus these *Wz* would:

> ... function like traces of which it is of the greatest importance to the psychical apparatus to know if they are traces of something or of nothing.

Thus, according to Le Gaufey:

> The *Wz* thus pose the question of the real to which it is possibly attached, and this partially disqualifies it as a "signifier".[14]

But we need to follow Lacan's argument a little further. He qualifies his statement that the *Wz* are signifiers by noting Freud's clarification that the *Wahrnehmungszeichen* must be constituted by *simultaneity*. Lacan then poses the question:

> What is this if it is not signifying synchrony?[15]

It should be noted here that the German *Gleichzeitigkeitsassoziation*, translated in the *Standard Edition* as "associations of simultaneity" is given in French as "association of synchrony".[16] Here we could propose then that the *Wz* might be the synchronic side of the signifier, that is, in one sense, the very structure of the signifying chain, and, as such, they no doubt touch upon the real.

By contrast, Lacan qualifies the other transcriptions in the psychical apparatus, those that we have noted that Freud speaks of as being arranged "in respect to other kinds of coincidence", "similarity and so on" as having:

> ... the same functions of similarity, so essential in the constitution of metaphor introduced by a diachrony.[17]

By contrast Lacan further elaborates this notion of the synchrony of the signifier, here from the *Subversion of the Subject and Dialectic of Desire* where he introduces the vector of the signifying chain in the graph of desire:

> … the *synchronic structure* is more hidden, it is the one that takes us back to the *origin*. It is metaphor in so far as the first attribution is constituted in it, that which promulgates "the dog goes miaow, the cat goes woof-woof", by which the child in one fell swoop, disconnecting the thing from its cry, raises the sign to the function of the signifier, and reality to the sophistry of signification and, through contempt for plausibility, opens up the diversity of objectifications to be verified, of this very thing.[18] [My italics]

To return for a moment to the *Letter 52* of the Freud-Fleiss correspondence in which we are left with a striking sentence right near the end of this letter. Here Freud proposes, concerning the hysterical phenomena in regard to which he has in part developed his schema of the psychical apparatus, that:

> Attacks of giddiness and fits of weeping—all of these are aimed at another person—but mostly the *prehistoric, unforgettable other* person who is never equalled by any one later.[19] [My italics]

Here we can discern, we might propose, precisely in this *prehistoric, unforgettable other*, a reference point which, in being *prehistoric*, is at once outside the diachrony of history, but also, in being *unforgettable*, pertains to the synchronic structure of language and therefore not subject to the usual repression and forgetfulness as are the later registrations, those attributed to the unconscious in Freud's schema.

In returning to the question of the *lost object* with which we began, even though we can discern in Freud's writings a distinction between the time of the lost object as a "prehistoric" and therefore synchronic referent, and history as pertaining to the diachrony of the signifier, there remains nonetheless a vacillation in Freud's ability to separate these. For instance, in the section entitled "Regression" in Chapter VII of the *Interpretation of Dreams*, he refers to his earlier work with Breuer, and notes that:

... when it was possible to bring infantile scenes (whether they were memories or phantasies) into consciousness they were like hallucinations ...[20]

... the emphasis that we are making here being the conflation of memories and phantasies. Phantasies, we would propose, in contrast to memories or history, having been reworked by the signifier, are then outside of history. After all, it is specifically the separation of history and fantasy that Freud makes in the establishment of psychoanalysis through Freud's famous letter to Fleiss of 21st September 1897 in which he states that:

I no longer believe in my *neurotica* ...[21]

Similarly, Freud's positing that there was a time in which the satisfying object was attained, even if this functions as a structuring referent, nonetheless is posited in temporal terms and thus holds out the illusion that such an object might once again be retrieved. We could say that the fact that the object was put forward in these terms, perhaps the only terms available to Freud, has contributed to the deviations that psychoanalysis has undergone.

Jean Allouch in his work *The Erotics of Mourning in the Time of Dry Death*, makes a parallel critique of the notion of the object in Freud's *Mourning and Melancholia*.[22] He questions the conception that Freud puts forward there of the object as substitutable, in so far as according to Freud in that paper, mourning can only be resolved by the taking of a new love object. If such resolution were to take place then effectively there would be no loss, but simply the substitution of one object for a new one. That is, according to what we began with, a lost object would in effect be re-found. Against this Allouch proposes the notion of a "dry loss", in other words "a loss without any compensation whatsoever".[23] In the early Lacan, for instance in his seminar *The Object Relation* with which we began, the object is construed as a "metonymic object", in other words a substitutable object, at least to the extent that there can be a displacement from one signifier to another. It is only with Lacan's later invention of the object *a* that we can take the object as an empty place, as inexistent.

So then if the mother's breast or nipple is the prototype of every relation of love as Freud proposes, it is only in so far as this sexual object is the first imaginary one that comes to occupy this empty place for the child and gives a particular form, a particular shape, to the structure of desire for the child.

Notes

1. Freud, S. "Three Essays on the Theory of Sexuality". *SE* VII, p. 221.
2. *Ibid.*, p. 221.
3. Lacan, J. *La Relation d'Objet*. Le Séminaire Livre IV. Seuil, Paris, 1994, p. 15.
4. Freud, S. "Project for a Scientific Psychology". *SE* I, p. 328.
5. Freud, S. "The Interpretation of Dreams". *SE* IV, p. 565.
6. Allouch, J. "The Mirror Stage Revisited". *Papers of the Freudian School of Melbourne* 21 (2000): p. 121.
7. Freud, S. "Project for a Scientific Psychology". *SE* I, pp. 352–359.
8. Aristotle. *Prior Analytics* (Book II, Chapter 18, 66a, 16).
9. Freud, S. "The Interpretation of Dreams". *SE* IV, p. 536.
10. *Ibid.*, p. 538.
11. *Ibid.*, p. 538.
12. Freud, S. "Letter 52. Extracts from the Fliess Papers". *SE* I, p. 233.
13. Lacan, J. *Les Quatre Concepts Fondamentaux de la Psychanalyse*. Éditions de l'Association Freudienne Internationale (Publication hors commerce), Paris, 1999, p. 53.
14. Le Gaufey, G. *L'Incomplétude du Symbolique*: de René Descartes à Jacques Lacan. E.P.E.L., Paris, 1996, p. 170.
15. Lacan, J. *Les Quatre Concepts Fondamentaux de la Psychanalyse*. Éditions de l'Association Freudienne Internationale (Publication hors commerce), Paris, 1999, p. 54.
16. Le Gaufey, G. *Op. Cit.*, p. 170.
17. Lacan, J. *Les Quatre Concepts Fondamentaux de la Psychanalyse*. Éditions de l'Association Freudienne Internationale (Publication hors commerce), Paris, p. 54.
18. Lacan, J. "Subversion of the subject and dialectic of desire". In: *Écrits*. Seuil, Paris, 1966, p. 805. I have used my own translation of this passage, as, amongst other things, the published translations of *Écrits* replace the French word *origine* with "source" (Sheridan) or "beginning" (Fink) which elide the specific notion of origins in question here.
19. Freud, S. "Letter 52. Extracts from the Fliess Papers". *SE* I, p. 238.
20. Freud, S. "The Interpretation of Dreams". *SE* IV, p. 545.
21. Freud, S. "Letter 69. Extracts from the Fliess papers". *SE* I, p. 258.
22. Allouch, J. *Érotique du Deuil au Temps de la Mort Sèche*. E.P.E.L., Paris, 1997, p. 115.
23. *Ibid.*, p. 9.

CHAPTER THREE

On *Nachträglichkeit*

Christiane Weller

> [...] one cannot say that we have cause to be entirely satisfied
> with its translation. There are some peculiar inaccuracies, which
> go right to the limit of impropriety. Some of them are astonishing.
> They all tend in the same direction which is to efface the sharp
> edges of the text. For those who know German, I cannot recommend
> referring to the original text too much.[1]

Here, in Seminar I, Lacan refers to the French translation of Freud's
paper on "The dynamics of transference" but his words may also apply
to the English translation of Freud's entire oeuvre.

The adjective *nachträglich* and the noun *Nachträglichkeit*, which Freud
uses first in his "Project" of 1895,[2] engender a conceptualisation of the
effects of time and the production of history/memory in regard to
meaning. It is often translated into English as either deferred or delayed
action, as retroactivity or sometimes as belatedness, Lacan continues to
use the German term but translates it as *après-coup*. While Freud is normally credited with the "invention" of the term, Harold Bloom contends
that it is derived from the Jewish Kabbalah. The term *Nachträglichkeit*
has come to play an important role in German historiography and soci-
ology, particularly in the fields of memory and trauma studies as they

21

have emerged in the past twenty years or so. The differing translations of the term into English have long rendered it unspecific and delayed a theorisation in the English-speaking world.

The echo of two other more commonly used words reverberates in the term *nachträglich* or *Nachträglichkeit*. On one hand we have the noun *Nachtrag* which can be translated as postscript, amendment or supplement (a term which incorrectly appears in the English translation of "The Signification of the Phallus" while in the German edition of that paper which was presented in German Lacan uses the term *Nachträglichkeit*), on the other hand, we have the adjectival attribute *nachtragend* translated as unforgiving, and the verb *nachtragen* which is oriented towards the noun as well as the adjective, translated on one hand as "to add", or—on the other hand—as "to bear a grudge". In *Zur Psychopathologie des Alltagslebens* (*Psychopathology of Everyday Life*) Freud recounts an observation made by Ferenczi who refers to the unconscious as "*nachträglich*" (belated, post-mortem) and "*nachtragend*" (unforgiving).[3] In these terms the aspects of *Nachträglichkeit* as a retroactive effect directed towards a past, and an after-effect or affect projected into a future come into play.

Here I would like to explore the concept of *Nachträglichkeit* firstly with reference to Freud and Lacan, and secondly through a reading of Walter Benjamin. I believe that the somewhat covert interface between the Freudian and the Benjaminian notion of history and memory has been extremely productive after 1945, and continues to shape the present debate on memory and history. Benjamin was well acquainted with Freud's writing, and it can be argued as some commentators have done recently (Sigrid Weigel, Sarah Ley Roff, Rainer Nägele) that while Benjamin might not make explicit mention of it, his work particularly in later years has been infused by psychoanalytic concepts. The theoretical intersection between Freud and Benjamin is most obvious in the theorisation of concepts like dream, myth, the law, melancholia, trauma, memory/remembrance, and history, but also in language and telepathy. Also interesting, I think, is the recourse taken by Freud and Benjamin, particularly in their later years, to Judaism and to the Jewish Kabbalah. One of the texts Benjamin mentions in his reading list is Freud's *Beyond the Pleasure Principle*, which he had first read in 1928 and returned to once more in 1939. In a letter to Benjamin, Adorno notes: "Perhaps without being aware of the fact [...] you find yourself [...] in the most profound agreement with Freud; there is certainly much to be thought about in this connection."[4]

Benjamin who translated Baudelaire's poetry and had while in Paris in 1926–27 worked on a translation of Proust's *A la recherche du temps perdu*, went into exile in Paris in 1933. Possible points of contact between Lacan and Benjamin might have arisen between 1937 and 1939, when Benjamin became an active member of the *Collège de sociologie*, founded by George Bataille, Michel Leiris and Roger Caillois. He was also involved with Bataille's secret society *Acéphale*. Benjamin, in developing close ties with Surrealism, published regularly in the surrealist journal *Cahiers du Sud*, edited by Jean Ballard.

While is it not my intention to trace possible personal contacts between Benjamin and Lacan—I would like to suggest that there are correspondences between Freud's and Lacan's psychoanalysis and Benjamin's philosophy of history particularly in regard to meaning and temporality to which the notion of *Nachträglichkeit* is central.

The concept of *Nachträglichkeit* (belatedness) as Freud develops it in his 'Project' is intrinsically linked to the production of an individual history. A first scene is attributed with (sexual) meaning through a second scene. The past or the meaning of a past event arises from a moment in the present. What is articulated here is the notion of trauma as the unassimilated experience, brought to the fore through the effects of *Nachträglichkeit*.

In his 'Studies on Hysteria' Freud shifts the emphasis of his concept of *Nachträglichkeit* slightly. Freud recalls a woman who nursed her dying husband and other family members. These experiences are stored in memory, but attention is given to them only after the death of the "loved ones". The work of memory is, as it were at liberty to construct them as traumatic or—in the case that the family members had recovered—it could have discarded them. Freud speaks of the "*nachträgliche Erledigung*,"[5] the retrospective fulfilment and/or disposal of trauma, traumas which, as Freud says, were collected before the death of the loved ones. The operation described in this case is one that memorialises and monumentalises these deaths. This work of memory, termed *Erinnerungsarbeit* by Freud in the "Studies on Hysteria", will lead him to the formulation of the work of mourning (*Trauerarbeit*) in "Mourning and Melancholia". It is the "*nachholende Träne*",[6] the tear which is making up for something which has been missed in the presence

of the death. This link between *Nachträglichkeit* and melancholia is one
that is also taken up by Benjamin.

Lacan notes that *Nachträglichkeit* "by which trauma becomes involved
in symptoms [or maybe more accurately 'is cloaked in symptoms'],
reveals a temporal structure of a higher order."[7] In current sociological
and historical debates on trauma and memory the connection between
the second and the first scene is often conceived of as a causal connection between an earlier event which can be verified historically and a
second re-working through the operation of a narrative. This apparently is supported by Freud's account of the Wolf Man case where it
seems that reality, i.e., total objectification of proof is at stake for Freud.
Lacan contends that the *causa* cannot easily be dispelled as a phantom
since that which it perpetuates here is "the reason that subordinates the
subject to the signifier's effect."[8] One might say that the "retroaction
of the signifier"[9] brings about an appearance of causality. In the Wolf
Man case the on-going restructuring of the subject through the various re-workings (possibly re-imaginations) of the event runs counter to
the claim of establishing "reality" and verifiable causality. While *Nachträglichkeit* points to temporality in Freud's Wolf Man case the interval
between the first and the second scene is according to Lacan collapsed in
a moment of concluding, annulling the time for understanding.[10] *Nachträglichkeit* not only gestures retroactively towards an event as memory
but it also anticipates an evocation of meaning which will arise in the
future, i.e., as a future perfect. Lacan in his misreading of the Freudian
text, captures this moment of recognition from the future to the past,
and the illusion of a cause located in the past determining the future, in
the term *zeitlich-Entwicklungsgeschichte*. While Freud separates *zeitlich*
(temporal) and *entwicklungsgeschichtlich* (developmental history), Lacan
collapses the two Freudian terms into an ambiguous one, commenting
that history cannot be easily reconciled with development. For Lacan,
history can never be anything other than retroactive.

> There is a connection between the imaginary dimension and the
> symbolic system, so long as the history of the subject is inscribed
> in it—not the *Entwicklung*, the development, but the *Geschichte*, that
> is, that within which the subject recognizes himself, correlatively
> in the past and in the future. [...] The past and the future corre-
> spond precisely to one another. And not any old how—not in the
> sense that you might believe that analysis indicates, namely from

the past to the future. On the contrary, precisely in analysis, because its technique works, it happens in the right order—from the future to the past.[11]

This recognition of the subject in *Geschichte* (history) is made possible through the universality of the symbolic. Ferenczi's[12] assumption that the unconscious is at the same time *nachträglich* and *nachtragend* goes to the heart of Lacan's idea of a "mobile relation"[13] between the subject and history, between the inaccessibility of the unconscious and the unconscious being realised in the symbolic. The return of the repressed does not come from the past but from the future, "through its symbolic realisation, its integration into the history of the subject."[14] "Literally, it will only ever be a thing which, at the given moment of its occurrence, *will have been*."[15]

Returning to Freud's Wolf Man case, what then is the status of the first scene, a scene constructed through the analysis which only develops its pathogenic effect retrospectively, in the moment (sexual) meaning can be attributed to it? This meaning only arises in the dream some years after the supposed observation of the child. The moment in which the subject simultaneously recognizes and represses something/its own desire marks a passage, moving the subject into the field of meaning through the construction of the past as its own history. "History"—Lacan says—"is not the past. History is the past in so far as it is historicised in the present—historicised in the present because it was lived in the past."[16]

However, what is essential to note here is not the re-living or remembering but the re-construction and re-writing.[17] The restoration of the past is what lends the subject the appearance of wholeness. The subject communicates with and adopts this past as having "truly lived through it."[18] Lacan, referring to Freud's "Studies on Hysteria", contends that the present lends the past possibility.[19] But what is at stake here is not so much the notion of a past, or a past relived, but the subject which "assumes his own lived experience."[20] A claim laid to the past is a claim laid to the subject as that which can pronounce the *moi*,[21] or one might say, as that which can come into history.

The assumption of a history which is bound up in an original moment, an *Urszene* or primal scene, presents the subject with its mythical foundation. The symbolic integration of this moment, takes on—as Lacan concludes—the status of trauma, it presents itself to the subject as a shock. It forces its logic onto the subject, something which, at the moment it appears, immediately demands a detachment.

At this point I would like to draw Benjamin into the discussion. In his essay of 1939 on Baudelaire ("On Some Motifs in Baudelaire", "Über einige Motive in Baudelaire", 1940 (1939)) Benjamin develops a reading of Freud's "Beyond the Pleasure Principle" and Proust's notion of a *mémoire involontaire*, a memory which is involuntary and accidental. For Benjamin the crucial point in Freud's paper is the idea that consciousness comes into existence in the place of the memory trace.[22] The excitation accompanying the memory trace quasi evaporates in the moment in which it becomes conscious. Only that which has not been "lived" or "experienced" at the conscious level can appear as *mémoire involontaire*. The traumatic effect of the shock which bursts onto the scene without being halted by the defences of the conscious system presents the subject with an *Erlebnis* (event, or experience). The greater the moment of shock accompanying an incident, the more vigilant the conscious defences have to be, which for Benjamin means that the incident fails to become an experience (*Erfahrung*) but presents at the level of event (*Erlebnis*). *Erlebnis* here has a different quality than *Erfahrung* (both are normally translated with experience). *Erlebnis* carries the mark of suddenness and immediacy while *Erfahrung* is a result of reflection and cognition. The achievement of the defence against shock becomes apparent when the incident, while sacrificing the integrity of its content, is located at a particular temporal position within the consciousness, and thereby becomes event (*Erlebnis*).[23] When Lacan takes up the term *Erlebnis* (event or experience) in *Seminar I*, he throws open the question of a memory which is "lived or not lived,"[24] a memory which can be evoked and recognized as a possibility from the point of the present. This connects *Erlebnis* (as lived or unlived memory) via its constructedness to the movement of *Nachträglichkeit*.

While *Nachträglichkeit* has so far been discussed in terms of the history of the individual or the subject I would like, in one final observation, to introduce the concept of an understanding of collective or cultural history. In his last work "Über den Begriff der Geschichte" ("On the Concept of History"), written in 1939, Benjamin develops the notion of a history which is constantly trying to hold catastrophe, i.e., trauma at bay.

One of the most notable ideas of Benjamin's conception of history is the notion that it is not the past which engenders an understanding of the present but, conversely, the present which makes an understanding of the past possible. Benjamin calls this a "Copernican turn". For Benjamin the past is always passing by. One event, fleetingly glanced at, is immediately replaced and superseded by another. The past is multi-layered and reveals itself only momentarily, in fleeting images, it is marked—according to Benjamin—by a rupture or a shock. Only in the moment of arrest can the past be seized. History constitutes itself by this very rupture, in this dissolution of narrative[25]. The moment these fleeting images come to a standstill, in this moment of arrest, remembrance—Benjamin's *"Eingedenken"*—can take place. "Articulating the past historically does not mean recognizing it in 'the way it really was.' [Leopold von Ranke] It means appropriating a memory as it flashes up in the moment of danger."[26] The relation between past and present is neither based on causality, nor on analogy, but on affinity—not given but chosen. This points to a moment of construction of the past as history, as well as to the illusion of a cause. Lacan's moment of concluding and Benjamin's *Eingedenken* transfer the image into the symbolic. The process of the present choosing its past, constructs its own history by a gesture of *Nachträglichkeit*[27]. But this operation of *Eingedenken* is always endangered by the experience of history as an overwhelming catastrophe. It seems as if the subject must constantly seek to negotiate the excess of the past with the demand of the present. One might conclude that for Benjamin the process of historicising the past, of inscribing it with the specificity of the traumatic event, rescues the subject from the overwhelming catastrophe of seeing it all. While something is fixated it can at the same time be forgotten. Benjamin's *Angelus Novus*, the Angel of History defies his name and attests to the danger of not being able to construct a history to which the illusion of a cause is integral. Benjamin's Angel sees it all:

> His face is turned toward the past. Where a chain of events appears before *us*, *he* sees one single catastrophe, which keeps piling wreckage upon wreckage and hurls it at his feet. The angel would like to stay, awaken the dead, and make whole what has been smashed. But a storm is blowing from Paradise and has got caught in his wings; it is so strong that the angel can no longer close them. The storm drives him irresistibly into the future, to which his back is turned, while the pile of debris before him grows toward the sky.[28]

In the gesture of *Nachträglichkeit*, in this moment in which one can say "it will have been", history arises out of the past. Punctuating the past situates the subject in a field of meaning. This punctuation forces its traumatic effect onto the subject. It is relying on the illusion of a cause. While it engages the subject in this first scene it at the same time separates it. Benjamin's Angel creates the apocalyptic vision of a past which can no longer be structured from the position of the future perfect. The past presents itself as mere debris. The Angel driven with its back into the future cannot organise the past by anticipating its conclusion in the future. While *Nachträglichkeit* allows for the particularlity and singularity of a trauma, or traumatic cause; the seeing-it-all exposes the subject—or society—to the limitless catastrophe. It comes as no surprise that the question of *Nachträglichkeit* and meaning is posed anew after 1945.

Notes

1. Lacan, J. *Seminar I, Freud's Papers on Technique*, 1953–1954, New York, London: W. W. Norton, p. 38.
2. Freud. S. "Entwurf einer Psychologie", Nachtragsband. In *Gesammelte Werke*, ed. Angela Richards, Frankfurt a.M.: Fischer, 1999: 375–486.
3. Freud, S. *Zur Psychopathologie des Alltagslebens*, vol. IV. In *Gesammelte Werke*, ed. Anna Freud, Frankfurt a.M.: Fischer, 1999, p. 36.
4. Letter from Adorno to Benjamin, June 1935. Cited in: Ley Roff, Sarah. "Benjamin and Psychoanalysis", In *The Cambridge Companion to Walter Benjamin*. Ed. David S. Ferris, Cambridge: Cambridge University Press, 2004: 115–133, p. 115.
5. Freud, S. "Studien über Hysterie", vol. I. In *Gesammelte Werke*, ed. Anna Freud, Frankfurt a.M.: Fischer, 1999, 75–312, p. 229.
6. *Ibid.*
7. Lacan, S. "Position of the Unconscious", In *Écrits'*, tr. Bruce Fink, New York/London: W.W. Norton, 2006, 829–721, p. 711.
8. *Ibid.*
9. *Ibid.*, p. 712.
10. Lacan, J. "The Function and Field of Speech and Language in Psychoanalysis", In *Écrits*, op. cit. 237–268, p. 213.
11. Lacan, *Seminar I*, op. cit. p. 157.
12. Freud, *Psychopathologie des Alltagslebens*, op. cit., p. 36
13. *Ibid.*, p. 158.
14. *Ibid.*, p. 159.

15. *Ibid.*
16. *Ibid.*, 12.
17. See *ibid.*, p. 14.
18. See *ibid.*
19. See *ibid.*, p. 36.
20. *Ibid.*, p. 37.
21. *Ibid.*
22. Cf. Benjamin, W. "On Some Motifs in Baudelaire", In *Selected Writings*, vol. IV, 1938–1940, eds. Michael W. Jennings et al., Cambridge Mass.: The Belknap Press of Harvard University Press, 2003, 313–355, p. 316ff.
23. *Ibid.*
24. Lacan, *Seminar I*, op. cit. p. 35.
25. Benjamin, W. "On the Concept of History", In *Selected Writings*, vol. IV, 1938–1940, eds. Michael W. Jennings et al., Cambridge Mass.: The Belknap Press of Harvard University Press, 2003, 389–400, p. 390f.
26. *Ibid.* p. 391. ["Vergangenes historisch artikulieren heißt nicht, es erkennen "wie es wirklich gewesen ist". Es heißt, sich einer Erinnerung zu bemächtigen, wie sie im Augenblick der Gefahr aufblitzt." Benjamin, W. "Über den Begriff der Geschichte", vol. I,2, In *Gesammelte Schriften*, eds. Rolf Tiedemann and Hermann Schweppenhäuser, Frankfurt a.M.: Suhrkamp, 691–704, p. 695.]
27. Moses, S. "Zu Benjamins Begriff des Eingedenkens", In *Bucklicht Männlein. Walter Benjamin—Theoretiker der Moderne*. Gießen: Anabas Verlag, 1990, 100–101, note 1.
28. Benjamin, op. cit. p. 392. ["Er hat das Antlitz der Vergangenheit zugewendet. Wo eine Kette von Begebenheiten vor *uns* erscheint, da sieht *er* eine einzige Katastrophe, die unablässig Trümmer auf Trümmer häuft und sie ihm vor die Füße schleudert. Er möchte wohl verweilen, die Toten wecken und das Zerschlagene zusammenfügen. Aber ein Sturm weht vom Paradiese her, der sich in seinen Flügeln verfangen hat und so stark ist, daß der Engel sie nicht mehr schließen kann. Dieser Sturm treibt ihn unaufhaltsam in die Zukunft, der er den Rücken kehrt, während der Trümmerhaufen vor ihm zum Himmel wächst." Benjamin, "Über den Begriff der Geschichte", op. cit. p. 697f.]

CHAPTER FOUR

Time out of number

Peter Gunn*

In *The Goon Show*, a BBC radio comedy of the 1950s, Bluebottle, the earnest boy-scout character, asks a seemingly straightforward question: "What time is it?" If the response which Eccles, another child-like character, gives to the question is equally straightforward, it nevertheless upsets our expectations: "Err, just a minute. I've got it written down here on a piece of paper." A nice man wrote the time down for me this morning.'

Why, after all this time, do we laugh? In part this has to do with our recognising that this exchange falls into a well-known genre, that of the comic double act. In such acts the one who is questioned is the funny man and the one who poses the questions to the other is the stooge. In our example Bluebottle is the innocent abroad who, by his interrogation of the funny man Eccles, functions as the stooge.

But Eccles also bears a resemblance to that creature which we call the clown. The clown is something else again. With the entry of the clown, the comic genre no longer holds; something disturbing now creeps in. The clown is absolutely certain about his position, so much

*Analyst Member, The Freudian School of Melbourne.

so that, with his air of unconcern, he may begin to make us concerned about something regarding which, up till then, we ourselves had had the assurance of common sense.

It is this creeping uncertainty which is the basis for our tendency to relegate the clown to one or other category of pathological otherness. In the case of Eccles, if it was not clear from the dialogue itself we would already be aware, especially if we had been a regular listener to *The Goon Show*, what this category is: idiocy. Eccles' place in the comedic structure of *The Goon Show* was that of the idiot.

But Eccles cannot be dismissed so easily. If he is an idiot, he remains other; to use the common tongue, if he is a clown, he is also a weirdo. His weirdness designates something we cannot recognise. Yet it is for this reason that we do not immediately dismiss what he has to say. There is something for us in the way Eccles responds to Bluebottle's interrogation. And yet, even though it is given articulation in the grammar and syntax of our language, what Eccles says does not quite make sense. For this reason, by his questioning Bluebottle speaks for us all.

Indeed, it is by the unfamiliarity of this conjunction, the conjunction of the demotic familiarity of Eccles' tongue with the rigour of his logic, that, through the medium of Bluebottle, this clown returns the question to us. The question which he returns to us is a question of knowledge, in this instance, one which concerns time. Eccles makes us question what it is each one of us does when, as the saying has it, we "tell the time". That is, he makes us question what it is we do when we say the number which we take to be the number of the time.

We see now that if we laugh we are also a little anxious. This is something Freud pointed out long ago in Jokes and their Relation to the Unconscious. By our laughter at the nonsense of the comic duo we implicate ourselves as the third party in an articulation around something we would rather know nothing about.

But Eccles himself appears to have no anxiety. Why is this?

It is here, I think, that we have resort to what we suppose of Eccles' time. We must suppose that at any instant his time has a constant face and number. It has the face of that nice man he met, and its number remains the one that same man wrote down on the piece of paper which he gave him. In his encounter with any other, Eccles, we assume, will always be in the comfortable position of already knowing the time; he will always already have been told the time.

Let us come then to time in psychoanalysis. What does Eccles have to tell us? I suggest that he speaks to us of time in its essential function in psychoanalysis. This function is in being the support for the subject, not in order to have a number to trot out, but in introducing the necessity of which numbering itself speaks. This a necessity which, by the agency of discourse articulated in the transference, arrives by way of an hiatus encountered in the ordering of history, an hiatus, that is, in the ordering of time supposed as already known.

Let me try to give a preliminary justification for this. What we have done so far is trace what we suppose of the imaginary of Eccles' position in this dialogue on time. But we have also indicated that for us something in that position lies beyond the imaginary; it is here that there is something which addresses us. Those of us who have not had the benefit of having met Eccles' nice man cannot rest with this imaginary certainty but, from that imaginary, the terms of Eccles' nonsense articulate a question to us: What is the face and number of my time?

Now that it is articulated this strange question will not let us rest. It poses time as that which addresses us. It makes fun of universal time, the time of the big Other, and confronts us with subjective time, the time of *this* subject.

On this reading we can say that the time of the subject is at once something imposed from elsewhere as hiatus, and yet also something which must be instituted. That is, if this time supports the subject by introducing the necessity of which the impasse of the chronology speaks, it also introduces the necessity of inventing that time, of, in effect, writing its number. To follow Levinas, by this act of naming I am returned to the signification of my face, that One from which I speak.[1]

Indeed, I would now like to propose that for psychoanalysis the subject *is* that time, that event. That is, the subject is that time which, out of the necessity which discourse imposes, must be designated, albeit always retrospectively and in fading, as founding event.

In the remainder of this paper I want to make a case for this proposition. I will do so by addressing the ad-vent of the subject with that logic which is exhibited in certain mathematical antinomies. To put this another way, what I want to do now is look at the logic of the time of the impossible, that being the encounter to which psychoanalytic praxis is directed.

In this endeavour we already have a lead from Lacan. In his 'Proposition of the 9th of October 1967 on the Psychoanalyst of the School'

Lacan speaks of the position of the analyst in the transference. He says that what the analyst "has of what is to be known can be traced out upon the same relationship 'in reserve' according to which all logic worthy of the name operates."[2] Here then we have the tracing or writing of the discourse of the analyst. It is in its adherence to the logic of a knowledge held "in reserve" that this writing tends to the designative function of the name.

Lacan then goes on to say that it by the desire of the analyst, evident in the writing of this logic, that a surprising thing happens: something is indeed found which is worthy of the name. This raises the question of the temporal and existential status of such a find: What was it before? Lacan seeks to indicate the order of such a find by citing the case of the nineteenth century mathematician Georg Cantor, and his discovery of the transfinite numbers. In naming him here Lacan is well aware that in the aftermath of his find Cantor spent much time in psychiatric institutions.

Let us consider the case of Cantor. He pursued knowledge of the infinite in order to place a limit on it by naming it. His find, his discovery of the transfinite numbers, may be seen as the product of his preoccupation with extending the imaginary consistency of the natural number series to the infinite. By numbering the infinite continuum with his transfinite numbers he produced an infinite, but an infinite which was determinate or actual.

Cantor went on to postulate his famous continuum hypothesis. This states that the transfinite numbers themselves form an ordered series, with the transfinite number which names the continuum of the real numbers being the successor to the transfinite number which names the series formed by the natural numbers. The effect of the continuum hypothesis is to ground the production of these pure transfinite numbers in what is taken to already exist, this being the familiar territory of the natural, the grounding of which is given by perceptual intuition.

According to the mathematician Paolo Zellini, Cantor never shook off the feeling that his work transgressed the Thomist and Aristotelian prohibitions against making the infinite actual.[3] In its theological form this view denies existence to any infinite as a totality except for God; in the world, that is, in God's creation, the infinite is indefinite. This was a view widely held in Cantor's time, including by his teacher Kronecker. Put philosophically it says that something of the One cannot function as limit in order to make determinate the Many. And this is of course precisely what Cantor's theory of numbered infinite sets claimed to do; out of the indefiniteness of the infinite it makes a definite succession of ones.

Cantor made several attempts to prove his continuum hypothesis. He failed, and the effort seems to have caused him considerable distress. It would appear in fact that it triggered the first of a series of psychotic breaks. We can speculate that if Cantor's only resort in his endeavour was to the imaginary of God's creation, the impossible of he, Cantor, so-named as subject, became insupportable.

It is, in retrospect, a great irony that in 1939 Kurt Gödel showed that, whether or not it is true, Cantor's continuum hypothesis could not be disproved, at least from the standard axiomatic model within which the hypothesis is formulated. That is, Gödel showed that the continuum hypothesis could not be demonstrated to be false within its own axiomatic system.

Drawing on Gödel's work, in 1963 the American mathematician Paul Cohen showed that if the continuum hypothesis could not be demonstrated to be false neither could it be demonstrated to be true. Together Gödel and Cohen showed that within the standard set-theoretic model a demonstration of either the truth or falsity of the continuum hypothesis is *impossible*. In mathematical terms, Gödel and Cohen together showed that the truth of the continuum hypothesis is independent of its axioms.

We could say that what this demonstrates is an opening on to the impossible from within the discourse of mathematics.[4] Logically this demonstration of an impasse is of the same order as that which arises in the saying of an analysis. But what is opened in an analysis is the gap between knowledge and that absolute otherness wherein the truth of the subject lies; in the end this truth is independent of knowledge. And again, for psychoanalysis this opening is not something static but an encounter, an event.

But even here the mathematical antinomy can continue to inform us. Cantor's transfinite numbers can themselves be understood as exhibiting the infinite as an event. To quote the mathematician Paolo Zellini, the transfinite numbers exhibit 'the actual infinite as a concrete event; [it is] an entity capable of limiting a potential infinity of objects of which it is not a part.'[5]

In order to establish the independence of the truth of the continuum hypothesis from what it is possible to demonstrate on the basis of its own axioms Paul Cohen did something quite remarkable. His strategy relied on finding an axiomatically consistent extension of the standard model of set theory.

As one mathematician puts it, a model of a theory "interprets the language of the theory in such a way that the axioms of the theory are true in the model."[6] Within the model of a theory all the theorems of that theory are true. Thus, if a given statement can be shown to be false in the model this demonstrates that the statement cannot be proved from the axioms of the theory.

What Cohen was able to do was find a method of constructing an addition to the standard model of set theory in which the axioms of that theory remain true but where the continuum hypothesis can be shown to be false. The success of this strategy was not guaranteed in advance. As the same mathematician describes it, the required addition had to be pulled out of thin air as a kind of imaginary object. But Cohen nevertheless found it, and in so doing demonstrated that, within the confines of the original model, the continuum hypothesis can neither be proved or disproved.

Cohen called his technique "forcing" and the supplement to the standard model a "generic" set or object. To attempt to grasp the implications for psychoanalysis of this act of imposing from outside a nevertheless generic object it may be helpful to follow Derrida's figurative usage of set-theoretic terms when proposing what he calls his law of the law of genre.

Derrida says of this law that it is,

> ... precisely a principle of contamination, a law of impurity, a parasitical economy. In the code of set theories, if I may use it at least figuratively, I would speak of a sort of participation without belonging—a taking part in without being part of, without membership in a set.[7]

This parasitic law of participation without membership, which I read as a homologue for Cohen's generic object, is, says Derrida, "the law of overflowing, of *excess*":

> The trait that marks membership inevitably divides, the boundary of the set comes to form, by invagination, an internal pocket larger than the whole; and the consequence of this division and of this overflowing remain as singular as they are limitless.[8]

By making determinate what is otherwise indeterminate or independent the generic object also transgresses God's prohibition against making the infinite actual. It thus has a designative function which is quite similar to Cantor's transfinite numbers.

But if it designates the generic object this is a curious kind of naming. Rather than functioning at the level of set theory itself, that is, in reference to the objects of that theory, it functions at the level of the *model* of set theory, that is, at the level of the *language* of that theory. At this level, in order to mark belonging, it takes part without being part of. It is a naming of what, in the terms of what it attaches itself to, remains indeterminate.

This is thus a naming which is both radically supplementary and parasitic. From that which, from within its own terms, its own language, overflows and slips loose and is unnameable, to take the step of encountering it as such is to be subjected to the parasitic and infinite outside of that language. Thus if, having been determined from this encounter as one, this one now functions as that supplement which names, it remains nevertheless a forced entry of that which, otherwise, overflows.

This description might recall Lacan's topological re-construction, in his seminar *Le Sinthome*, of the unconscious as a slip or fault in knotting, a fault which is 'corrected' by that fabrication which he calls the sinthome. In order to signal these resonances and, in so doing, to bring us back to life and, in particular, to the clinic, allow me to quote just one passage from that seminar:

> There is … at once sexual relationship and non-relationship. Except for the fact that where there is relationship it is in the measure that there is sinthome. *Namely* where, as I *said*, it is from the sinthome that the other sex is supported. I *allowed* myself to *say* that the sinthome is very precisely the sex to which I do not belong, *namely*, a woman. If *a* woman is a sinthome for every man it is quite clear that there is a need to find *another name* for what is involved in the case of a man for *a* woman since precisely the sinthome is characterised by non-equivalence. One may *say* that man is for a woman anything you please, namely an affliction, worse than a sinthome, you may well *articulate* it as you please, a devastation even, but if there is no equivalence you are *forced* to specify what is involved in the sinthome.[9]

If we read this in conjunction with the previous discussion we can re-formulate Lacan's proposition of 1967. We can say that the continuum of the imaginary of the transference, when traced out, that is, articulated rigorously on account of the signifier as an unbroken series of letters, necessarily leads to an impasse. Looked at from another perspective we can say that this is an encounter with what enters as limit to the infinity of interminable, serial metonymy. This limit is both of time and enters from outside.

In other words, this is an encounter with a gap in time, one which ex-ists to the infinite time series which is articulated in the signifier. To put this yet another way, by rigorously ordering the not-known as the border of knowledge this articulation leads to the encounter with that order of the impossible, the parasitic non sexual relation. In short, it leads to the encounter with the real. It is only from the articulation of that-which-is-not that this real can be said to be held in reserve.

As such this order is the same, I suggest, as that of Cantor's transfinite numbers. It was this order, this impossible and parasitic time out of number which overflows and slips out there, which he could not bear. And yet, speaking of the order of Cantor's transfinite numbers, it is in speaking of this that Lacan makes reference to a lucky find.

I take this to indicate that, through the speaking of an analysis, it is only in being seized by this time out that there is the possibility of it presenting itself out of thin air as *my* time. This possibility is given then not by following Cantor and obsessively seeking to specify the ordering of the interminable not-known by reference to God's imaginary, but rather in the allowance given, and given in an analysis by the desire of the analyst in alliance with the transference, to encountering that limit from the interminable articulation of the symptom as that which does not stop writing itself.

From the articulation of the symptom which, though it repeats, never quite finds the terms to say what is the full truth of it, this is, at the limit, an articulation or, truthfully now, a writing, a writing literally out of those terms, a writing of that-which-is-not. This is the lucky event of the 'stops not being written.'[10]

For those of us who do not have the good fortune of having our time writted this is our only possibility. But for this time to be appropriated as *my* time there remains the necessity of a forcing, a forcing by which my name is imposed.

In the first instance this forcing is supported. In an analysis it is supported by the transference through the medium of the analyst functioning not as God or as Eccles' Nice Man but in his own name, and as no more than *semblant* of that impossible and excessive object which Lacan calls *objet a*. It is by the analyst functioning in this way as supplement for that object that it might, at the limit, come to be found intruding as the subject's very own, its own invention.

But however I might name it, whether as sinthome or with another name, this time, this time of the subject, remains a writing from the outside, of the Not-All-To-Be-Written. If I am to have any luck it is inasmuch as I can allow that I am not relieved by this name. I am, perforce, left with the necessity of it incessantly imposing itself, now from outside, yet as my most proximate truth as subject.

Notes

1. Levinas E. (1996). Proper Names. Michael B. Smith (Trans.), Stanford: Stanford University Press.
2. The Proposition was originally published in Lacan, J. (1968). Proposition du 9 octobre 1967 sur le psychanalyste de l'École. Scilicet, Number 1. The English translation from which I am quoting (and which I have modified) is Lacan, J. (1995). Proposition of 9 October 1967 on the Psychoanalyst of the School. Analysis, Number 6, 1–13. Geelong: The Australian Centre for Psychoanalysis in the Freudian Field.
3. Zellini P. (2005). A Brief History of Infinity. David Marsh (Trans.), London: Penguin Books, p. 58.
4. Cf. Zellini (2005), p. 177.
5. Zellini (2005), pp. 153–4.
6. Jech T. (2008). What is Forcing? *Notices of the American Mathematical Society*, 55, 4, 688–689. The article is available online at http://www.ams.org/notices/200806/tx080600692p.pdf.
7. Derrida J. (1992). The Law of Genre. In Derek Attridge (Ed.), Acts of Literature (pp. 221–252). New York: Routledge, p. 227. I am indebted to my partner, Dr. Helen Dell, for alerting me to this work.
8. Derrida J., The Law of Genre, *op. cit.*, p. 228.
9. Lacan J. (1976). *Le Sinthome*. Seminar of 1975–76, lesson of 17th February 1976, unpublished English translation by Cormac Gallagher; my emphases.
10. Lacan J. (1990). Television. In Joan Copjec (Ed.), *Television: A Challenge to the Psychoanalytic Establishment*, (pp. 3–48). New York: W. W. Norton & Co, p. 39.

CHAPTER FIVE

The origin of language

Michael Plastow

> And out of the ground the Lord God formed every beast of the
> field, and every fowl of the air; and brought *them* unto Adam to see
> what he would call them: and whatsoever Adam called every liv-
> ing creature, that *was* the name thereof.[1]

This is one account of the origin, of the genesis of language, a type of
traditional or naïve account in which it functions as a series of signs
that stand in for things, or referents. The beginnings of the discipline of
linguistics were also imbued in the notion that one could find an origin
to language, an original language. Modern linguistics, with Chomsky
for instance, has returned to such a notion through universal grammar,
which gives rise to a generative grammar steeped in genetics, another
type of assumed genesis or origin.

Ferdinand de Saussure warned against the notions of such origins.
He wrote:

> The question of the origin of languages does not have the impor-
> tance given to it. The question does not even exist. Question of the
> *source* of the Rhône: puerile! The moment of genesis is not in itself
> able to be grasped: it can not be seen.[2] [My italics]

41

Here we can see that Saussure is categorical: the question does not even exist, it is impossible. And furthermore to sustain such a question is puerile or childish. The effort to find the origin or the *child of language* is in itself childish. From psychoanalysis, we could say that what can not be seen is the primal scene, the moment of one's parents' enjoyment through which one originates, but from which one is excluded.

What I would like to propose is that this and other pronouncements are put forward by Saussure, and others, as a type of prohibition, a *necessary* prohibition for the study of language. It is this that might allow us to examine the place and function of the concept of the origin of language in reference to psychoanalysis. In doing so I would like to give emphasis to the writings of Saussure in their pertinence to psychoanalysis.

Saussure and linguistics

Saussure has been known mainly through the *Course on General Linguistics* which was put together by his contemporaries, and not exclusively those most favorable to his teachings, in a manner that often distorted his thought.[3] It is also based upon the notes of his students, and not the best students![4] Clearly enough of Saussure's theorisation of language was able to be transmitted to give rise to a whole generation of thinkers. However, if it weren't for the discovery of Saussure's writings in 1996 in the *orangerie* of the family property in Geneva, Saussurism might have died out and linguistics willingly swallowed up by the cognitive sciences and the sciences of communication. However thanks to new readings of his texts, and, according to linguist François Rastier,[5] "favored no doubt by the theoretical and practical failure of Chomskyism, the descriptive weakness of cognitivism and the anecdotism of ordinary pragmatics", we are now witness to a resurgence of interest in Saussure's thought, albeit mostly through French-speaking scholars.

Lacan also gives utterance to a prohibition akin to that of Saussure:

> I reminded you that something worthy of this linguistic title as science, that only something that seems to have language as such or even speech as its object was sustained, that it was only sustained on the condition of linguists swearing amongst themselves to never, to never ever again—because that's all they had done for centuries—to

never ever again, even distantly, to make allusion to the origin of language. This was, amongst others, one of the watchwords I had given to this form of introduction that was articulated in my formula *the unconscious is structured as a language*.[6] [My italics]

Here we can say that Lacan concords with Saussure in attributing to the origin of language a place as impossible, an impossible that underwrites Lacan's thesis of the unconscious as structure. But what is it that Lacan is referring to here?

The Linguistic Society of Paris had an internal rule which excluded any communications on the origins of language. Here is article 2 of the statutes of that Society from 1866 and revised in 1876: "The Society does not allow any communication concerning, either the origin of language or the creation of a universal language".[7] With this in mind, we will not be surprised then to find that when Saussure arrived in Paris in 1880, he frequented the Linguistic Society of Paris and in fact had previously travelled from his studies in Leipzig to give a paper at that Society.[8]

Here we have a confident epistemology based on linguistics as a descriptive and historical science, which refuses such false problems as imagining the first or the last of human languages. The notion of origin and the universal are of course related, as we have noted already regarding the generative and universal grammars of Chomsky. The original language is in fact a universal, as is the simplistic notion of any future universal language whether we might consider that this would take the form of English, Esperanto or any other language. François Rastier proposes this exclusion of origins by the Linguistic Society of Paris as a *"founding privation* decisively distinguishes [linguistics] from metaphysics".[9] [My italics]

With such a statement we are not far from Lacan's aphorism that there is no metalanguage. The Norwegian philosopher Arild Utaker also proposes something similar in distinguishing the comparative linguistics of Saussure to the generative grammar of Chomsky. He notes:

> A more interesting concept of language can be found in the grammar that indeed must be seen as the opposite of generative grammar, the comparative grammar of the last century. Here there can be no universal language.[10]

Nonetheless, Utaker distinguishes between two structuralisms: one starting from Saussure that is semantical, the other with Roman Jakobson, with his point of departure in phonology, that is, in something physical, thus returning to the old metaphysics of the division of the material and the spiritual. In this Jakobson reverses Saussure's radical step of separating the linguistic sign from any connection with the **referent**, or matter. It is the structuralism of Saussure that Utaker chooses, that which refuses the traditional metaphysics.

Origin as metaphysics

Let us endeavour to elucidate a little further this question of metaphysics in relation to linguistics. Giorgio Agamben asserts that Saussure:

> ... experienced in an exemplary manner and up to the very end the *impossibility* of developing a science of language in the heart of Western metaphysics.[11] [My italics]

Saussure attributes this impossibility to the very nature of language itself. This is what he calls the "sliding substance of language" for which no term is ever adequate, including the term "term". No term is able to be properly defined. For Saussure this impossibility also was a barrier to be able to write of it and to publish. He wrote the following to a student in 1909: "As for a book on this subject, one cannot even dream of it: it must give the definitive thought of its author".[12] And the writings that were discovered are fragmentary, containing many gaps, many words that have been barred. And although his writings also contained many question marks, these have been converted into full stops by the editors of *Writings on General Linguistics*,[13] attempting in some way to render his writings more definitive.[14]

Nonetheless, in regard to an examination of language, Saussure notes that "there is not a single point that might be the obvious point of departure". *The Double Essence of Language*, the most important text of his writings on general linguistics, opens with the following:

> It seems *impossible* in fact to give a pre-eminence to this or that truth of linguistics, in such a way to make of it the central point of departure: but there are five or six fundamental truths which are

so tied together that one could start indifferently from one or the other and one will logically arrive at all the others and to any small ramification of the same consequences by starting from any one of them.[15] [My italics]

In this logical structure that Saussure articulates, we can hear something not far from Freud's description of the navel of the dream. Rastier sees in this statement the refusal of the ontological tradition which has dominated Western thought. The opposition between potential (*dunamis*) and act (*ergon*) is one of the foundations of western ontology in that it permits to safeguard the invariable unity of Being and to reduce action to the manifestation of a pre-existing potential. We can find the same ontological division in Chomsky's opposition of competence and performance.[16] This schema applies to how production of language is conceived but also to what we could call a general schema of objective science. The Freudian unconscious is construed in similar terms and no doubt this is how much of psychotherapy and psychoanalysis outside the Lacanian field is constituted, that is, as a revealing of some prior or original truth, through a developmental and aetiological bias. We inevitably attempt to explain the surface structures by the supposed deeper structures.

Saussure ruptures such a schema firstly by separating speech from language by proposing two linguistics, and secondly, by inverting the relation between the potential and the act. Thus:

> ... linguistics, I dare say, is vast. Notably it is comprised of two parts: one is closer to the *tongue*[17] [*langue*], passive deposit, the other is closer to *speech* [*parole*], active force and veritable origin of the phenomena that are then perceived bit by bit in the other moiety of language [*langage*].[18]

Here speech is conceived as being the "active force" and the tongue is the passive deposit that ultimately experiences the effects of what happens in speech. Thus, in Saussure's schema, what was considered an effect becomes primary and original, and what was considered *original* (tongue or *langue*) becomes a secondary effect. The paradigm of science consisting of *cause*, taken as origin, and *effect* becomes subverted. Such a movement, we can say, is homologous with that which Lacan subsequently effected in the field of psychoanalysis, the unconscious becoming an *effect* of speech and not a *cause*.

The search for the origin of language

Let us return now to the question of the prohibition of speaking of the origin of language and what to do with it. Clearly, this prohibition has mostly been ignored. Here we can examine the results of some of the lines of argument that stem from this.

The nineteenth century linguistics that Saussure initially studied, not only privileged written language over spoken, it also privileged ancient languages over modern ones, and dominant languages over dialects. The emphasis was to attempt to discover an original language from which all modern languages derived. Thus there was a postulated Indo-European language whose closest known representative was Sanskrit. Saussure noted that this fictional Indo-European did not have any phonetics: it was never spoken. This "made Saussure say that the geographical origin of Indo-european, usually situated at Pamir in Central Asia, could equally have been found in deep Germany",[19] in other words, that one cannot locate a specific origin. This of course did not prevent the proposition of other original languages, or the attempt to push the origin of languages further back by the proposal of other great language families such as Altaic and a common proto-language currently referred to as Nostratic.

Another means through which this prohibition has been ignored is through a search for the genesis of language by attempting to locate a "language gene". This type of research starts naturally from the conception of language as a biological function. Thus a language gene was proposed on the FOXP2 site on chromosome 7, thought responsible for hereditary aphasia in an English family. This proposition has, however, been subsequently discredited by the discovery that the FOXP2 gene is also associated with the song of certain birds, as well as certain mutations of this gene affecting the vocal performance of mice. Hence this gene has no specificity to human language and thus the search must be directed elsewhere.[20]

Following the postulate that any function must be underpinned by an anatomical faculty, the search for an origin of language also becomes that of the origin of the organ of language. Here once again an act must be explained by an underlying potential: in applying nominally naturalistic and teleological thinking, psychical attributes must be underwritten by organic functions. Thus it is the function that creates the organ and any circumscribed mental function must be allocated a cerebral localisation. As Rastier comments:

> ... if the faculty of language is a faculty for acquiring language, its exercise presupposes the existence of languages; in this case human nature presupposes culture, which goes against the initial naturalistic hypothesis.[21]

The results of such flaunting of the prohibition of the origin to language are, in the end, derisory. In addition, any endeavour to locate an origin to language seems doomed to fall, not only into a developmental mode of thinking, but also one imbued with the prejudice of those who believe they possess a superior form of language. This is evident from studies of language acquisition of the child, the deficits of the deaf, or Creole and pidgin forms of language.[22] Thus the child, the handicapped, blacks or those from more traditional societies, in this schema, are only able to speak supposedly primitive forms of language.

The function of prohibition

In his paper *The Third*, Lacan refers to Parmenides' interdiction of speaking of non-being. We are of course also reminded of other forms of prohibition that effectively establish an exception upon which the set of what is knowable, or what is possible, is established. We are reminded of the murder of the father of the primal horde in "Totem and Taboo" that is able to establish the law of desire. Or of the primal scene we referred to earlier in this paper. Or primary repression which, in a logical sense, is able to establish repression proper in the Freudian schema.

Parmenides' interdiction of speaking of non-being effectively establishes ontology and in this we can place the birth of Western metaphysics. Saussure's "fundamental privation" has the same form of a categorical injunction as that of Parmenides. It differs in that Saussure's prohibition effectively concerns an interdiction of speaking of *being*, for the question of origin, as we have seen, effectively participates in an ontological position. Thus the originality of Saussure was to go against the whole weight of the metaphysical tradition in order to permit the elaboration of the structure of language.

Saussure's lack of ontology is also his means of conceptualising language. In his schema there are no positive terms, only opposition and difference, whether it is on the side of the signifier or that of the signified. Saussure links this to what he calls "THE fundamental difference".[23]

It is only when we are able to take up Saussure's proposition that we might be able to locate an origin, albeit of a different nature, to language. We have already noted his proposition that speech is an "active force and veritable *origin* of the phenomena" that are then perceived bit by bit in the other moiety of language. And Lacan adds that:

> What we have to understand is that it is the deposit, the alluvion, the petrification [i.e., *langue*/tongue] which differentiates itself from the usage by a group of its unconscious experience,[24]

… that is to say, from speech.

Saussure's refusal of an ontology is also expressed in the following statement:

> Is it not ridiculous and even intolerable to be constantly enclosed in one's particular ego [*moi*] and subjected to this very little me [or ego: *moi*]?[25]

Here Saussure goes against the whole stream of Western metaphysics in putting paid to the notion of a self-reflective subject identical to him or herself. In his writings we can find different notions of the subject but one of interest is that of a subject *subjected* to language. This is a notion of the 'accidents' of language in which the expression of thought is: "at the mercy of the most ridiculous accident of a vowel or an accent".[26] Here Saussure criticises the pretensions of cultures that promote a notion of a supposed "genius", in which we also hear "genesis", of their language:

> The "genius of the tongue [*langue*]" weighs *zero* in the face of the sole fact such as the suppression of a final *o*, which is in each instant capable of revolutionising from top to bottom the relation of the sign[27] [signifier] and the idea [signified], in whatever form of language.[28]

Here we can locate the germ of a notion of language as creative through its autonomy in regard to any pre-formed ontology. This creativity is not truly able to be conceived according to the Aristotelian tradition and hence the failure of Chomskyism to give an account of it. This creativity can only be accounted for by a theory of action, whether of speech or of writing, and not one of representation.[29]

The originality of speech

So here we might be able to move from a theory of creation to one of creativity, from origin to originality in language. That is, if we are to locate an origin to language, it is in the poietic power of speech. The writer Raymond Queneau also proposes that:

> Nothing is more striking than the vitality of a language: how aware its speakers are that they're speaking that language, how they suffer when they see some unbearable wrong done to it, how able they are to develop and enrich it, leaving it more beautiful year after year, always producing new harvests.[30]

If the jouissance of the primal scene is one to which the subject owes his existence, it is not a temporal origin, but rather a structural one. We could say however that the task of analysis is the question of how to deal with this impossible, the impossible of the prohibition, the impossible as real. How then to "speak *lalangue*",[31] as Lacan says, or to speak thetongue, when this tongue is no longer just an idiom but also the embodiment of a forbidden jouissance, a tongue that speaks, that cajoles, that licks, that protrudes, that tut-tuts and many other things besides? This mother's tongue is the source of one's enjoyment; *lalangue* then is thetongue inhabited by an enjoyment, a jouissance to which we are subject, an enjoyment that consequently manifests as symptom.

In noting the primacy of spoken language over the written, Raymond Queneau warns:

> … lose sight of the source and your tongue will go dry: you'll die of thirst, and soon wither away altogether.[32]

This source of originality is nonetheless a traumatic one: it cannot be represented. In Saussure's schema the voice is not only outside the field of representation, it is also outside of the domain of signification, being encompassed by neither the signifier, nor the signified. With Lacan the voice is one form of the object *a*, an object through which "it enjoys" (*se jouit*), "an object of which there is no idea".[33]

But how to hear in one's speech, in one's own voice, one's debt to *lalangue* in order to apprehend something of this creative power of language? The only way to approach the impossible of this jouissance is through the symptom, the symptom then as necessary, or as Lacan says, "it is something which in the first place does not cease from being written from the real".[34] For Freud "a symptom is a sign of, and a substitute for, a drive satisfaction which has remained in abeyance".[35] Here again we encounter the symptom as standing in for the forbidden jouissance, the enjoyment of origins.

It is this drive, this enjoyment, which is the true origin of speech, the effective source of jouissance and of the production of signifiers that stand in for it. Here surely is the origin of creativity if we are able to harness it through the symptom, to be able to put to work this Other source of the Rhône.

Notes

1. The Holy Bible. Oxford, Oxford University Press, 1878. Genesis II, 19.
2. Saussure, F. Cited in: Arrivé, M. *À la Recherche de Ferdinand de Saussure*. Presses Universitaires de France, Paris, 2007, p. 20.
3. Engler, R. "The making of the Cours de linguistique générale". In: *The Cambridge Companion to Saussure*. Cambridge University Press, Cambridge, 2004, pp. 47–58.
4. Rastier, F. "Saussure et la science des texts". Podcast: http://podcast1. univ-lyon2.fr/podcastserver/evenementslyon2/ICAR/
5. Rastier, F. "Saussure au futur: Ecrits retrouvés et nouvelles receptions". *Texto!* http://www.revue-texto.net/index.php?id = 1816. p. 1.
6. Lacan, J. *Le Savoir du Psychanalyste*, Séminaire 1971–1972. Lesson of 3rd February 1972. Éditions de l'Association Freudienne Internationale (Publication hors commerce), Paris.
7. Cited in: Rastier, F. "Le langage a-t-il une origine?" *Texto!* July 2007, Vol XII, no. 3. http://www.revue-texto.net/Dialogues/Dial_index. html p. 10. Also published in: *La Revue française de psychanalyse* 2007; 71: 1481–1496.
8. Sanders, C. "The Paris years". In: *The Cambridge Companion to Saussure*. Cambridge University Press, Cambridge, 2004, pp. 30–31.
9. Rastier, F. "Le langage a-t-il une origine?" *Op. cit.*, p. 10.
10. Utaker, A. "Form in Language: Wittgenstein and Structuralism". http:// www.revue-texto.net/Saussure/Sur_Saussure/Utaker_Wittgenstein. html p. 205. Also in: Henry, P. and Utaker, A. (eds). *Wittgenstein and Contemporary Theories of Language*, Bergen, 1992, p. 205.

11. Cited in Rastier, F. "Le silence de Saussure ou l'ontologie refuse". In: Bouquet, S., ed. *Saussure*. L'Herne, Paris, p. 26.
12. *Ibid.*, p. 25.
13. Saussure, F. *Écrits de linguistique générale*. Éditions Gallimard, Paris, 2002.
14. Rastier, F. "Saussure et la science des texts". *Op. cit.*
15. Saussure, F. *Écrits de linguistique générale. Op. cit.*, p. 17.
16. Rastier, F. "Saussure, la pensée indienne et la critique de l'ontologie" (2006). *Texto!* http://www.revue-texto.net/index.php?id = 1820. p. 3.
17. Here I have used "tongue" to translate *langue* since "language" is already used to translate *langage*. In Saussure's schema, *langage* is an overarching notion that comprises both *langue*, or "tongue", and *parole*, or "speech". "Tongue" is also preferred here as it also conveys the bodily notion of *langue* as an organ of speech.
18. Saussure, F. *Écrits de linguistique générale*. Éditions Gallimard, Paris, 2002, p. 273.
19. Flournoy, O. "Sigmund Freud, le psychanalyste, Ferdinand de Saussure le linguiste: Deux contemporains de génie. Convergences, divergences". (Lecture given at the University of Geneva, 11th January 2007, organised by the Centre de psychanalyse Raymond de Saussure de Genève). http://www.cprs.ch/modules.php?name = Downloads&d_op = getit&lid = 36.
20. Rastier, F. "Le langage a-t-il une origine?" *Op. cit.*, p. 8.
21. *Ibid*, p. 8.
22. *Ibid*, p. 9.
23. Saussure, F. *Écrits de linguistique générale. Op. cit.*, p. 65.
24. Lacan, J. "The Third" (La Troisième). Unpublished lecture of 01/11/1974. Accessible at: http://www.ecole-lacanienne.net/documents/1974-11-01.doc
25. Rastier, F. "Saussure, la pensée indienne et la critique de l'ontologie" (2006). *Op. cit.*, p. 6.
26. Saussure, F. *Écrits de linguistique générale. Op. cit.*, p. 216.
27. Although the terms 'signifier' and 'signified' were introduced by Saussure, he only used them right at the end of his career, in his third year of lectures on general linguistics. I have placed them in brackets in this citation to clarify what Saussure is referring to here.
28. Saussure, F. *Écrits de linguistique générale. Op. cit.*, p. 216.
29. Rastier, F. "Saussure, la pensée indienne et la critique de l'ontologie" (2006). *Op. cit.*, pp. 9–10.
30. Queneau, R. *Letters, Numbers, Forms: Essays, 1928–70*. Urbana and Chicago: University of Illinois Press, 2007, p. 82.

31. Lacan, J. "The Third" (La Troisième). Unpublished lecture of 01/11/1974.
32. Queneau, R. Op. cit., p. 84.
33. Lacan, J. "The Third" (La Troisième). Unpublished lecture of 01/11/1974.
34. *Ibid*.
35. Freud, S. "Inhibitions, Symptoms and Anxiety" (1926). *SE* XX, p. 90.

PART II

THE LACANIAN CLINIC TODAY

CHAPTER SIX

The necessity and impossibility of interpretation

David Pereira

The question of whether interpretation continues to play a significant part in the practice of psychoanalysis today has been the subject of considerable debate. Arguments which have been advanced that it is no longer adequate to speak of interpretation in terms of the clarification of hidden meaning, or rendering what was unconscious conscious, carry considerable weight. Within the context of this debate appears the following: "The age of interpretation is behind us. This is what Lacan knew but did not say."[1] Such a statement, as it stands, would be difficult, if not impossible to defend either in terms of Lacan's teaching or indeed any serious examination of our practice. What is perhaps more important about such a statement, however, is that within it resides the very problem which has plagued the theory and practice of interpretation.

Attempting to decipher what Lacan knew but did not say places us in a difficult zone somewhere between paranoia and mysticism. To speak of a post-interpretative era signals the birth of a problematical concept of psychoanalytic interpretation which concerns itself with the intuition of thoughts—of knowledge—without reference to the saying.

For my part, my practice is oriented by sticking as closely as possible to what is said/to the saying. This is something I understand to be emblematic of the practice and transmission of psychoanalysis within the Freudian School of Melbourne, and certainly of my training as an analyst within that School—to stick to the saying; to interrogate Lacan at the level of his saying rather than what he knew but did not say. To this extent, it is true that the way in which Lacan speaks of interpretation, what he in fact *says* about it, changes somewhat.

Let's consider now what necessitated this change and the consequences which ensued from it.

From about 1970 onwards, and I will refer in detail to some of the Seminars of this time, we note in Lacan an insistent questioning of analysis based on interpretation as referred to meaning and the elucidation of meaning. In the lesson of 26th November, 1969 Lacan signals this change by indicating, "... how much analytic interpretation itself goes against the grain of the ordinary meaning of the term."[2] By ordinary meaning we might understand here the exercise of elucidation and ordering of meaning in the context of what becomes known of the analysand's history. In itself, such an enterprise departs somewhat from the saying, in a manner not dissimilar to imputing to Lacan a knowledge which did not make its way into a saying.

Now, a change in the theory of interpretation is given impetus and acquires a formal theoretical status in reference to the concept of *lalangue*[3] which, by the time of the *Intervention at the Discourse of Rome in 1974*, is clearly articulated as a significant theoretical entity. It is worthwhile noting that some twenty one years had elapsed since the first Rome Discourse in 1953 on the *Function and Field of Speech and Language in Psychoanalysis*. In the 1974 *Rome Discourse* Lacan unequivocally states that "it is *lalangue* which operates interpretation."

Lalangue appears in a way which causes us to specify something else at work in the function of speech and the field of language. Whilst remaining within this function and field, in being the "key to incomprehension"[4] *lalangue* separates the operation of interpretation in psychoanalysis from that relationship of truth to knowledge which has a psychology of meaning as its effect.

The Seminars leading to the 1974 *Rome Discourse* accord an increasing importance to the concept of *lalangue*. In the Seminars, *The Reverse of Psychoanalysis, Ou Pire,* and *The Knowledge of the Psychoanalyst,* for example, we find being developed a movement from the purely representational dimension of the subject as given by a relation between truth and knowledge from which meaning arises, to the importance of jouissance, enjoyment, as the substance of thought underlying any relation between truth and knowledge.

If the structure of interpretation is defined as a "knowledge qua truth"[5], and if what we expect from a discourse is the work of truth, then there is no discourse from which the question of jouissance can be excluded.[6] Any reference to discourse, a discourse in which the subject is caught up, is necessarily also caught up in a jouissance, thereby installing a fundamental relationship between knowledge and jouissance which is priviledged as a marker of the "efflorescence of the signifier."[7]

The concept of *lalangue*, therefore, and particularly as it comes to be articulated in the *2nd Rome Discourse*, brings a certain emphasis, not to the side of meaning and representation in the field of language, but to an embodied jouissance. It is where "jouissance deposits iself".[8] At the limit of the question of meaning is encountered the problem which man's jouissance poses for him. In this sense there is no interpretation given through the operation of *lalangue* that does not address the link between speech and jouissance. Interpretation in psychoanalysis, then, is always a gain at the level of jouissance.[9]

Lalangue, therefore, becomes significant within the theoretical articulations concerning interpretation when interpretation is addressed not simply to the meaning of speech, but to jouissance embodied in speech. *Lalangue* takes up the living structure of language—the visceral structure of language in which meaning is tied to jouissance.[10]

How does interpretation touch on that form of knowledge—resident in a jouissance—which defies the categorical arrangement of knowledge from which meaning finds its subsistence? How does interpretation approach a knowledge which it is impossible for the subject to rejoin?

This begins, of course, to sound somewhat mystical; such that we may once again find ourselves in the field of the intuition of thoughts. I am going to be very clear about why this is not the case. Against mysticism, the question we must now pose is: what designates the subject in the vicinity of this knowledge?

In the lesson of 4th November 1971, in *The Knowledge of the Analyst* Seminar, Lacan tells us that, for psychoanalysts, for those who have to deal with the unconscious, the useful aspect of the function of *lalangue*, is logic.[11] Here then we find the second importance of the concept of *lalangue*; in addition to its embodiment of jouissance, it now "incarnates", Lacan contends, a certain logic. It won't have escaped us that terms such as "embodiment" and "incarnate" continue to remind us that *lalangue* has a certain fleshy presence, a certain visceral density.

Such a logic finds its origins in the *logos*, in that which is defined as the art of producing a necessity of discourse. *Lalangue*, as the operator of interpretation, as an embodiment of jouissance and the incarnation of a logic, allows us now to define the logic of interpretation as the art of producing a necessity of discourse.[12] The term of this necessity is to be read as that which is capable of designating the subject in its encounter with a limit to meaning and knowledge.

"It is going to be *necessary* for us to produce", Lacan says, already invoking this logic in the *Ou Pire* Seminar, "a signifier that can be written by the fact that it bars the capital A"[13]—that it bars the Other.

There is only one signifier which is able to designate the subject in the vicinity of this knowledge. It is a signifier which is not produced at the level of the Other, the Other as the locus of meaning, but at the level of logic as the production of a necessity of discourse. At the level of this logic it will be necessary to produce a signifier which bars this Other; to produce it as a "One missing" at the level of the Other, at the level of meaning.[14]

Such a distinction articulates a difference between a grammar of interpretation and a logic of interpretation. The former constitutes what was earlier referred to as the "ordinary meaning" of interpretation.

This very difference is well articulated by Jacques Nassif in a detailed and lengthy intervention he makes in Lacan's Seminar *The Psychoanalytic Act*.[15] In relation to the phenomenon of judgment pertaining to negation, Nassif argues that negation as commonly understood operates at the level of grammar. At this level there is an interdependence, a relation, between negation and affirmation. For example, the negation of {BLACK} is {NOT BLACK}. The negation {NOT BLACK} is all that is excluded from the set {BLACK}. Such a negation maintains the predicative status of the sets, maintaining them as mutually exclusive and without contradiction in a complementary relation.

Differentiated from this is a form of negation said to be logical rather than grammatical. It is distinguished by the fact that it does not operate at the level of the predicative, at the level of the mutual exclusion of categories, therefore producing an encounter with a certain contradiction. Nassif notes that Lacan refers to this form of negation as a "not without"—we find it in the assertion, anxiety is *not without* object, for example. With this operation of negation, we note the presence of a certain contradiction and most importantly for our consideration of interpretation, the dissolution of grammatical categories which guarantee the complementary structure of meaning and knowledge.

Whilst the grammar of interpretation works in the field of meaning, given by the fixity of categories as mutually exclusive, the logic of interpretation moves to the dissolution of such categorical distinctions in language in order to assert the power of a contradiction—an encounter with an impossible at the level of knowledge and meaning.[16] It is at this level that we find interpretation able to address man's relation to his jouissance at the limit of meaning, and an impossible at the level of knowledge.

This logic of interpretation involves the production of a signifier capable of designating the subject at this point. Such a signifier is named by Lacan, and written, not without a certain element of artifice, as *Y a d' l'Un*—there is something of One.

This "One" is emptied of its meaning, emptied of its being, of its function of predication. It is a designative, denotative "One". To this extent, the "One" is referenced against Plato, Kripke and Frege respectively.

Now, what becomes Lacan's specific contribution to this? What becomes Lacan's saying beyond the imputation of all this gathered knowledge? His contribution concerns exactly the specifics of the saying; the necessity of a saying, a saying which makes its way into writing.

In not being able to be deduced, the "One" is to be produced. It is in this production, that it **is** to be produced, that the function of necessity resides. If, as Lacan reminds us, the only necessity is the one that is said, then **it is in the saying of this "One"** that the logic of interpretation is realized. The saying of this "One" breeches the categorical structure of language given by grammar and supportive of the complementarity and integrity of meaning.

As we stated at the outset, this is some distance from the province of what is known but not said. The logic of interpretation as the art of producing a point of necessity in discourse, necessarily moves the discourse of the analysis to an encounter with a real, a knowledge that it is impossible for the subject to rejoin. At this point, a saying, a designation is to be made—it is necessary, as we have noted elsewhere, for the angel not to simply stay, but to say. Therefore, the logic of interpretation arises, not out of the possibility of producing meaning, but of a saying of this "One" when faced with an impossibility which calls for the necessity of a response.

Notes

1. Miller, J. A. "Interpretation in Reverse", in *Psychoanalytical Notebooks 2, 1999. The Unconscious.*

2. Lacan, J. *The Reverse of Psychoanalysis.* 1969–1970. Translated by Cormac Gallagher from unedited French manuscripts. Lesson of 26th November 1969.

3. Lacan, J. *The Third. Intervention at the Rome Congress.* 31.10.74 & 03.11.74. Personal translation.

4. Lacan, J. *The Knowledge of the Analyst.* 1971–1972. Translated by Cormac Gallagher from unedited French manuscripts. Lesson of 2nd December 1971.

5. Lacan, J. *The Reverse of Psychoanalysis.* 1969–1970. Translated by Cormac Gallagher from unedited French manuscripts. Lesson of 17th December 1969.

6. Lacan, J. *Ibid.* Lesson of 11th February 1970.

7. Lacan, J. *Ibid.* Lesson of 26th November 1969.

8. Lacan, J. *The Third.* Op.cit.

9. Lacan, J. *The Knowledge of the Analyst.* Op.cit. Lesson of 4th November 1971.

10. Lacan, J. *The Third.* Op.cit. "The living structure of language is not given because it is in usage … It is not because the unconscious is structured like a language that *lalangue* does not have to play against it's jouissance, since it is made of this jouissance itself."

11. Lacan, J. *The Knowledge of the Analyst.* Op.cit. Lesson of 4th November 1971.

12. Lacan, J. *… Ou pire/… Or worse.* 1971–1972. Translated by Cormac Gallagher from unedited French manuscripts. Lesson of 19th January 1972.

13. Lacan,. J. *Ou Pire. Ibid.* Lesson of 8th March 1972.

14. Lacan, J. *The Psychoanalytic Act.* 1967–1968. Translated by Cormac Gallagher from unedited French manuscripts. Lesson of 28th February 1968.

15. Lacan, J. *Ou Pire.* Op.cit. Lesson of 12th January 1972.

CHAPTER SEVEN

Maltreating the individual

Peter Gunn

I would like to begin by quoting from a commentary on the state of psychoanalysis today:

> The patients of the 1990s are quite different from those of earlier days. They mostly present with narcissistic or depressive symptoms and suffer from loneliness, instability and loss of identity. They no longer wish to undergo long courses of treatment, and refuse to see their analyst regularly enough for the treatment to be useful. Either they skip sessions or they agree to attend only once or twice a week. As soon as they see an improvement in their condition they break off the treatment, invoking a kind of ego omnipotence. When new symptoms appear they go back to their analyst. In short, they treat analysis as a kind of medicine.[1]

This passage comes from an article entitled "Psychoanalysis at the End of the 20th Century: The Situation in France: Clinical and Institutional Prospects". It was written by Elisabeth Roudinesco, the French historian of psychoanalysis, and was published in 1997.

Now I must admit that when I first read this litany of complaint it struck a chord with me. Indeed, if I were to take up Roudinesco's banner, I think I could come up with a few additions to her list of charges concerning the "patient of today". I suspect also that what Roudinesco says will find a reverberation with some readers.

But before we get too comfortable with our concordance on the delinquency of today's patient, I would like to cite another list of charges. Because it comes from a different period, this list is not directed at the patient of today, nor indeed is it directed at anyone identified as a patient. However, the way in which time is positioned in this complaint is not so different to Roudinesco. Neither, as it turns out, is there much difference in the object which is the target of complaint.

> No one can say of the modern English girl that she is tender, loving, retiring, or domestic. The old fault so often found by keen-sighted Frenchwomen, that she was so fatally romanesque, so prone to sacrifice appearances and social advantages for love, will never be set down to the girl of the period. Love indeed is the last thing she thinks of, and the least of the dangers besetting her. ... For all seriousness of thought respecting the duties or the consequences of marriage, she has not a trace.[2]

You might recognise the author from that catchphrase "the girl of the period". In fact, that is the title of the essay: "The Girl of the Period". It is by the nineteenth century English novelist and essayist Eliza Lynn Linton. It was first published in 1868.

Now, not surprisingly, in her lament Linton does not provide us with a list of what we would identify as the symptoms of her girl's delinquency. But her essay is full of warnings about the moral danger in which the girl places herself. In her dress and demeanour she is alleged to model herself on the female denizens of the London demi-monde. According to Linton, for the girl of the period these wantons have everything for which her soul hungers.

But there is a price to be paid, a price for which the girl does not make allowance. This is a deficit the account for which is presented in the currency of morality. To quote Linton, the girl of the period "never stops to reflect at what a price [these wantons] have bought their gains, and what fearful moral penalties they pay for their sensuous pleasures.

Now whilst the ostensible topic of Roudinesco's article is the state of psychoanalysis at the end of the twentieth century the target of her complaint is in fact the same as Linton's: the shameful state of love today. In both cases it is love which does not measure up, a failure which is measured by the standard of the time before. That is, time here is located in a moral economy in which it is the old time which provides the gauge for the goodness of love.

On this measure Roudinesco's patient is as much an egotist as Linton's girl. The patient-of-today is also either unable or unwilling to make the sacrifices necessary for the love which is proper, that love being the love which conforms to the prescriptions of old-time morality. Indeed, what this love preserves is the upright father of sacred memory.

Roudinesco's complaint thus positions the analyst as representative of this ideal of old-time morality. It is precisely in upholding this father-ideal that the analyst finds that the patient's love, that is, her love for him, does not measure up. Yet we are also to imagine that it is by the impress of his authority that the analyst will make up the deficit which insists in the anomic patient-of-today.

Let me now give you an example of one of these brat-patients of today. It is an example which comes from my own practice. But I will in fact take the risk of using this case not to exemplify churlishness in the patient but rather failure in the function of the analyst.

A rather pretty young woman comes to see me. I will, for the moment, call her a girl (and in doing so I confess that I am more than old enough to be her father). It is her first and only visit. Fifteen minutes before the appointed time she rings the doorbell of my consulting room. I receive her. When I do I realise that this is the same girl who, fifteen minutes before that, I had noticed walking past the building and stopping out-side it for a few seconds. I suppose that she had been checking to see whether she had the correct address.

Once seated in my consulting room she has considerable difficulty speaking. Eventually she says that whenever she goes home to see her parents she feels she doesn't fit in. She has fights with them; she doesn't know how to behave around them. She speaks in similar terms both about her childhood and about her present group of girlfriends. She thinks she avoids getting too close to these girls for fear that she will be rejected in the same way that she was rejected by classmates in school.

She is studying, but feels that her parents don't approve of her choice of subjects. They do however support her with an allowance. In order to try to pay her own way she has been trying to find work. Shortly before coming to see me she had found a job selling trinkets to tourists in a market. After a day or two however her boss tells her he does not want her. She thinks this was because she didn't really believe in the job. She was trying to sell things to people who did not really want them. It was this incident which led her to look for someone to talk to.

Her allowance is given to her by her mother who has a small business. Her father's work means that he is often away. When, in reference to who pays her allowance, I say, "Not your father?", she says, "No, I guess he's got other things that he's paying off." But, she says, her father has threatened to take away her allowance, describing her as a spoilt brat.

At the end of the session I invite her to come back and talk further. She says she will telephone me. She does not.

Now in considering the relevance of this material to Roudinesco's complaint allow me, as I have said, to lay that complaint at the address of the analyst rather than at the address to which the patient attends. And at this point I need to add a caveat.

If I am to lay the complaint at that address, the one of the analyst, what I am now going to say about this particular woman (as I will now refer to her) who came to see me should not be understood as some kind of diagnosis, one by which she is reduced to being no more than the contemporary representative of the girl of the period.

As a corollary, I would also like to make it clear that I do not equate the function of the analyst with the imposition of discipline. Rather, in making an example of my patient I aim to make a breach in the moral universe of discipline. If I instance my patient it is in order to elucidate how it is that, in the clinic of today, it is the analyst who continues to reduce his function to that of representation.

I now feel emboldened to propose to you that, in retrospect, my reception of this girl at my door provides her with another allowance, an allowance for the failure of love. It constitutes a fitting-in, an accommodation of the historical economy of wantonness. As such it is a retreat from the logic of lack.

By coming early the girl propositions me. By my appearance I fit myself into the terms of that proposition. This girl's question can then continue to be: What am I worth in that time, in that moral economy of time which the authoritative but absent Father dispenses?

It is, I suggest, into this economy of complaint that this girl of the period places herself, and in the very moment of her refusal to attend to periodic time. Her actual father does not want to pay her time; he has other fish to fry, others for whose time he pays. She feigns indifference, but in order to obscure another question, one which the otherness of her father's desire raises for her.

With what does her own wantonness address her, and with what will she pay for that discovery? Such a question is not without its share of anxiety for both analysand and analyst. This share is not however a debt of a moral kind. My patient indicates this herself. If she comes early to my address and disdains to continue to attend, she does at the same time address me with the untimeliness by which she is herself addressed.

In the light of this perhaps we can say that if the one who comes to the door of an analyst today often absconds, perhaps he has his reasons in what he finds there. Could it be that what he enters into on these occasions is not transference love but an economy of imaginary exchange? In this economy time is the time of the father of the period, and love is the token of appearance, one to be given at the door, whether in the coming or the going.

And if love is here such an imaginary dispensation, a dispensation which the father-analyst assumes in his person, is the patient not already spoken for, documented in his status as individual? In this reception names function only as labels of the kind Roudinesco lists: ego-omnipotence, narcissism, loneliness, depression, instability; the so-named patient herself.

This is not the place for naming as an appropriation from what might be encountered in and through analytic discourse. Names aplenty are already installed in the good sense of the father-analyst. In other words, there is no place for chance. With nothing to lose the so-called patient looks, he (or she) looks to the main chance which the so-called analyst, by appearing, personifies. He looks to what he can take from what is on offer. What is on offer is the address of the so-called analyst in terms of the medicinal seriousness of his thought.

For all the attention given to the individual in this dreary pharmacy some one nevertheless skips the scene for not being attended to. The one who skips away is, I suggest, not this well-known one, which we may label, indifferently, as "individual" or "patient", but the one of speaking, that more obscure one by which the subject is designated.

Now, having said this, it is the case today that such atoms of nothingness do often come to our door, and they do often demand that we dole out medicinal thought. I have, I think, given you an example. But again, we should not fall into the trap of making the particular, contemporary form of this phenomenon an alibi for impotence in the face of what is in fact constitutive for the subject.

It is of course Freud who, already in the nineteenth century, begins to foment the revolution which overthrows the seventeenth century Cartesian notion of the unified subject, that One for which thought functions as a prophylaxis. By 1935 we have the French writer Roger Caillois giving an explicit account of subjective dislocation in the surrealist journal *Minotaure*.

For his account Caillois draws on both his own experience and that of the incorrigibly psychotic. Along with the work of Freud himself, it is this account which, in turn, Lacan drew on in 1936 with the first version of his proposition of the mirror stage.[3] As Lacan developed it, this is nothing less than a new conception of the subject, one in which dislocation is made structuring.

In effect, what Lacan found enabling with Caillois is the way in which that same epidemic of anomie which Roudinesco reports in the neurotic patient-of-today is made to intersect with the endemic. That is, anomie is re-situated in the intersection of the experiential and the structural. Caillois' formulation is worth quoting because of the hallucinatory dimension which it lends to this intertwining:

> To these dispossessed souls, space seems to be a devouring force. Space pursues them, encircles them, digests them in a gigantic phagocytosis. It ends by replacing them. Then the body separates itself from thought, the individual breaks the boundary of his skin and occupies the other side of his senses. He tries to look at himself from any point whatever in space. He feels himself becoming space, dark space where things cannot be put. He is similar, not similar to something, but just similar. And he invents spaces of which he is "the convulsive possession."[4]

Making, as we are, a distinction between the individual, unified by thought and good sense, and the subject, separated forever by the non-sense of speaking from the original unity of the body, one sentence in this passage seems particularly pertinent: "Then the body separates itself from thought, the individual breaks the boundary of his skin and occupies the other side of his senses."

Likewise for Lacan, the sense of the symptom of the individual must be referred to that other side which is structuring for the speaking being.

In his 1948 paper "Aggressiveness in Psychoanalysis" the symptomatic aggregate which he labelled the "emancipated man of modern society" is presented in just this way. Yet in its phenomenal dimension Lacan's characterisation of this "fractured" individual of sixty years past does not seem so different to the one Roudinesco complains about:

> In the "emancipated" man of modern society, this fracturing reveals that his formidable crack goes right to the very depths of his being. It is a self-punishing neurosis, with hysterical/hypochondriacal symptoms of its functional inhibitions, psychasthenic forms of its derealization of other people and of the world, and its social consequences of failure and crime.[5]

But whilst it is true that Lacan is, like Roudinesco, scathing about this individual's so-called "ego omnipotence", his attention to the structural means that he does not make of this an alibi for the analyst. That is, he recognises in this beautiful soul a dispossession which is endemic to the speaking being: the state of dispossession from one's own place, in which state the relation with the little other is experienced as at once rivalrous and phagocytotic.

Let me quote Lacan again:

> It is this touching victim, this innocent escapee who has thrown off the shackles that condemn man to the most formidable social hell whom we take in when he comes to us; it is this being of nothingness for whom, in our daily task, we clear anew the path to his meaning in a discreet fraternity—a fraternity to which we never measure up.[6]

As I read this passage in the light of Lacan's later work, in being addressed by the analysand's demand it is the analyst who is implicated in the anxiety of "not measuring up". This is, again, the "not measuring up" to the little other which is endemic to the speaking being. But in occupying the position of semblance of that absent place of wholeness which the little other represents for his analysand, the function of the analyst is to nevertheless insist on the one of the does-not-measure-up. It is this one which gives the possibility for the subject to arrive at an assumption of his own dis-possession.

This is not the re-possession of identity which the beneficent father-analyst vouchsafes, but the subject's own possession, one which is arrived to from the cutting logic of non-being. It is the subject's own *jouissance*. And, need it be said, this is a form of identification which is beyond the relation of similarity to the other in which narcissistic love is couched.

This of course is easier said than done. With our resituation of Roudinesco's grievance from what appears at the door of the consulting room to that of the position of the analyst as such we are left facing a double exigency. On the one hand there is the obdurate and inescapable demand of the individual. This is a demand for a measure of medicinal love. But the satisfaction of this demand, leading as it does to identification to the analyst, forecloses any possibility of the subject.

On the other hand there in this demand another side. This is a not-known demand but one which is equally obdurate. It is a hating demand which is also a demand to be treated with hate. In anticipating that we will not measure up, this demand also anxiously demands that we not measure up; it demands that we not know in order that we not measure the subject by the units of that first demand for love.

This demand demands, in fine, that rather than responding to that bell,[7] signalling by this sign of love our continuity with the beforehand-time of this one called the individual, we instead exact from that one something which does not cease to insist as hiatus in his relation to love. Only by such mal-treatment might that one come to be subjected to the *jouissance* of the time-at-hand, his own one time of speaking-to-be.

Notes

1. Roudinesco E. (1997). Psychoanalysis at the end of the 20th Century: The Situation in France: Clinical and Institutional Prospects. *http://www. ipa.org.uk/newsletter/97-1/roudin.htm*
2. Linton E. L. (2006)., The Girl of the Period. In Stephen Greenblatt, M. H. Abrams, Carol T. Christ (Eds.), *The Norton Anthology of English literature*, 8th Edition, Volume E: The Victorian Age. New York: W. W. Norton. Thie text is also available at http://erc.lib.umn.edu/dynaweb/victorian/lintgirl/@Generic__BookView
3. For an account of the vicissitudes of Lacan's attempts to put forward his theory of the mirror stage see Gallop J. (1983). Lacan's "Mirror Stage": Where to Begin. *SubStance*, *11*, 4: 118–128.

4. Caillois R. (1983). Mimicry and Legendary Psychasthenia. *October*, *31*, Winter: 16–32, p. 30. The article was originally published in 1935 in the surrealist journal *Minotaure*.

5. Lacan J. (2006). Aggressiveness in Psychoanalysis. In Bruce Fink (Trans.), *Écrits: The First Complete Edition in English* (pp. 82–101), New York: W. W. Norton, p. 101.

6. Lacan J. (2006), p. 101.

7. In addition to its more familiar reference the word "bell" can also refer to the cry of a stag or buck at rutting time.

CHAPTER EIGHT

The child and seduction[1]

Michael Plastow

At the beginning of the twenty-first century, we are witness to a culture of the blame of the Other for one's suffering. Amongst some of our colleagues we hear cries of "sexual abuse" or any other variety of "abuse" on the basis of particular symptoms or certain clinical presentations such as anorexia nervosa or "borderline personality disorder" which is said to be "emerging" when the presentation does not conform to the manual and the patient is a minor. In such cries we note an excessive insistence on history, as well as a conflation of history with the cause of the suffering of the child.

Such an insistence on history is also found in Freud's formulation of the seduction hypothesis. Here we can examine the relevance and place of the seduction hypothesis and its abandonment to psychoanalysis and clinical practice today. In doing so we can assert that these are essential components of each and every analysis.

Let us then revisit the seduction hypothesis and its abandonment from this angle. In 1896, in a series of papers, Freud presented a theory about hysteria which became known as the "seduction hypothesis".[2] According to this hypothesis the existence and symptomatology of hysteria found their origin in infantile sexual experiences. These "experiences" though were not able to be remembered by Freud's patients but were "unconscious" and elicited through his treatment of them. Nonetheless it was the father of the patient who was primarily implicated in such scenes of seduction.

In proposing such a theory, Freud believed he had found the aetiology of hysteria in the early history of the patient, a history obscured by amnesia, which he later came to refer to as "infantile amnesia".[3] Here we can define the seduction hypothesis as an attempt to define one's suffering through a reference to one's history.

However in 1897, specifically in his letter of 21st September to Wilhelm Fliess, Freud abandoned his belief in the seduction hypothesis with the following words: "I no longer believe in my *neurotica*",[4] that is, in his theory of the neuroses.

Whilst elaborating this theory, Freud was also conducting his self-analysis. In fact it has been proposed that Freud's self-analysis is one that he undertook primarily in his correspondence to Fliess,[5] in transference to Fliess, whom he took to have a special knowledge of neurotic suffering. Even if this conceptualisation of Freud's self-analysis is open to question,[6] we must take note of these two parallel aspects of his writings to Fliess, that of the personal in which Freud recounts his own neurotic suffering, his "little hysteria"[7] as he calls it, and the clinical and theoretical side through which he expounds the beginnings of psychoanalytic theory.

Freud gives three reasons for no longer believing in his "*neurotica*". The second of these is:

> ... the surprise that in *all* cases, the *father*, not excluding my own, had to be accused of being perverse.[8] [My italics]

Here we see this parallel between the results of Freud's self-analysis and the theory expounded from his clinical practice which makes of the seduction hypothesis a *universal*. Hence seduction necessarily has to be posited in "all" cases in order to account for the symptoms of hysteria by reference to history.

Of course the critiques of Freud's abandonment of the seduction hypothesis are well known, from Jeffrey Masson's *Assault on Truth*,[9] to the feminist and trauma theory critique.[10] These posit that Freud denied the reality of the sexual abuse of children. Such critiques place their insistence on an historical truth. In any case, according to Laplanche and Pontalis:

> Right up to the end of his life, Freud continued to assert the existence, prevalence and pathogenic force of scenes of seduction actually experienced by children.[11]

In other words what is in question here is something quite different.

On the other hand, psychoanalysts have maintained that Freud's abandonment of the seduction hypothesis was a defining moment in psychoanalysis in Freud's discovery of unconscious fantasy and the Oedipus Complex. Indeed Freud states in this letter that:

> ... there would remain the solution that the sexual fantasy invariably seizes upon the theme of the parents.[12]

... thus noting that it is the Oedipus Complex, as he came to call this later on, rather than seduction *per se*, that is invariable, or universal. Here the Oedipus Complex refers to something beyond the individual history, something one then comes to inhabit. "[Freud] placed seduction", note Laplanche and Pontalis, "in the last analysis, amongst the "primal phantasies" whose origin he dates back to the pre-history of humanity",[13] in other words *outside* of history as lived.

In Freud's letter of the 21st September 1897, he gives as his third reason for no longer believing in the seduction hypothesis:

> ... the certain insight that there are no indications of reality in the unconscious, so that one cannot distinguish between truth and fiction ...[14]

So here the distinction of fact and fantasy, truth and fiction, is not one that exists in the unconscious and thus not a relevant division for psychoanalysis. Hence fantasy becomes a necessary fiction, but at the same time the fantasy is what carries the truth of the subject's encounter with the enigma of sex, however encountered. Thus fantasy structures one's existence including what is taken for one's history, therefore determining what one takes as "reality".

So if for psychoanalysis the distinction between truth and fantasy does not function, how then can we read Freud's seduction hypothesis and its abandonment? If there is a distinction to be marked it is surely the one to which we have already alluded, that of the history of the subject as a *lived history*, and the seduction hypothesis as a distant inaccessible *time*, a time outside of this lived history which is struck by amnesia.

In other words this remote time is a logical posit, a structural necessity which grounds the individual history by marking that which lies outside of that history, that which is not able to be accounted for by that history. We have already noted that one of the ways by which Freud refers to this is in terms of a "pre-history", that is, a *time* outside of history. He also writes of the "phylogenetic inheritance" as that which lies outside of the individual history. Here we can cite Freud from the *Wolf Man* case:

> All that we find in the *prehistory* of neuroses is that a child catches hold of this phylogenetic inheritance *where his own experience fails him*. [My italics][15]

In this way Freud places a limit on history in its determination of the individual psychopathology. In other words, not all of one's suffering is able to be explicated by reference to one's own history.

Here I would like to take up this differentiation of *history* as lived, and *time* as a structural referent outside of history, by reference to the contemporary Italian thinker, Giorgio Agamben, particularly in reference to his paper *In Playland*.[16] Here he opposes the two notions of *play* and *ritual* through an analysis of a section of Collodi's novel *Pinocchio*. Agamben proposes that:

> Every conception of *history* is invariably accompanied by a certain experience of *time* which is implicit in it, conditions it, and thereby has to be elucidated.[17] [My italics]

Let us then attempt to use this differentiation to explicate the notion of *time* in reference to *history*. Now Agamben, drawing on the writings of Claude Lévi-Strauss, has something quite interesting to say about play and ritual. For Agamben ritual and play both keep a relation to time (calendar) and history, but this relationship is an inverse one. He notes that rites transform events, that is, lived history, into structures, specifically the synchronic structure of time. Play on the other hand transforms structures into events.

So ritual fixes and structures the calendar, or "cyclical time";[18] play, on the other hand, changes it and destroys it. That is, again according to Agamben:

... play ... is a machine for transforming synchrony (time) into diachrony (history).[19]

Here we can interpose clinical practice and posit ritual as *repetition* which ensures that things structurally remain the same and therefore synchronous, such as we encounter in the phenomenon of *repetition compulsion*. It is also this same ritual by which the calendar, or timetable, of the obsessional is marked. Play, on the other hand, is what a child does in a session. For the adult, in reference to clinical practice, play is the play of the signifier, the speaking by free association as the method by which psychoanalysis proceeds.

But whether it is the play of the child or the play of speech of the adult, the effect of this play, to take up Agamben's proposition, is to transform structure into events. Now if the *time* of seduction, as we have spoken of it, is a structural referent, it is specifically this structure that would be transformed into an event in the psychoanalytic session. That is to say that the play of words tends to historicise this structure, to construct the seduction as an event.

Now Freud in his self-analysis, at least initially takes up the position that his parents are implicated in, and effectively responsible for, his suffering. Through the analysis of his own dreams and parapraxes, his proposition takes on a specifically sexual flavour and he reaches a provisional conclusion that he must have been subject to seduction at the hands of his father. Moreover, in regard to *all* of his patients, he provisionally reaches the same conclusion.

Such a complaint is also familiar to us in our daily clinical practice. We could summarise the position of the patient presenting for analysis in the following way: "If only I'd had a decent mother and father, if only they had treated me and loved me as I imagine I should have been, and not how they did, then I would never have turned out like this".

We can hear the very same sentiment in the words of the poet, in this case the British poet Phillip Larkin in a more succinct and franker manner. In the first stanza to his well-known poem *This Be the Verse* he notes:

> They fuck you up, your mum and dad.
> They may not mean to but they do.
> They fill you with the faults they had
> And add some extra just for you.

We can hear this proposition "They fuck you up", in at least three ways. Firstly that through their sexual act, their primal scene from which you are absent, they beget you. Secondly that "they fuck you up" literally, or in Freud's terminology they "seduce" you. And thirdly in the figurative sense "they" are the cause of your suffering. Just like Freud proposed in his abandonment of the seduction hypothesis, that "in all cases ... the father had to be accused of being perverse", here Larkin also proposes this, in reference to a "they" as a generalised proposition, as a universal. We might propose that this complaint, this form of the seduction hypothesis, is the universal complaint of the neurotic, a position from which any analysis might begin.

However if we are proposing that each analysis might begin with the seduction hypothesis, we might equally propose that the abandonment of the seduction hypothesis is the work, the movement required in order to be able to finish an analysis. We have examined this already in relation to both Freud's self-analysis and the movement in Freud's work with his hysterical patients. In order to finish his self-analysis, Freud has to both abandon his individual seduction hypothesis, as well as abandon his belief in Fliess' hypotheses regarding neurosis. Freud gives as his first reason for the abandonment of the seduction hypothesis:

> The continual disappointment in my efforts to bring a single analysis to a real conclusion.[20]

The abandonment of the seduction hypothesis then allows the possibility of concluding an analysis. This requires, amongst other things, the disinvestment in the Other's responsibility for one's suffering, which is the primordial aspect of the seduction hypothesis, posited in sexual terms, or given a sexual meaning. To abandon this position is to apprehend what lacks in this account, what fails in this historicised account of the event of seduction. It is also to take on the fact that one's history is not able to account for one's suffering. In this way we encounter the very limits of seduction and of history as a causal hypothesis. This is what we can refer to as castration.

The philosopher Emmanuel Levinas proposed that:

> My existence is a fact not reducible to evidence.

Here is connoted a point where the evidence of history fails, leaving a gaping chasm in the place of cause, and thus disarticulating cause from history.

So if the seduction hypothesis and its abandonment were both necessary steps in Freud's self-analysis and in the foundation of psychoanalytic theory, they are also fundamental steps in the possibility of beginning and of concluding each and every analysis. An analysis allows the repositioning of the primordial complaint regarding the Other, which can take the form of one's parents. Thus to abandon one's seduction hypothesis requires one to sustain a loss of the very hypothesis upon which the supposed evidence of one's existence has hitherto been based.

Notes

1. Paper presented at *International Congress of Psychoanalysis. The child and adolescent in the XXI century: psychoanalytic, political and social challenges*, in Recife, Brazil, Oct-Nov 2008, under the title *A criança e a sedução: o lugar da hipótese da sedução e seu abandono na psicanálise contemporânea*.
2. Israëls, H., Schatzman, M. "The seduction theory". *History of Psychiatry*, iv (1993), pp. 23–59.
3. Pereira, D. "The Infans and the (K)not of history". *Papers of the Freudian School of Melbourne* 20 (1999): pp. 59–71.
4. Masson, J. (ed.) *The Complete Letters of Sigmund Freud to Wilhelm Fliess: 1887–1904*. Belknap Press, Cambridge Mass., 1985, p. 264.
5. Anzieu, D. *Freud's Self-Analysis*. The International Psycho-Analytical Library, 118, 1986.
6. Porge, E. *Freud Fließ: Mythe et chimère de l'auto-analyse*. Anthropos, Paris, 1996.
7. Masson, J. (ed.) *Op. cit.*, p. 261.
8. *Ibid.*, p. 264.
9. Masson, J. *The Assault on Truth: Freud's Suppression of the Seduction Theory*. New York, 1984.
10. Herman, J. L. *Trauma and Recovery: from Domestic Abuse to Political Terror*. Harper Collins, London, 1992.
11. Laplanche, J., Pontalis, J. -B. *The Language of Psycho-Analysis*. The Hogarth Press, London, 1985, p. 406.
12. Masson, J. (ed.) *The Complete Letters of Sigmund Freud to Wilhelm Fliess: 1887–1904*. Belknap Press, Cambridge Mass., 1985, pp. 264–265.
13. Laplanche, J. & Pontalis, J. -B. *Op. Cit.*, p. 407.

14. Masson, J. (ed.) *The Complete Letters of Sigmund Freud to Wilhelm Fliess: 1887–1904*. Belknap Press, Cambridge Mass., 1985, p. 264.
15. Freud, S. "From the History of an Infantile Neurosis". *SE* XVII, p. 97.
16. Agamben, G. "In Playland: reflections on history and play". In: *Infancy and History: on the destruction of experience*. (trans. Heron, L.) Verso, London, 1993.
17. Agamben, G. "Time and history: Critique of the instant and the continuum". In: *Infancy and History: on the destruction of experience*. (trans. Heron, L.) Verso, London, 1993, p. 99.
18. Agamben, G. "In Playland: reflections on history and play". Op. cit., p. 73.
19. *Ibid.*, p. 74.
20. Masson, J. (ed.) *The Complete Letters of Sigmund Freud to Wilhelm Fliess: 1887–1904*. Belknap Press, Cambridge Mass.: 1985, p. 264.

CHAPTER NINE

How to do a psychoanalytic clinic: a recipe for madness

Peter Gunn

There are many manuals for treatment, not the least of them being the *Diagnostic and Statistical Manual of Mental Disorders* (DSM), the fifth revision of which is slated to appear in 2013. The DSM could be described as providing a categorisation of madness in the service of treatment, treatment being directed to managing madness, frequently with the assistance of medication. In a psychoanalysis, by contrast, it is madness itself, that particular form of madness known as the transference, which serves the treatment.

It is said, however, that transference is a form of love. If then we were to take our lead from the catalogue of the seducer would not the treatment which the psychoanalyst proposes also be amenable to just such a categorisation?

To begin to explore this question let us, to start with, see what Socrates has to say about manuals of seduction in the generality.

At the beginning of Plato's *Phaedrus*[1] Socrates has a chance encounter. He meets Phaedrus who is about to walk to a quiet spot by the river Ilissus, apparently to memorise a speech he has just heard by Lysias concerning love. Lysias' thesis is that it is better for a good-looking boy to give in to the advances of a non-lover than to those of a lover because, unlike the lover, the non-lover is not mad.

On hearing about Lysias' speech Socrates is keen to hear it. Phaedrus is however reluctant to repeat it, saying that he hasn't as yet learnt it by heart and that, in any event, he could not do justice to the work of such a master as Lysias. He is however persuaded to do so by a little story which Socrates then tells.

In the story Phaedrus, so-named but now referred to in the third person as a character in the story, has already memorised Lysias' speech. He has done this only by having listened to Lysias repeat it several times and, finally in some desperation, by borrowing Lysias' written scroll.

This Phaedrus' reluctance to repeat the speech is feigned. He is in fact in such a frenzy to practice what he has just memorised that he is prepared to force anyone who he comes across to be his audience. Going for a walk outside the city walls he meets such a one. Fortuitously this one happens to be a lover of discourse and "sick with passion" to listen to speeches.

At the end of his story Socrates returns quite abruptly to direct speech. He makes a demand of the real Phaedrus saying, "Show me what you've got in your left hand under your clothing". At this injunction Phaedrus produces the scroll and confirms the truth of Socrates' story.

Claiming to be bewitched by Phaedrus dangling this scroll in front of him,[2] Socrates then accompanies Phaedrus to the spot by the river in order, apparently, to listen to him read from Lysias' scroll. As they arrive Phaedrus conjectures that it may be the very place that figures in one of the myths. He asks Socrates whether he thinks this myth is true.

In response Socrates says that the myth is in fact set at another place, one which is further downstream. He takes this as an opportunity to criticise those who interpret myths in order to make them conform to what is probable, wanting, for example, to "correct" the appearance of such impossible hybrid creatures as the Centaur and the Chimaera.

Socrates then makes the following declaration: "As for me, I never have time to spend on these things, and there's a good reason for this, my friend: I am still incapable of obeying the Delphic inscription and knowing myself."

What I've presented here of the Phaedrus is taken from only a part of the first two hundred or so lines of the dialogue. It is clear nevertheless that Socrates is moving to take up a different position on this madness of love than that of either Phaedrus or his master Lysias. In particular, by following his dismissal of Phaedrus' question regarding the truth of the myth with this reference to the Delphic oracle Socrates already indicates that for him it is truth itself which, being at once external and yet also quite personal, is maddening.

It is this maddening truth which Socrates has time for. And it is, I think, also this maddening truth with which psychoanalysis is preoccupied. But before we move on to some direct speaking in order to take up this preoccupation, let us try to abstract something further about this truth of which Socrates speaks.

The things which Socrates has no time for include those interpretations which have as their end conformity, conformity to the probable. He dismisses those who would reduce myth to this status, attempting to assign them meaning by reference to the standard of the already given, whether in the form of a true story, a veritable piece of history, or in the form of the image of the familiar. And we can see as well that with his gentle, tongue-in-cheek ridicule of Phaedrus' project of memorising and repeating Lysias' speech Socrates is also dismissing the already given whether as already written or as already said.[3]

Furthermore, Socrates rejects Lysias' thesis. In doing so he quotes one line from a poet by the name of Stesichorus. Story has it that this Stesichorus had been made blind by the gods for telling a false tale about them. When he recants he uses the same words which Socrates quotes: "False was the tale". At that point his sight is restored.

It may seem paradoxical that Socrates should present his rejection of Lysias' thesis in the form of a repetition of the words of another concerning truth. But Socrates seeks here to indicate that his difficulty with Lysias is not one which could be resolved empirically, for example, by doing some fieldwork on the best technique for seducing boys, but has rather to do with the very order of truth which Lysias' thesis promulgates. By contrast with the truth of the gods, the truth of Lysias' thesis has the same blinding or mesmerising effect as any such repetition, including the kind of repetition to which Phaedrus would reduce myth.

Thus if Socrates quotes these words of the poet at this point it is only to highlight that it is this order of truth which, as the restoration of sight at the moment of his declaration indicates, they had for the poet. This is not a truth which concerns the veracity of the tale about the tale about Stesichorus, or indeed of any tale in which the gods make an appearance, but one which concerns the falsity of any such tale *per se*.

This quotation of the words of the poet is an interpolation in the dialogue. As such it is has the same status as the tale Socrates himself tells about Phaedrus. In being set out from the dialogue in this way these interpolations are granted the status of propositions, propositions whose truth is not to be assessed by reference to any supposed reality but by their designation of something at once personal and beyond.

But if Socrates does not have time for the kinds of things of which Phaedrus' repetition is an example, why then does he have time for Phaedrus? We might conjecture that he is in fact putting into practice with Phaedrus some recipe of his own for seduction. But here we need to return to what Socrates' does have time for: a repetition, but one bearing on his own inability to know himself. What Socrates discerns in Phaedrus' mania to repeat is this other kind of repetition.

All of Socrates' propositions to Phaedrus undercut the comfortable linking of his mania to repeat with his mesmerised love of what, in the form of the phallic scroll, the other supposedly possesses. In particular, it is by what Socrates says directly to him concerning this scroll that we can see that Socrates' approach to Phaedrus is indeed fully that of a lover. And it is fully that of a lover because of what, in its very directness, this approach lacks. Direct speech carries indirection in the very speaking of it; this is both its madness and its truth.

What Socrates is possessed *by* is the madness of love, *eros*, a contagion which is a variety of what the Greeks called *enthusiasmos*, that is, the inhabitation of a human soul by a god.[4] This *enthusiasmos* is of the same order as those things which are told of in myth; if myths can be said to be "tales" in the telling they remain impossible injunctions from the gods. What Socrates is inhabited by then is of the order of this impossible, one which both inhabits the subject in his very speech and is yet external and beyond. Socrates is a lover of discourse of this kind, where impossibility rewrites itself.

It is also clear from the dialogue that if Socrates is inhabited by this God-given force, this "enthusiasm", if we can take the liberty of translating the Greek word in this way, it is only inasmuch as he himself is shown, in the face of questioning by the gods, to be incorrigibly lacking. If he remains incapable of obeying the Delphic injunction, "Know thyself!" it is inasmuch as he is possessed by such enthusiasm that he is driven out of his mind.[5]

What Socrates actually demands therefore from Phaedrus is not the scroll possessed by Lysias but rather, we might say, Phaedrus' account of his own not-the-scroll. In other words, given that, in the face of the question "What have you got?", Phaedrus has been shown to lack, Socrates demands that he nevertheless articulate that lack.

When Socrates propositions Phaedrus by reference to what he possesses hidden under his clothes he does so as a lover. If in so-doing he gives the appearance of inviting Phaedrus to embrace him bodily, this is only a ruse. In its formality as a proposition, this approach takes the form of an invitation to Phaedrus that he too be possessed by the subjective disparity of which, oddly enough, Socrates himself speaks with such enthusiasm.

Let us now leave Plato and go directly to Freud. We know that, with an irony rather reminiscent of that of Socrates, it is to hearsay that Freud assigns the means by which psychoanalysis, that is, psychoanalysis in the abstract, might be known: "... you cannot be present as an audience at a psychoanalytic treatment. You can only be told about it; and, in the strictest sense of the word, it is only by hearsay that you will get to know psychoanalysis."[6] This is, Freud tells us, hearsay in the "strictest sense of the word"; this is a knowing by hearing, and then ... saying.

At first glance then what Freud appears to be promulgating is Phaedrus' "method" of knowing: one falls in love with what one hears and then repeats it. And here, as we have seen, truth is of the order of that which might be known from repetition of the said; that is, it is reduced to what can be abstracted from the already known.

It would seem then that what is called for is an "abstract" or manual of psychoanalysis, perhaps akin to the scroll of Lysias' speech on seduction. For it is also true, is it not, that you cannot be present as an audience at a seduction; two's company, three's a crowd! Yet Freud never produced such a manual. But neither did he lose his enthusiasm for attempting to transmit something about the value of psychoanalysis.

Indeed, it is not coincidental that Freud says these words at the commencement of one of his more concerted attempts to transmit something about psychoanalysis to a general audience, the *Introductory Lectures*. We might recall also what he says at the beginning of the lecture on transference love. Referring to the method of psychoanalysis he says, "I shall not ... tell it to you, but shall insist on your discovering it for yourselves."[7]

The position Freud adopts in not stopping in his attempt to transmit something of this value of psychoanalysis, is not unlike that of Socrates: that of the seducer. And like Socrates, and as with any seducer, there is some dissimulation, some artifice, in this. But this is only similarity, a similarity which refers to what we might call "normal" seduction, that is, to the seduction of the ortho-dox. What sets this method of Socrates and Freud apart is its para-dox.

Like Socrates, as a seducer Freud acts only as a pimp, a tell-tale. He is an agent for that One which really has It and of whom he too is a lover. In this contradictory position he is coy. "I might tell you about it", says Freud in effect, "because I might know it", he says, "but then if I did it would not be 'it', but hearsay. So I refuse to tell you. If you want to know, you'll have to discover 'it' for yourself."

Freud in effect differentiates hearsay from an It whereby another order of truth is designated. This truth is the paradoxical, impossible kind characteristic of the tales of the gods. Thus Freud's 'I shall not tell it to you' is not an assertion made within the bounds of a truth already given, but is itself a negation of such bounds; it is, we might say, a NOT-assertion, that is, an assertion of negation, of the order, "that's not it". We could say then that such an assertion designates a truth that lies beyond, or, to be at once more succinct, more precise, and more personal, it designates a truth that lies: tales told according to the imperative of this order of truth are always false, but because impossible.

Now I must confess that in preparing to write this paper, and indeed, even as I wrote, I did not know what I would write. I did consult some written material. Also, strangely enough, I had with me a kind of scroll, what in common parlance is called an abstract. And so now, with "these things" in mind, let us return, finally, to where I began before I began to write this paper: to that abstract.

Let me take the risk of quoting from this abstract here: "To offer the possibility of a psychoanalysis is not to represent something for someone; it does not sustain the Other. Nevertheless there is a function of representation, an artifice, which is necessary. This paper will explore the paradox which lies at the conjunction of the proposition of a psychoanalytic practice and the necessary style of any such practice."

Now, if this abstract means anything it is that the founding of a psychoanalytic practice constitutes an offer, a proposition; a proposition to some one that they might themselves be present at a psychoanalytic treatment. But what is it then that, in the abstract, is being proposed? What is it that is offered when, logically, any psychoanalytic treatment can be no more than supposed?

Like Socrates proposition to Phaedrus concerning the falsity of Lysias' thesis, this proposition of a psychoanalytic treatment, or indeed, to begin with, of a psychoanalytic practice, should, as a proposition, be taken in the abstract, that is, it should be read formally, in terms of logic. In itself this proposition does not represent psychoanalysis as being this or that; in particular, it does not represent psychoanalysis as offering a therapeutic counterpart to any demand for a cure.

The offer of an analysis is a proposition which makes an offer but does not offer anything in particular, except, that is, what one might suppose of an analysis at which one is not present and, by extension, what one might suppose of the one, a psychoanalyst, who makes such an offer. What is of significance here is what is entailed for some one, in their particularity, in being addressed by another, and addressed under the auspices of psychoanalysis.

Now, as Lacan reminds us in *Le Sinthome* seminar, what might be supposed of psychoanalysis and the psychoanalyst bears on the link between what is supposed of two other, quite famous suppositions: the psychoanalyst's couch and the bed of the sexual relationship.[8] But if there is a seduction involved in the link between these two suppositions, it is, as Lacan suggests with a play on words in French, by way of being a *lie*.

Whereas the first of these suppositions, concerning the psychoanalyst's couch, bears on the possible of the imaginary, the second, concerning the sexual relationship, bears on the impossible of the real. And it is in this lie, a lie which is of the order of a paradox or impasse, that there lies the truth of a psychoanalysis. This proposition of a psychoanalytic treatment then is akin to Socrates' question to Phaedrus: it is an address to some one concerning what they have upon them, but concealed. That is, it concerns the symptom which lies hidden, as it might be, under the clothes, but only inasmuch as it bears, in its articulation, on a truth by which they are possessed, being upon them, yet which lies elsewhere.

And if some one is seduced by the offer to be present at their own psychoanalysis then the psychoanalyst will also be present. And this is where the real art enters the picture. The psychoanalyst will indeed be present, presenting all of his or her imaginary attributes, including, perhaps, a couch. But in being present the psychoanalyst will, if they are a psychoanalyst, necessarily also make present in their practice that consistency which is the mark of a particular style.[9]

This is the same necessity, the same enthusiasm, to which Socrates alludes when talking about the things he has time for. This necessity engenders a very personal repetition which, strangely enough, is borne on a negation. Like Socrates, the psychoanalyst is, still, NOT capable of knowing himself. And it is precisely because of the *enthusiasm* engendered by the encounter with this impossible that he is able to put his style into practice, style which the seventeenth century naturalist Le Comte de Buffon identified, despite himself, as being the symptom of man; that is, nothing, nothing ... other than ... the man himself.

Notes

1. I am primarily relying on the translation in Plato (2002). *Phaedrus*. Robin Waterfield (Trans.), Oxford: Oxford World Classics, Oxford University Press. My reading of the *Phaedrus* draws to some extent on Waterfield's introduction and, to a somewhat greater extent, on Andrea Wilson Nightingale's essay on the *Phaedrus* entitled "Alien and Authentic Discourse" (in Nightingale A. W. (1995). *Genres in Dialogue*. Cambridge: Cambridge University Press, pp. 133–171). The rather tendentious reading which I offer here is however my own.
2. I have taken a slight liberty here; Socrates does not refer to being bewitched by the scroll until a little later in the dialogue.
3. See Nightingale (1995).
4. See Nightingale (1995), pp. 159–60.
5. See Nightingale (1995), p. 160.
6. Freud S. (1916–17). Introductory Lectures on Psychoanalysis. *Standard Edition XV*, p. 18.
7. Freud S. (1916–17). Introductory Lectures on Psychoanalysis. *Standard Edition XVI*, p. 431.
8. Lacan J. (1976). *Le sinthome*. Seminar of 1975–76, lesson of 17th February 1976, unpublished English translation by Cormac Gallagher.
9. Cf. Etkin G. (1992). The Lacanian Clinic. In Felicity Bagot, Linda Clifton, David Pereira (Eds.), *Papers of The Freudian School of Melbourne, 13*, 125–132. Melbourne: The Freudian School of Melbourne.

CHAPTER TEN

The Gospel according to Saint Jacques

Rodney Kleiman

In the year 1921, Sigmund Freud and his wife suffered the tragic and unexpected loss of their daughter. She was twenty-six years of age, mother of two and a young and healthy woman; dead from influenza.

Freud wrote to his friend Ferenczi:

> Since I am profoundly irreligious there is no one I can accuse, and I know there is nowhere to which any complaint could be addressed. The unvarying circle of a soldier's duties, and the "sweet habit of existence" will see to it that things go on as before.

Is there a greater obstacle that could be placed in the path of life and work than such grief, so outside of the natural order of generation? What can question life as to its meaning more intensely than the tragic intrusion of untimely death? Are Freud's words sufficient to provide adequate explanation as to what allowed him to continue his work under these circumstances? As he did keep working, when confronted with the perils of war, the loss of his life savings, his own cancer and the years of pain that accompanied it and finally his expulsion from his homeland. I think he had more than just the force of habit, however sweet, to drive him.

What allows one to keep going and working in the face of life's losses and turmoil? How do we deal with the bereavements and all those more frequent aspects of life; sickness, aging, disappointment?

God in his various incarnations has provided many with consolation. He has held out the promise of future happiness whether in this life or the next and the prospect of a reward for perseverance, decrying therein the attractions of the various forms of suicide, the quick and the slow. God has provided the meaning to guide us through these travails in the company of a religious morality, tempted by a karmic future and a more bounteous reincarnation as recompense for good behaviour. But without God, godless like Freud, what will motivate our endeavours?

I ask because these are as much my questions as anyone's but also because, of course, as an analyst, these are the questions one hears asked daily in various forms in a psychoanalytic clinic. What's the point of it all? Why bother? It remains no doubt a temptation to reply with words of support, disguised in a humanistic veil, but espousing nonetheless some religious sentiment. In those many moments where someone speaks of the overwhelming loss and grief that accompanies human existence, it is tempting to turn to some other form of consolation. What better form of consolation than to believe in a higher purpose, a divine enterprise, a meaning from without, outside the lived experience.

One is tempted to reply thus: "Have faith! Believe in the intrinsic goodness of mankind. Believe life has some extrinsic meaning." It is tempting but ultimately leads to the same problematic as the promises of the preacher. "Didn't you say I would be happy in the end?" comes the retort.

What differentiates the psychoanalytic approach from the religious? What keeps the godless psychoanalyst working? Does the analyst just believe in a different god, in the truth of the unconscious and therefore proffer that as the place of ultimate meaning? Are we then any different to the priests, who at least are open about their belief in the place of the Almighty. Is psychoanalysis a religion, albeit with a different god, the all-powerful unconscious?

It's a reasonable question since no amount of loud and public avowal of atheism provides any guarantee. The most vociferous atheists believe the most strongly in their own personal moral code and their own personal religion.

God has not been truly removed from the equation by negation but persists in disguise, made in one's own image. How does an analyst truly avoid the moralizing which is at the heart of all religion?

A quotation of Lacan to assist our thoughts.

> And as long as things are said, the God Hypothesis will persist. That is why, in the end, only theologians can be truly atheistic, namely, those who speak of God.[1]

Thus we will need to speak of God, openly, in order to aspire to be atheists. Not just any God, not the white bearded human version, but the concept of God which has been defined in numerous ways over the ages and by many characteristics. God has been conveyed by terms such as omnipotence, the creator, the unmoved mover, the all loving, pure thought, etc. I will approach the concept of God through the question of knowledge. Omniscience, an absolute relation to knowledge, could well be the most important defining characteristic of God. It is, after all, questions with which we begin our researches, sexual and otherwise and who knows the answers?

> Who then knows whence it has arisen
> Whence this emanation has arisen,
> Whether God disposed it, or whether he did not, -
> Only he who is its overseer in highest heaven knows.
> Or perhaps he does not know!

These words from Hindu scriptures have been dated to 1500 B.C. thus exposing a chronology which emphasizes that these questions are somewhat long in the answering.

Citing another sentence from Lacan.

> It is indubitable that the symbolic is the basis of what was made into God.[2]

In the beginning was the word. Language presides at the entry of man into symbols and speech. And the word was God. Is not the word still God? We can surely render a quite servicable icon for our religious inclinations out of the image of the unconscious. Does not the unconscious possess attributes which could easily be the same as those of the religious God?

The unconscious as God is the creator, for the word gives substance to the thing. Also God the moral guardian named as the ravaging punitive superego. God, the source of all love and meaning, is unconscious desire. The unconscious knows what we do not know, it knows all about us. The unconscious is all knowing, omniscient, a God. As an all powerful force, it leads us on the path to our neurotic destiny, like Oedipus, victim of fate. It controls our desires, inhibits our lust, and it forces us to repeatedly go in directions contrary to the dictates of conscious rationality.

Before Freud recognised this power of the unconscious, that lies within yet is exterior to our being, man had already named it, this unconscious. And its name was God.

It is because man has been subjected to the power of speech and the world constructed thus by words, that God as a concept has come into being.

> It is indubitable that the symbolic is the basis of what was made
> into God.[3]

Of this fact, Lacan states, we should take note, for it is beyond doubt, indubitable. What does it mean to go beyond doubt? If psychoanalysis deals with the unseen forces which dictate our live's paths, how is an analysis different from "getting to know God", as they say. To know God is to know yourself. It is to know the Truth. But the truth can only be half said. Should we not be wary and attempt to avoid the apparently certain beliefs of religion? Should we not be wary of someone, even Lacan, saying the word, "indubitable". What makes him so certain? Why does he even use such a term as indubitable? If he is so certain should we not follow the word that is his word?

The good news, the gospel, is the news of the truth of God as spoken on earth by Jesus. Is this the new gospel, the word of the truth, of the analyst, of Lacan? No. But why not?

It is my assertion that psychoanalysis and religion can be and should be ultimately logically differentiated according to important principles. Psychoanalysis is not a religion.

This does not preclude, in fact probably it dictates, the occurrence of a type of practice calling itself psychoanalysis, which is but a disguised religion.

When this distinction is lost we have lost the real possibilities of psychoanalysis, for this religious analysis has neither more nor less to offer than any other creed or belief structure. I'm not saying psychoanalysis is a better answer to life's dilemmas but it is a different one, better for me, but not for everyone. Many have and will prefer the religious variety of answer. Its up to each to choose.

If Lacan, the analyst, speaks at times with an apparent certainty then it is not a matter of simply believing him. He is not the source of true knowledge such that he should be deified. But it doesn't mean we should discount his apparent certainty , as simply his style of narcissism.

In fact, my question will be posed by the nature of the status of certainty, the indubitable and the beyond doubt by consider ing the place of certainty for the analyst and for psychoanalysis.

God proffers a certainty based upon his absolute knowledge. To dispute certainty is thus one mode of avoiding the religious approach. Everything is uncertain and to be ongoingly questioned. We perhaps then should avoid ever being certain of our knowledge in psychoanalysis and continue to question everything. If we become certain then we have strayed to the path of religious righteousness.

Should there be no certainty in psychoanalysis? Is that the correct path? We shouldn't say indubitable. It is an assumption to which I do not subscribe. This is where I'll get into trouble but so be it.

I suggest and I will try to justify the suggestion, that certainty is precisely the possibility that differentiates psychoanalysis and religion. Surely, you might say, certainty should be a dirty word. We must forever question and the truth can only be half said. To be certain is to be a believer and religious or psychotic and delusional. I propose not. It is this proposition which is my focus in attempting to justify it. My proposition is thus posed: *There is certainty to be attained through psychoanalysis. It is a certainty very different to that of religious knowledge and the delusional belief.*

Jean Allouch, the French analyst, writes about transference in his book *Lacan Love.*

In considering the transference after Lacan, thus the subject supposed to know, he suggests that we move away from the known/unknown dichotomy of Freud. The Freudian unconscious was an unknown knowledge which could become known thus solving its problematics. But such a revelation is precisely what religion offers and better. Instead, after Lacan, we work around the question of supposition/desupposition thus the supposed subject of knowledge. This produces a different attribution of knowledge which is irrelevant to the priests because it is not a matter for them of supposing that God has the knowledge since it is certain that he does. God knows, as we are all often prone to say.

The problem and the challenge faced in an analysis is thus not simply coming to know but of de-supposing the Other as knowing. What does one become via this de-supposition? Not so much more knowledgeable, which is one thing, but certain, which is something very different. One is certain that the Other does not know it all.

Allouch also writes the following which is ripe for our consideration:

> As radically not supposed, true knowledge equals certainty. A subject is constituted as such in reaching a local point of certainty- not simply of truth. Such are, for example, the Freudian interpretation of dreams, the "I think therefore I am" of Rene Descartes, Godel's theorem of incompletude: and the fainting of Champollion at the exact moment when he knew for certain that he had solved the mystery of Egyptian hieroglyphics.[4]

This passage is worth dwelling on. The important reference here is to certainty. These are interesting examples, examples of the acquisition of a knowledge which is beyond doubt, indubitable. Note the emphasis on "a local point of certainty". These examples show how through thought and the application of logic each was able to arrive at a local point of certainty. Local because it is theirs, their own, and as such does not rest on the Other as knowing. Note also, that it is certainty that is privileged not the truth. This is because the truth can be only half said whereas certainty is no half measure. Here is the aim and the possibility of the termination of an analysis; a subject, certain locally.

If Freud was able to keep working without false gods, it was because he had attained this point of certainty, his certainty. His certainty was the interpretation of dreams. A certainty which required the interpretation of his own dreams, thus localising it. This led to his suggestion that there should be a plaque on the wall of the house where was revealed to him the secrets of dreams.

> Insight such as this falls to ones lot but once in a lifetime.

Certainty is a very singular thing. Thus it was not first and foremost the truth that Freud produced but certainty. Here he reached his point of certainty. It is not a divine revelation except that it was divined by his manner of approach to the matter of language as contained in the dream. It is not that he is certain of the total interpretation of each dream, notably his own dreams, not that they are completely interpretable since the navel, the unknown, remains at the core of the dream, something beyond meaning and interpretation.

Dreams are interpretable even if incompletely. Of this fact Freud is quite certain and it keeps him going for the next forty years through all the tribulations of the psychoanalytic movement, the world chaos and the personal traumas. This is his certainty, of which he is subject, and which allows him little choice but to persevere as one must if one is to not knowingly give up on one's desire.

So Freud was the non believer since he didn't believe in the interpretation of dreams. He was certain of it. This is a difference which may or may not be subtle, but it is essential.

If you are certain you can never become uncertain. If you simply believe you can become a nonbeliever. It happens everyday. People believe one thing and then the opposite. If you know something you can forget it or find yourself mistaken. But if you are certain you can never become uncertain. Freud could never doubt psychoanalysis because of his conviction regarding his discovery of the interpretation of dreams. An analyst may doubt the future of psychoanalysis but not the certainty of psychoanalysis arrived at via their own locality.

Lacan under lines this in his seminar.

> It is because Freud declares the certainty of the unconscious that
> the progress by which he changed the world for us was made.[5]

The major term, in fact, is not truth. It is certainty. The question is, "Of what can one be certain?"

It was and is insufficient to preach the truth or to demand belief. Freud's method spread because of his unswerving loyalty to what was certain.

Lacan in his turn discovered that the unconscious is structured like a language. Can this discovery be added to the above list of Allouch? This knowledge can be questioned, reconsidered but it never becomes uncertain, at least not for Lacan. It is his local point of certainty. Local because only one can make such a discovery, as Freud did.

These are the discoveries of moments of genius. What can be the relevance of such moments to we who, if you will excuse me, are not so gifted nor so lucky as to stumble upon a great discovery?

Is it possible to arrive at certainty, a true knowledge without the status of the Freudian discovery? Precisely this is my assertion.

The end of the analysis corresponds with such a possibility. It is not simply a matter of discovering the truth of your history. It is a case of being certain of your place in respect of that history. Not to extract and thus escape from its truth but by avowing this certainty to persevere with life, in spite of it all. The all of life being all its limits and its impossibilities and its lack of external meaning. The meaning of life being only; to live.

In speaking in an analysis one can recognise one's place in history, ones own particular place. It doesn't have a meaning beyond that recognition.

It is a discovery that is not necessarily of any interest to anyone else and constitutes one's local certainty. This is what gives life meaning. Which is why an analyst who is one, is certain of the possibility of an analysis arriving at the necessary point of certainty since he or she has and experienced this place. The locality, not of the whole truth but of the true knowledge equals certainty. This is what gives the analyst that face of certainty which is the essential element required for an analysis. Never giving up because without that the analysis will never reach its conclusion.

There of course is danger, because the priest, even the one who without collar, calling himself analyst, can present the facade of certainty by mistaking it for the truth, that is, the truth they believe in. The truth professed as being "according to Lacan" or another Other who has written the gospel. The truth, to be read, understood, believed and followed. That is not the certainty of which I speak but a matter of belief and faith. Since religion is more acceptable to the majority why not a version of psychoanalysis as a new religion? Perhaps psychoanalysis can be a better religion than some but it threatens to destroy the possibility that psychoanalysis holds, that of concluding an analysis.

A conclusion wherein the Other no longer exists, when God, one's own Gods have fallen, and a point of local certainty emerges from the ashes which can sustain the work to come. What is an example of true knowledge? Perhaps the Ratman clearly caught in the unconscious repetition of repayment of his father's debt? The true knowledge being his history and his certain place in it.

Down the generations one can recognise the effects of this aspect of history repeating. Local certainty might mean nothing to anyone else, but one can be certain of it. This is why one must speak, to struggle against the silent servitude that our fate dictates. One speaks in order to make a noise in the cosmos. God is not listening. But someone might hear. Certainly, it is possible, that you might hear yourself.

Notes

1. Lacan, J. *Encore The Seminar of 1972–3.* Norton Press [1998].
2. Lacan, J. *ibid.*
3. Lacan, J. *ibid.*
4. Allouch, J. *Lacan Love* Ed. M-I Rotmiler de Zentner and Oscar Zentner Lituraterre 2007.
5. Lacan, J. *The Four Fundamentals of Psychoanalysis* Penguin 1979.

PART III

PSYCHOANALYSIS AND THE CHILD

CHAPTER ELEVEN

Psychoanalysis and the child

Tine Norregaard Arroyo and Michael Plastow

T he psychoanalysis of children was, from the outset, a domain of female analysts, being designated as such by Freud himself. Such women, moreover, were generally non-medical analysts, for no less a reason than by virtue of the fact that women were barred from studying medicine at the time. These women also took up the place of educators of children, both in the sense of raising children, but also literally as teachers. Such was the case of the woman whom we can situate as the first psychoanalyst of children, Hermine Hug-Hellmuth. These beginnings open up a question regarding the place of the analyst in regard to a child, the maternal relationship tending to be conflated, in the first instance, with the transference.

In addition, as is well known, many of the early analysts analysed their own children. Most prominent amongst this trend was Anna Freud's analysis by her father Sigmund Freud. Melanie Klein also situated herself as analyst of her own children. The analysis of little Hans by his father, who was a member of Freud's circle, is also a case in point.

Freud explicitly articulates this position in relation to the case of little Hans, but puts it forwards as necessary:

> It was only because the authority of a father and a physician were united in a single person, and because in him both affectionate care and scientific interest were combined, that it was possible in this one instance to apply the method to a use to which it would not otherwise have lent itself.[1]

Thus from the very beginning of the clinical practice of psychoanalysis of children, the analyst was placed right at the centre of the family drama.

Hence this family drama is introduced as an actual phenomenon, and not a symbolic one along the lines of the Oedipus myth. Like the transgressions in the symbolic form of the Oedipus drama, the family dramas occurred as transgressions of relationships between parents and children by the very manner in which the sons, daughters, nephews and so on, became both objects of observation for psychoanalytic research on infantile sexuality, as well as analysands of their own fathers, mothers and aunts.

Hug-Hellmuth's life and work were marked by questions of legitimacy: she never revealed the illegitimacy of her half-sister, offspring of the father's previous liaison. Her sister gave birth to an illegitimate child known as Rolf. Despite the fact that his symptoms, dreams and other phenomena were studied and written about by Hug-Hellmuth in numerous papers, the family relation was obscured. Hug-Hellmuth had a falling out with her half-sister who later died prematurely. Whilst not nominated as guardian for her nephew, she did nonetheless assume some maternal care for him. Hermine Hug-Hellmuth tragically met her end when she was murdered by Rolf in the context of his attempting to steal money and valuables from her.

Questions were also raised about the legitimacy of the book *A Young Girl's Diary*[2] that she published, presented as a journal of an anonymous adolescent girl, but to all evidence a fabrication by Hug-Hellmuth based upon her own experiences and memories. Freud came to Hug-Hellmuth's defence in support of the legitimacy of this work.

Hermine Hug-Hellmuth presented her paper *On the Technique of Child-Analysis* at the Sixth International Psychoanalytic Congress at The Hague in September 1920. In the audience was Sigmund Freud. Towards the end of her paper, she threw out what we can consider a challenge to Freud: "I consider it impossible for anyone to analyse properly his own child".[3] Despite, or because of, her own studies of the phenomena of her nephew, Hug-Hellmuth is able to draw a line here regarding a fundamental difficulty in the beginnings of child psychoanalysis, that is, the place of the parents. We can propose that Hug-Hellmuth was thus able to introduce a certain "legitimacy" into the practice of the psychoanalysis of children such that with her that it was able to move away from being a family affair.

We can see Hermine Hug-Hellmuth as the forerunner to two divergent streams of psychoanalysis with children. On the one hand, the educative aspect of her work was taken up by Anna Freud, principally through her assumption of a pedagogic stance in the treatment and her emphasis on the ego, or character, with the later weight that she gave to the defence mechanisms and prescriptive developmental lines. On the other hand we can see the more properly analytical stream in Hug-Hellmuth's work as having been taken up by Melanie Klein, including Hermine's conceptualisation of the transference of the child. In her work Hug-Hellmuth followed the child in his or her use of play in the analysis. This long preceded Klein's use of play, which became reified into a "technique" in her hands.

Hug-Hellmuth's analytical work with children preceded both Anna Freud's and Melanie Klein's by many years. In 1912 Anna Freud was still at school whilst Hug-Hellmuth published psychoanalytic papers. It was not until 1927 that Anna Freud and Klein began to publish their first important papers. This chronology and the contributions made by Hermine Hug-Hellmuth have been deliberately obscured. Take for instance Explanatory Note by the Melanie Klein Trust which is an appendix to her work *The Psycho-Analysis of Children*:

> *The Psycho-Analysis of Children* [...] is a classic text of child analysis. It sets out the psychoanalytic play technique Melanie Klein pioneered in Berlin in the early 1920s at about the time that Doctor H. B. Hug-Hellmuth ("On the Technique of Child Analysis", 1921) and Anna Freud ("Introduction to the Technique of Child Analysis", 1927) founded a different line of development.[4]

In addition, Anna Freud, who gave scarce recognition to Hug-Hellmuth's developments in the field, took credit for this work herself.

Indeed, as McLean and Rappen note, "every concept outlined by Hug-Hellmuth in 1920, 1921, and 1924 is later described as a basic element of the child psychoanalytic technique of Anna Freud".[5] Each of Hug-Hellmuth's two successors criticised aspects of her work that they identified with the rival. Thus Hug-Hellmuth was caught in the crossfire between Anna Freud and Melanie Klein, each of them burying her legacy under the rubble.

One of the significant advances made by Hug-Hellmuth was to indicate the place of the parents in regard to the analysis of the child. Her articulation of the request by mothers of children in analysis for "active therapy" has a very contemporary ring about it in the context of current calls by parents, and offers by therapists, for "strategies". We can also see Hug-Hellmuth's indication of a separate place regarding the function of the mother and that of the father, in contrast to a modern tendency to conflate these by converting the noun "parents" into a verb by talking of "parenting".

In Hug-Hellmuth's view, parents look upon psychoanalysis as a last resort. Despite this they nonetheless expect a miraculous cure. In Hug-Hellmuth's opinion, from the outset parents often have a time limit in their minds and break off the treatment halfway through, despite this resulting in a considerable waste of time, trouble and money. Following Hug-Hellmuth, we can take this as a wish of the parents, in particular that of the mother, to retain the *status quo* of a particular jouissance in regard to the child. Whilst Hug-Hellmuth's primary concern in seeing the parents was to support the analysis of the child, her comments regarding the sessions with them are perspicacious and open up this area with a richness that was ignored by the child analysts who followed.

Hence we put forward that the very life and work of this pioneer of psychoanalysis of children has been obscured. In fact it has been proposed that it was Anna Freud who intentionally erased Hermine Hug-Hellmuth's role in the beginnings of the psychoanalysis of children in order to promote herself, illegitimately, as the principal pioneer of this field.

It is our assertion that Hermine Hug-Hellmuth's work has undergone two "rescues". The first of these was an historical rescue by George McLean, a Canadian psychoanalyst, and Ulrich Rappen, his German colleague. In 1991 they published a work entitled *Hermine Hug-Hellmuth: Her Life and Work*.[6] This volume contains a brief biography, the scant result of exhaustive research on the part of the authors, as well as a selection and translation of Hug-Hellmuth's papers, many previously unpublished in English. Through this they were instrumental in bringing forward Hug-Hellmuth's place in recent years and rescued her work from historical obscurity.

A few days before her death, however, Hug-Hellmuth wrote a will expressing a wish that no account of her life or her work should appear. Rarely are such injunctions followed with persons of such historical and theoretical interest. Nonetheless, MacLean and Ulrich Rappen, in researching their book, wrote to Anna Freud seeking to elaborate upon her history. She responded to this request suggesting that the authors abide by the injunction. Thus, to even be able to speak and write of Hug-Hellmuth is to transgress a prohibition, to overcome a certain illegitimacy.

Jean Bergès and Gabriel Balbo, in their book *The Child and Psychoanalysis*,[7] effected a theoretical "rescue" of the work of Hug-Hellmuth. In particular, through an analysis of the demand and transference of both the child and the parents, they were able to re-formulate Hug-Hellmuth's propositions in a way that allowed them to precisely situate the place of the mother and father, not only in regard to the analysis of the child, but also in regard to their child's suffering and their consequent demand for treatment. Indeed, Bergès and Balbo put forward, based on their reading of Hug-Hellmuth, that "[the parents'] narcissism pushes them to accept the analysis of the child only if, by this means, their own childhood returns in the child".

For Bergès and Balbo the negotiation of an analytic contract with the child and his or her parents bears upon the possibility of formulating something of the demand of the child by working with this demand and dissociating it from the transference that is at play in the demand of the parents. As we have seen, these central questions of demand, transference and the analytic contract with the parents have also been played out through the history of the psychoanalytic movement regarding the child.

Thus the place of the analyst in relation to a child cannot but confront the history of psychoanalysis of the child. Erik Porge[8] offers us a tool to further examine this question. The practice of the early analysts of analysing their own children, he writes, is directly inspired by a fusion of the places of the Name of the Father and the Subject Supposed of Knowledge, the latter being Lacan's notion of the transference. This fusion is precisely what is at heart here, the con-fusion of the place of the mother or father, each differently intertwined to the Name of the Father, with that of the analyst.

Porge, in his examination of Freud's correspondence with Fliess, puts forward that the conflation of these two entities is something that marks the very beginnings of psychoanalysis through Freud's transference to Fliess. As we have seen, Freud put forward that this fusion was necessary in the case of little Hans at the very beginning of psychoanalysis of the child. We might say then that if such a fusion of the two were necessary for the establishment of the domain of psychoanalysis of the child, as Freud suggests, it is our task as the inheritors of this legacy to tease apart these two strands that nonetheless maintain a structural relation to each other. Hence we can propose that if the differentiation of the Name of the Father from the Subject Supposed of Knowledge is essential in examining the history of psychoanalysis of children, it also something crucial in each and every psychoanalysis of a child.

Notes

1. Freud, S.: "Analysis of a Phobia in a Five-Year-Old Boy" (1909). *SE*: X, p. 149.
2. Hug-Hellmuth, H. (1924) *A Young Girl's Diary*. Boston: Milford House, 1971.
3. Hug-Hellmuth, H. "On the Technique of Child-Analysis". *International Journal of Psychoanalysis* Vol. 2, 1921, p. 287.
4. In: Klein, M. The Psycho-Analysis of Children. London: Vintage, 1997, p. 283.
5. MacLean, G. & Rappen, U. *Hermine Hug-Hellmuth: Her Life and Work.* Routledge: New York, 1991, p. 279.
6. MacLean, G. & Rappen, U. *Op. Cit.*
7. Bergès, J. & Balbo, G. *L'Enfant et la Psychanalyse: Nouvelles perspectives.* Paris: Masson, 1996.
8. Porge, E. *Freud Fliess: mythe et chimère de l'auto-analyse.* Paris, Anthropos, 1996.

CHAPTER TWELVE

The treatment setting: demand, transference and the contract with the parents and for their child

Jean Bergès and Gabriel Balbo

Introduction

The paper published here is a translation of the first half of Chapter Five "*Le cadre de la cure: demande, transfert et contrat avec les parents et pour l'enfant*" of the book *L'Enfant et la psychanalyse: Nouvelles perpectives* (*The Child and Psychoanalysis: New perspectives*), 2nd edition, by Jean Bergès and Gabriel Balbo, published by Masson, Paris, 1996. Gabriel Balbo is a psychoanalyst and founder of *Libre Association Freudienne*. Jean Bergès, deceased in 2004, was a neuropsychiatrist and psychoanalyst, member of the *Association Lacanienne Internationale*. Within the framework of that Association he founded the *École de la psychanalyse de l'enfant à Paris* (*Paris School of Psychoanalysis of the Child*). He was the director of the *Unité de Psychopathologie de l'Enfant et de l'Adolescent* (*Child and Adolescent Psychopathology Unit*) of the Sainte-Anne Hospital in Paris for 35 years.

Bergès and Balbo collaborated on a number of works pertaining to the psychoanalysis of children, including the one from which this extract is taken. This paper gives an historical overview of the demand, transference and contract with the parents in analyses with children, with particular emphasis on the work of the early child psychoanalyst

Hermine Hug-Hellmuth. Gabriel Balbo has kindly given his agreement for publication in this form.

Michael Plastow

* * *

Following a brief historical account of the original nature of the demand for analysis of the child, the contract established with the parents and the place and function that the transference had in the direction of the treatment elaborated by the analyst, we will take up the problem posed by the current nature of the demand and its effects in the negotiation of the analytical contract with the parents and their child. Consequently we will more precisely define the demand and the non-demand in order to demonstrate the inevitably conflictual nature of the relation between the two. This conflict, having its origin at the heart of each case that we take on, will lead us to consider the question of the master of jouissance during an analysis of a child, as well as something of the fundamental question of symbolic anticipation when a treatment with a child has been decided upon. Further, it allows us to clarify the nature of the demand of transference as distinguished from the transference of the demand, and to conclude, to consider the question of transference in the child's treatment itself.

Historical Perspective

Freud

If the psychoanalyst, thanks to his practice with adults, is able to formulate hypotheses regarding infantile sexuality, he may wish to hear the formations, which construct the not yet completely unconscious desires, directly from the child, and before they are completely repressed. It was for this reason that Freud created child psychoanalysis, and it was hence from him that the demand originally emanated:

> With this end in view I have for many years been urging my pupils and my friends to collect observations on the sexual life of children [...] Amongst the material which came into my possession as a result of these requests, the reports which I received at regular intervals about little Hans soon began to take a prominent place.[1]

An incitation, a request: Freud's demand was thus answered by that of the child's parents thanks to whom an analytic contract was knotted all the more easily, since the child's analyst, to the greatest satisfaction of the Master, was none other than his father.

Demand, contract and transference therefore seemed to join together in an ideal manner. Freud thus thought that no person other than the father could more legitimately undertake the analysis of his son:

> It was only because the authority of a father and a physician were united in a single person, and because in him both affectionate care and scientific interest were combined, that it was possible in this one instance to apply the method to a use to which it would not otherwise have lent itself.[2]

For a child, not only is the transference optimal with his father, but furthermore there is no risk of suggestion. Eliminating this risk thus allowed the associations to be freer and much more frank.

Freud was not a man to think, conceive of or to put forward just any old thing. Nothing could therefore cast doubt on his rigour and his scientific conviction, nor on his sincere concern. Moreover he regularly supervised the analysis undertaken by the father with his son, and from the place of symbolic third. He himself analysed his own daughter Anna. And even in 1935, if he did not advise Eduardo Weiss to contemplate the analysis of his own son, nor did he forbid him from doing so:

> … with my own daughter, I have succeeded very well, with a son one confronts particular misgivings […]. Obviously all depends on the two people and the relationship between them. The difficulties are well known to you. Nonetheless I will not be surprised if you succeed.[3]

Are parents good therapists?

When it was her turn to become a psychoanalyst, Anna Freud always maintained that the child could only develop a transference with the parents. Melanie Klein, who also analysed her own children, objected that on the contrary, with a child an analytic transference is always possible like with the adult and quite independently of the parents. The practice of analysing one's own children took place more than just occasionally, particularly in the English speaking countries. There it was also the object of an extraordinary theoretical development by Donald Winnicott who returned, fundamentally, to Freud's inaugural position: parents are excellent therapists for their children and it is sufficient for them to give an account to a psychoanalyst in the position of symbolic third for the transference not to be short-circuited by closing upon itself. The analysis of the little Piggle gives us an example of this.

Hermine Hug-Hellmuth

Hermine Hug-Hellmuth, in charge of the column in *Imago* entitled *The True Essence of the Child's Soul* which was created by her in 1912, nonetheless declared the following as early as 1920 at the Congress of The Hague, at the end of her lecture devoted to the technique of the analysis with a child:

> I consider it impossible for anyone to analyse properly his own child. This is so not only because the child hardly ever reveals its deepest desires and thoughts, conscious or unconscious, to father and mother, but because in this case the analyst is often driven to reconstruct too freely, and also because the narcissism of the parents would make it almost unbearable to hear from their own child the psychoanalytic revelations.

The argument opposes point by point that of Freud's, and it is declared in all its "frankness" in his presence, during a congress. Perhaps Hermine Hug-Hellmuth knew what she was speaking about, she who unsuccessfully attempted to analyse her own nephew, fatally in her case. Is it for this reason that her work had so little currency amongst the adherents of psychoanalysis with children of the time? It is unlikely given that the principles set out by Freud in 1909 remained prescriptive for all. In what way do they remain so, at heart, and what is it that has fundamentally changed since?

The Freudian symbolic triangle

We have to acknowledge that in regard to the treatment of very young children, indeed of infants, as well as the treatment of the psychotic children, indeed of the autistic, we find today the implementation of the same "parent(s)-child-psychoanalyst" triangle as in Freud's time. However, the real arrangement is no longer quite the same since the parent is no longer the official analyst of the child. The parent, however, participates no less in the child's treatment, and actively moreover, as he or she has a place during the sessions, just as the other two nominally have their places. This implementation of the real presence leaves in suspension that of the symbolic absence from which it should maintain itself. But why the theoretical justification of such a real technical arrangement of the places (although it is far from unanimous since the practice of treatment in words with the baby alone does in fact occur)? The often detailed justification essentially asserts that the mother-child separation is impossible (for example when the child is an *infans*, very little or very impaired), is never very convincing, seems false and evokes those "tricks" used by Hermine Hug-Hellmuth in order to gain the collaboration of young reticent patients. It is not convincing because it always seems to be nothing but the alibi of the analyst who takes his technical scaffolding as a substitute for what is at stake psychically and in the transference that he still misapprehends [*méconnaît*], but with which he is confronted without knowing. Hence it is sound to maintain that, in the absence of another, of a new clinical and theoretical elaboration as rigorous and relevant as that of Freud's, the principles he put forward in 1909 remain valid, their prescriptive nature being strengthened by the multiple and less probing techniques invented since.

Mother treatments

Nonetheless, something which is far from insignificant has fundamentally changed since the analysis of little Hans. Where Freud maintained that only the father was qualified to participate in the treatment of the child, the mother now takes her place and prevails over the father. Anything goes in all the explanations put forward to claim that this is the way it has to be, and that without such an arrangement not only would the results of the treatment be compromised, but moreover the very future of the child would be threatened. The reasons put forward range from the absence of the father to the foreclosure of the name-of-the-father, from perversion to problematical repressions of the mother's ancestors, from the mirror stage to the optical schema. All of that and many other things besides, in order to end up with the irreplaceable mother, and, when the child is autistic, to the inevitable "mother-child" conjunction, whose unary trait is evidently one of union. When words no longer recall corresponding things, technical constructions are invented so that clinical practice does not appear too jumbled! It is never said that with an autistic child, a treatment with father *and* child would not be more congruent than a mother-child treatment, at least in regard to the real, if it is really upon this rather than the symbolic that technique should be sustained. The failure of all these mother techniques is once again to the advantage of Freud's ideas. Would it not be more economical to return to these, taking as backdrop for our theoretical elaborations with the child, the symbolic triangle of the places that Freud proposes for us? It is worth posing the question, even if it is disturbing: it is not every day that the phallic law diverts from castration.

The propositions of Hermine Hug-Hellmuth

Hermine Hug-Hellmuth does not beat around the bush and responds to this question with some very interesting ideas. She was the first, after Freud, to elaborate a rigorous theorisation of technique with children. Nonetheless her theorisation allows room for subtlety and subjective nuances, for the naivety of the child and the analyst alike, to their liberating astonishment. Formally, her article on the technique of child analysis develops in the following manner: aim of analysis, technical generalities, importance of the first session, subjective technical characteristics, function of the parental imago in the transference of the child during the treatment, transference of the analyst, transference of the parents and the analyst's work with the parents. However this text effectively deals with the demand, the transference and the analytic contract.

Demand and transference with the child

Hermine Hug-Hellmuth grasps the fact that with a child in analysis the main difficulty resides in the establishment of the very conditions required to sustain a setting for the transference that will, in the most spontaneous manner, make play possible. However, this setting is dependent both on the demand and the contract. And as far as both the parents and the child are concerned, neither the one nor the other present themselves to us with the best omens. From the outset, conditions conspire for the transference to be principally negative. And this author's genius is to have understood that it is of the utmost importance to start out from this transferential given, without too many illusions, in other words taking stock of this, knowing that this negativity will be a backdrop for the whole of the treatment, and that the work of the transference is nothing in the end but a work of mourning.

The child does not formulate any demand of the analyst and often attends against his will, knowing none of the aims of the analysis, but holding on to his suffering from which he gains jouissance in order to reinforce his sense of omnipotence and his narcissism of difference. It is consequently necessary to first of all create a transferential relation with the child, one that allows the emergence of a demand. And for that to happen, this relation is sustained in the first instance by narcissism. Thus it is better for the first few meetings with the parents to occur without the child, and for the treatment to begin at home.

- *The first session and the first reversal of the demand*

From the first session onwards, one should adapt the method to his person: his intelligence, his age, his temperament and his pathology decide the rules and the course to follow, utilising one after the other or simultaneously: games, verbal associations and symbolic actions as silent discourses. Giving evidence of an attentive and benevolent listening, the analyst coordinates his work with that of the child towards whom he formulates no prohibition nor suggestion: the young analysand consolidates his confidence in him, invests his treatment in him, and soon feels so little distrust towards his analyst that he formulates a first demand towards him: he wants to be able to have complete trust in him. This first demand consequently effects a remarkable narcissistic reversal through which the child is engaged, whist implicating his analyst in this, in a positive transference, but nonetheless of a purely specular nature.

- *The mirror: imaginary transference and imago*

Why does it come down to such a mirror to definitively break the ice [*glace*] between the analyst and his very young analysand? Precisely because the latter engages in an imaginary transference whose stakes are some imagos, in particular those of the parents. In order to take advantage of this in the treatment, such a transference requires, on the side of the analyst, that he himself is clear about his own imagos. "Analytic work takes place in the unconscious" declares Hermine

Hug-Hellmuth: and nowhere else, we can add. That means that the imago only takes on a symbolic and signifying value for a subject in analysis, even and especially if he is a *infans*, when what conceptualizes it puts to death the repressed thing that it images and represents. However this value is only taken, and the thing dies from its words, only if the treatment does without the real parents, only if the psychoanalyst does not "*real-ise*" them himself. For to really incarnate the imago to which they thus endeavour to make present, the psychoanalyst and parents, despite what they say, render its being put to death more than improbable. In this transferential game the analyst must therefore remain a third, to attend to the unconscious, in order to not fall into this real. From the imago, he can thus emphasise the signifiers of lack and thus allow the child to express his conscious and unconscious desires.

- *Second reversal of the demand*

In being expressed, these desires effect a second reversal of the demand: in the transference, the analyst does not respond to any of the childish desires by incarnating the imago towards which they are directed, but in not responding to the demand he nonetheless always incarnates this anonymous bit of the real upon which each imago is supported, in order to come to the place of the object *a* to be lost. The psychoanalyst thus incarnates something incorporable, and hence realizes a literally ablating incarnation, with which the imago seems to have no relation.

- *But who do you take me for?*

Concretely, each time the child transfers an imago upon the analyst, the latter brings forward the real which qualifies it, in such a way that no one is able to identify with it, to appropriate it, to incorporate it. It is as if he were enouncing to the child: "But who do you take me for?" The real allows him to dissociate himself from the imago, and through this to be able to reveal to his young analysand what desires his object is made of. The imago is this specious currency with which the child weaves the web of the transference. According to its sign, the analyst is either the ally of the parents against the child, his ally against the parents, enemy of all three or friend of them all. He is also at once the parental ideal or the best of children, the worst or the most fraternal … In short the young analysand, thanks to the treatment, progressively abandons his process of attributions and his black-and-white and anxiety-provoking divisions pertaining to images, in order to be able to come to symbolise the imago to which, not without a depressive effect, he can thus renounce as object *a*.

• *The passage from the imaginary to the symbolic through speech*

This symbolisation which undoes the alienation in his imaginary is produced from little bits of the real which are nothing other than words, these words which bring things to memory, remembering them by naming them, these words which have value only through their anonymous use, these words that only rhetoric can subvert and subjectify from the figures of style of the discourse used. When the analyst locates an imago in the transference and names its real, it falls into the repressed or is lost as a dead thing. This nomination in itself makes present what it names, absent nonetheless through having to be named. The passage from the imaginary to the symbolic is effected through the medium of the real of speech.

Demand and transference with the parents

Hermine Hug-Hellmuth notes that with the parents, the project of analysing their child does not present itself in the most propitious manner: even when they formulate it of their own will, their demand is made against their better judgement. The symptoms of their child, the lack of success of other treatment methods and the hope for a miracle all lead them only as a last resort to the psychoanalyst, towards whom they harbour nothing but mistrust and of whose chance of success they are doubtful given that all else has failed.

• *The narcissistic wound*

It is advisable in the first instance to gain the trust of the parents as well, then to maintain this throughout the whole treatment, knowing full well that the narcissistic wound is in play for them from one end of the treatment to the other. They present themselves as guilty of having failed and they already know for a fact that any improvement in the health of their child will essentially be due to the analysis and that it will have little to do with them. As with their child, consequently it will all begin with a negative transference, and it is necessary to create the conditions which will allow this to be freely played out, then to be transformed, but by dissociating it from that known to the child in the context of his treatment. In this regard Anna Freud was of the opinion that it was necessary to lead the parents to undertake an analysis in their own right.

• *The parents first*

This was not Hermine Hug-Hellmuth's approach. She saw the parents first in order to initially dedicate herself solely to them since it is principally with them that the analytic contract is negotiated. Then, due to their negative transference, from which she elaborated their demand with them, she started the child's treatment at their home. As soon as the transference no longer produced a narcissistic wound in them, she conducted the analysis in her own consulting room, where she saw them regularly. Thus their trust is established, their function and place are recognised as is their request to participate.

• *The specular reversal and its imagos*

But such is the specular reversal that occurs in their regard that, as soon as the analyst has their trust, they ask him to accept their active participation in the treatment of their child. They expect the analyst's trust in them to reflect the trust they give him. Just like with their child, this specular difficulty is only able to be resolved by the elaboration of the imagos that are carried by it. More precisely, the parents ask the analyst to identify with their own parental imagos. But their demand is also that he incorporate the imago of the child that is able to flatter the narcissism of the parents. Thus it is themselves, as they suppose themselves to have been as children, that they desire to re-find in the child: their child, in identifying with this ideal analytic imago in its turn, would be nothing but what they were in their childhood. Their narcissism thus pushes them to only accept the analysis of their child if, by this means, their own childhood returns in the child. The miracle that they expect from it is hence only a banal narcissistic return of the repressed ideal.

• *The advantages of the narcissistic return, mourning*

The advantages that they expect from such a return are multiple. In the first instance it is reparatory for them. Through becoming the child that they were, their child will help them forget that they might partly have been the cause of the child's symptoms. It reassures them that they no longer need to suffer from the jealously felt against a transference between the analyst and the child, experienced by them with as much envy and hate as a young child who observes the happy scene of his mother whose newborn suckles from her breast. It allows them to tolerate the improvements and the setbacks due to the treatment, as well as the duration of the treatment. However the parents must undergo the work of mourning of all this, a work that for them passes through the questions of weaning, privation and symbolic castration.

• *Contradictions, errors*

Hermine Hug-Hellmuth recognises that she has great difficulty in limiting the parents to their function alone, obliging them to keep to their places. But it is difficult to ask this of them when, moreover, she wants to meet with them in order to know more about their relations with their child, in order to establish the veracity of a memory (which we cannot help but put into question), in order to know about the child's early history, as if the child were not capable of speaking of it him or herself. She extracts herself from this as best she can, in other words by compromises. She explains to them that the positive transference of their child is transient, that moreover it does no harm to them, and that it is not the source of all good things since the success achieved with it has to be set against the price of scholastic difficulties …, but she explains this whilst asserting that, on the other hand, the parents must stay outside of the analysis of their child.

Conclusions

In his "Introductory Lectures on Psychoanalysis", Freud puts the same thing forward in regard to the parents and then goes back on this opinion in his "New Introductory Lectures". Melanie Klein never varied in her opinion but neither of them chose any half-measure: the treatment of the child is conducted without the parents.

• *Crucial transference*

Nonetheless, the work of Hermine Hug-Hellmuth is exemplary and to read it is enriching. She clearly shows that in the analysis of the child the transference is a crucial question, from which the questions of the demand and the negotiation of the contract must be elaborated. It is not just the conception and direction of the treatment that must be considered in relation to the transference.

- *The language of Aesop*

Since it is only the transference that marks psychoanalysis with this specificity, which excludes it from the field of all research that clearly dissociates the researcher from the object of his study, the principles stated by Freud during little Hans' treatment gain all their symbolic strength and all their radical relevance from it. In order to elaborate psychoanalytic technique with children, it is worth returning to this, without the prejudice of the superego and without the sort of zeal that produces repression. Here clinical practice can find the deeds of its nobility. Clinical practice is only what is transmitted from it by virtue of the transference of whosoever engages in it in order to transmit it. It only takes form through the transference, and gains meaning from the theory to which this same transference is articulated in a dialectical game. Outside of this game it is possible to make each one say everything or nothing at all, since each one in itself is only the language of Aesop.

Translated from French by Tine Norregaard Arroyo and Michael Plastow.

Notes

1. Freud, S.: "Analysis of a Phobia in a Five-Year-Old Boy" (1909). *SE*: X, p. 5.
2. *Ibid.*, p. 149.
3. Freud, S. and Weiss, E., *Sigmund Freud as a consultant: Recollections of a Pioneer in Psychoanalysis*, 1970.

CHAPTER THIRTEEN

Some cases of *"name of the father subject supposed of knowledge"*

Erik Porge

Introduction

Erik Porge is a psychoanalyst practising in Paris and member of *la lettre lacanienne, une école de la psychanalyse*. He is editor of the journal *Essaim* and author of various works including his most recent book *Des fondements de la clinique psychanalytique* (*Foundations of the psychoanalytic clinic*), published by Érès, Paris. The paper below is an excerpt from Chapter III "An unanalysed remainder of Freud by Lacan, in 1964" of Erik Porge's book *Freud Fließ: Mythe et chimère de l'autoanalyse* (*Freud Fliess: Myth and chimera of self-analysis*) published by Anthropos, Paris, 1996.

This book takes up the proposition initially raised by Didier Anzieu in his book *Freud's Self-Analysis* and perpetuated in psychoanalytic circles that Freud undertook his self-analysis in transference to Wilhelm Fliess. This is despite Freud's own avowal to Fliess that "True self-analysis is impossible; otherwise there would be no [neurotic] illness." It provides a critique of the notion of self-analysis as being a distortion of what transpired in the correspondence and the relation between the two men. Porge puts forward that the friendship between Freud and Fliess was what allowed Freud to ground his desire as analyst in the soil of science. This operation took place, nonetheless, at the expense of a more detailed examination of Fliess' madness, which Freud misrecognised. Porge proposes that Freud also played a part in maintaining Fliess' madness, prior to their rupture. He asserts, in the chapter from which this excerpt is taken, that the figure that Fliess incarnated for Freud has been transmitted to Freud's followers, precisely through the myth of Freud's self-analysis. Further to this, Porge proposes that this spectre played a role in the failure that Lacan encountered in holding a seminar on *The Names of the Father* in 1963. The passage translated here is central to Porge's argument of a fusion for Freud, in relation to Wilhelm Fliess, of the places of Name of the Father and Subject Supposed of Knowledge. Of particular interest for the psychoanalysis of children is the risk that Porge expounds of a conflation between the Name of the Father and the Subject Supposed of Knowledge, enacted, in Porge's view, by the early analysts who analysed their own children.

Michael Plastow

In Jean Jacques Rousseau's *Émile*, one encounters a figure of the Name of the father subject supposed of knowledge in the person of the governor. He is described to us as the qualified interpreter of Nature and as a master who must know everything in regard to the child:

> He [the child] must not want anything apart from what you want him to do; he must not take a step that you have not foreseen, he must not open his mouth unless you know what he is going to say,

… writes Rousseau in regard to his subject.

The person of the governor is in part linked with paternity and especially with Rousseau himself. It is in the same thrust as this passage, when Rousseau admits his regret for not having raised his own children, that he defines the qualities of a good governor.[1] The latter occupies an impossible place of ideal father. The governor must replace the father ("So who will raise my child? I have already told you, yourself. I cannot.") and at the same time it is an impossible task. Rousseau, moreover, refuses from the outset to accept such a job: "I will not put my hands to this work but rather to the pen and instead of doing the necessary I will endeavour to say it." Saying it is to write it, to publish it; this is also doing. This is perhaps the reason for which the publication of *Émile* corresponded to the triggering of a delusion in Rousseau. Delays in printing made him believe that the Jesuits had got hold of the text and had fomented a plot to add their own ideas under his name.[2]

It can be put forward that the publication of his saying in regard to the fiction of the governor triggered a delusion about the paternity of his works. The fiction of the governor must be considered as a Name of the Father for Rousseau.

The governor is not a preceptor, he does not give precepts as he must allow precepts to be found in his pupil and to guide him. Rousseau, speaking in the name of the governor, in order to accomplish his educational task, gives himself an imaginary pupil whom he tailors to measure: young, of good birth, of a similar culture, and who he names: Émile. The governor must become the friend of his pupil and never leave his side. In addition there is one essential condition: "Émile is an orphan."

The function of the governor is in competition with that of father and the two must be brought together in one person. The governor is a Name of the father subject supposed of knowledge. This is not the case, for example, in Fénelon's *Telemachus*.[3]

At the end of *Émile* it seems that Rousseau imagines a dissociation of these two functions, at the moment when Émile becomes a father in his turn, after having married that other imaginary being with whom Rousseau completed him, Sophie. Émile then addresses the governor:

> May it please God that I allow you to also bring up the son, after having brought up the father.[4]

Since Émile concludes on that point, it could be thought that this sentence situates what is at stake at the point to which Rousseau arrives in his book, and that this fiction will allow him to envisage the assumption of paternity, if not for himself, then at least for his fictional characters. After all, in this concluding moment, a shadow remains: the character answering to the Name of the father subject supposed of knowledge has not been dissolved, he is still solicited by Émile who has become a father.

> Remain the master of young masters. Advise us, govern us, we will be docile: as long as you live, I will need you.

... requests Émile of his governor.

The sequel to *Émile*, entitled *Émile and Sophie or the Solitary Ones*, ends in drama, quite in the Rousseau fashion. Émile loses everything: he separates from Sophie, loses his children and his parents-in-law die.

Everything was leading towards a nice life, everything was promising me a sweet old age and a peaceful death in my children's arms. Alas! What has become of this happy time of enjoyment and hope, where the future decorated the present, where my heart, inebriated with joy, drank a century of happiness each day? It has all vanished like a dream. Still young, I have lost everything, wife, children, friends, all in short, including contact with my fellows.[5]

Émile's complaint resonates with Rousseau's in *Les rêveries*:

An event as sad as it is unforseen has ended up wiping from my heart this weak ray of hope and has seen my destiny forever sealed with no return …[6]

Émile's story finishes by his accession to paternity. Beyond this, Rousseau is not able to sustain the fiction, the version. It fails for Rousseau himself who, at the point of publishing *Émile*, begins to be delusional. The fiction of the governor, figure of the Name of the father Subject Supposed of Knowledge, makes good a shortcoming of the Name of the Father and, at the same time, can be considered as an element of the delusion which reveals the insufficiency of this making good.

The shadow of the Name of the father subject supposed of knowledge can be found in a clinical domain in which it is particularly important to make the distinction between Name of the Father and subject supposed of knowledge, that of psychoanalysis with children. In his introduction to the case of "little Hans", Freud explains the success of the psychoanalytic method in the following fashion:

It was only because the authority of a father and of a physician were united in a single person, and because in him both affectionate care and scientific interest were combined, that it was possible in this one instance to apply the method to a use to which it would not otherwise have lent itself.[7]

The course of little Hans' treatment in reality demonstrates quite the opposite, in other words that the efficacious moments were the ones in which paternal authority was dissociated from medical authority. These included the moment of the visit of Hans and his father to Freud and the fact of Freud indirectly addressing Hans, through the intermediary of his father.[8] Apart from that, Hans was waiting precisely for some parental authority from his father (principally in relation to the mother) which could be neither too understanding nor that of a subject supposed of knowledge. As Lacan emphasised several times, Hans wanted his father to be jealous, to be angry with him, to castrate him. In allowing Hans to be the plaything of his mother's whims, his father did not fulfil this function and it was precisely the phobia that made up for it.[9]

The fusion of the Name of the Father with the Subject Supposed of Knowledge in our opinion directly inspires the practice of analysts analysing their own children, which was widespread in Freud's time. Anna Freud had two periods of analysis with her father and we are indebted to this analysis for the fantasy "A child is being beaten". Melanie Klein analysed her children and published accounts of these analyses: Erich (5 years old) became Fritz, Hans, Felix, Melitta and Lisa. To this mixture of functions was added the fact that the writings that arose from these experiences were used as passports to enter the psychoanalytical societies that their authors wanted to join. Anna Freud wrote an original article "Fantasy of 'being beaten' and daydreams"[10] following a lecture to the Psychoanalytical Society of Vienna, 31st May 1922, and Melanie Klein, in 1919, published the communication that she had presented to the psychoanalytical society under the title of "Der Familienroman in statu nascendi" in the *Internationale Zeitschrift für Psychoanalyse*. It has been said that Abraham and Jung also analysed their children. Hermine Hug-Hellmuth, a pioneer in the analysis of children, made use of material from her nephew whom she had raised and who, later, murdered her. The abandonment today of the practice of analysing one's own children indicates to us that we should also be in a position to separate the subject supposed of knowledge and the Name of the Father. The stakes are raised in the practice of psychoanalysis with children which necessarily confronts us with this distinction. In the simultaneous positions that the analyst occupies with the parents and the children he attends, the analyst must maintain a constant vigil to separate the registers of the Name of the Father and of the Subject Supposed of Knowledge in not conflating his authority as Subject Supposed of Knowledge with that of father, even if it is only in allowing the father of the child to say his name.

The case of Wilhelm Fliess furnishes a final example of a confusion between Name of the Father and Subject Supposed of Knowledge. The theory of periods, a veritable conception of the world ruled by an absolute determinism, leaves no room for any shortcoming in knowledge. Fliess invariably answered any criticism addressed to him that he was only revealing the laws of Nature, an infallible subject supposed of knowledge. We demonstrated in *Vol d'idées?* that Fliess, in his theoretical texts, does without the father in the very place where his system theorises upon the transmission from one generation to the next. The laws of the periods replace a law of the Name of the Father. This position that Fliess put forward from his delusion opened the doors to Freud's transference to him as manifested in a poem that the latter sent to him on the occasion of the birth of second son Charles, and which is a sort of hymn to the Name of he who is at once the father of Charles and father of a theory:

> Hail
> To the valiant son who at the behest of his father appeared at the right time,
> To be his assistant and fellow worker in fathoming the divine order.
> But hail to the father, too, who just prior to the event found in his calculations
> The key to restraining the power of the female sex
> And to shouldering his burden of lawful succession;
> No longer relying on sensory appearances, as does the mother,
> He calls upon the higher powers to claim his right, conclusion, belief, and doubt;
> Thus, at the beginning, there stands, hale and hearty, equal to the exigency of error, the father
> In his infinitely mature development.
> May the calculation be correct and, as the legacy of labour, be transferred from father to son and beyond the parting of the centuries
> Unite in the mind what the vicissitudes of life tear apart.[11]

Paternity and the theory of periods, which predicts the birth and the sex of the child, are coupled with "familial" paternity. The theory of periods is a sort of emblem of paternal potency. This poem clarifies the relation of Freud with Fliess for us. Fliess represents, in Freud's eyes, a Name of the father subject supposed of knowledge.

Translated from French by Michael Plastow.

Notes

1. Rousseau, J -J. *Œuvres complètes*. Paris, Gallimard, Vol. IV, 1969, pp. 263–266.
2. Rousseau recounted this afterwards in his *Confessions*. In: *Œuvres complètes*. Paris, Gallimard, Vol. I, 1969, p. 566. *Cf.* also p. 575 the accusation of plagiarism that he makes in regard to another book at the time of the release of *Émile*.
3. Fénelon. *The adventures of Telemachus* (1699). Preface by Le Brun, J. Paris, Gallimard, 1995. The Archbishop of Cambrai effectively exercised the responsibility of preceptor for the grandson of Louis XIV, the Duke of Burgundy, as well as for his younger brother Philippe, Duke of Anjou. Fénelon drew upon the texts he wrote for them in order to write *Telemachus*. In this story Mentor is not a pedagogue who takes the place of the father like Rousseau's governor. He teaches Telemachus but he also protects him in his adventures in so far as he incarnates Minerva, into whom he becomes transfigured at the end of the story. Mentor helps and accompanies Telemachus in search of his father. Ulysses, with whom the son has a missed encounter, since, although troubled by the encounter, he fails to recognise him. The pedagogical relationship serves as a support for the father-son relation of which there are other illustrations in the text (that of Idonmen). "Behind absent Ulysses appears the hidden Father who flees, the perhaps cruel Father who gave Fénelon's attempts at Christology their tragic character." (Preface, p. 13)
4. Rousseau, J -J. *Op. cit.*, Vol. IV, p. 867.
5. Rousseau, J -J. "Les rêveries du promeneur solitaire". In: *Op. Cit.*, Vol. I, p. 881.
6. *Ibid.*, Vol. I, p. 997.
7. Freud, S.: "Analysis of a Phobia in a Five-Year-Old Boy" (1909). *SE*: X, p. 4.
8. *Ibid.*, p. 71. "Hans: If he thinks it [that his mother would drop Hanna into the water and that Hans would be left alone with his mother], it is good all the same, because you can write it to the Professor." Freud adds moreover at that moment, in a note: "Well done, little Hans! I could wish for no better understanding of psycho-analysis from any grown-up."
9. Cf. Lacan, J. *La relation d'objet*. Paris: Seuil, 1994, pp. 322, 366, 402 (on the function of the father as a jealous God).
10. Published in French in: *Féminité mascarade*. Seuil: Paris, 1994, pp. 57–75.
11. Masson, J. M. *The complete letters of Sigmund Freud to Wilhelm Fliess 1887–1904*. Belknap Press: Cambridge Mass., 1985, pp. 393–394.

CHAPTER FOURTEEN

Father can't you see that I am burning?— interventions in the real of the parental couple

Tine Norregaard Arroyo

A 10 year old boy was brought to analysis due to his parents' concerns about his recurring accidents. Many of these accidents occurred when the boy was allowed to use the tools of his father, a welder, who, in the initial interview spoke of his disappointments not only with regard to his son, but also with his own father and life overall. The parents separated during the course of the analysis, after it was revealed that the father had incurred a longstanding gambling debt, which had caused major financial losses in the family.

The boy was no stranger to sexual matters, which he candidly spoke about in terms of his puppy, who had "all the works". For him it was rather a confusion between playing around with and making the tool work; his own and his father's. His symptoms, the accidents and burn marks on his body appeared at the crossing point of the knowledge about the "welds" of his own body and his attempts at "welding" the parents' relationship.

A necessary intervention enabled a turning point in the analysis, when the mother reported in a session that the boy had driven the family car into a tree, slightly injuring himself and two other boys. The mother, stressing her anger at the seriousness of the accident, and at the fact that the father had allowed the boy to play around in the car, demanded that the boy pay for the costs of the damage with his pocket money. The following intervention was offered to the mother and the son: *more than the cost of the car is involved in this accident as there is a difference between the age when a boy needs his parents to drive him and the age when the law in society allows him to drive a car by himself.*

After this the boy produced a series of associations about rules and regulations concerning the safety of fire-extinguishers in the big companies that his father had worked in; the unknown knowledge of the danger arising in the company of his father. The law of castration could then be supported by inviting him to search for his father's love in other ways than placing himself and his body in the line of fire. The symptom, the welding or the joining, was then also able to be questioned in terms of a difference between his own sexual *jouissance* and that of h is parents: *could he perhaps rather join in the games with his mates, like in a tennis team which included girls?* It was a matter of finding some tools that worked for him, like the "heavy metal music" that resonated with the metal used by the father in his trade, and making use of the team sports to "go for the ball, rather than go for the man".

In this case of an analysis with a boy and his parents, an intervention was necessary to support the paternal function for the boy and the mother. For the mother it raised a prohibition against assuming the boy in the same position as the father: *Thou shall not make thy son pay for the mistakes of the father.* For the boy it produced a cut in the deadly rite of the automaton by which his particular symptom enabled the accidental marks on his body.

As Freud also pointed out in the case of Little Hans and his father, an intervention which supports the paternal function has a particular status in the work of psychoanalysis with a child, in the sense that it may be an intervention which is required in the presence of one or both of the parents with the child. In this way we cannot speak of psychoanalysis with a child without also thinking about the place of the parents in this work. This paper will discuss the status of such an intervention in the field of psychoanalysis of a child with his parents.

The child, the symptom and the parents

Freud held that the superego in the child, which is not yet fully developed, is transmitted unconsciously from the superego of the parents. It is this assumption which made him consider the transference of the child in analysis as something which had to be handled in conjunction with the parents themselves. From this point around which the law of the Oedipus turns, we determine in what manner the paternal function has intervened in the discourse of the child by also knowing how this function has intervened for the parents themselves.

According to Lacan the family is a social bond determined by a series of complexes, the Oedipus complex being the one that most clearly situates the child as a subject in his own discourse through the manner in which he attempts to answer the question of what a sexual being is.[1] The clearest articulation of the child's symptom is when it speaks of the place where the child is trapped in the encounter with his own sexual *jouissance* and the sexual relation of the parents. This is what Lacan refers to as the child being situated in regard to the real of the "parental couple".[2] But, when the child's symptom rather speaks on the side of an object that supports the mother's phantasm, the discourse in which the child is presented is one where the jouissance of the mother appears as an All, not mediated by the paternal function, and where there is no representation of the "parental couple". From this position the means of an articulation by the child of his own symptom is made more difficult.[3]

In making use of Lacan's words Maud Mannoni states that the specific nature of the symptom of the child is that it is at the same time "hooked" onto the symptom of the parents, and that we are required to intervene at this place to clarify what the demand of the child is:

> It is evident that if, apart from the fact that the neurosis of the child is his own affair, the neurotic child is at the same time the symptom of the mother or the parental couple, as a consequence we are then required to modify the technique.[4]

So, this modification of the technique in the analysis of the child does not divert from the ethics of psychoanalysis, that is, to listen to the unconscious of the transference, but, it is rather directed at the specific manner in which we listen to the transference of the child, as it is tied with the transference of one or both of the parents who bring the child to analysis.

The father and the paternal position

When Freud introduced the case of Little Hans in 1909 he made an appeal to the role of paternal authority:

> No one else in my opinion could possibly have prevailed on the child to make any such avowals; the special knowledge by means of which he was able to interpret the remarks made by his five-year-old son was indispensable, and without it the technical difficulties in the way of conducting a psycho-analysis upon so young a child would have been insuperable. It was only because the authority of a father and of a physician were united in a single person, and because in him both affectionate care and scientific interests were combined that it was possible in this one instance to apply the method to a use to which it would not otherwise have lent itself.[5]

In the scientific interests that Freud underlines we can discern a blurring of boundaries in a father, who observes and treats his son as an object of science, and who also has a strong transference to the Professor Freud, the subject supposed of knowledge for the father himself.

We hear then Freud's famous interpretation as something which made a knotting possible of the paternal position because of this transference in the father to Freud: *"long before you were born, I knew that a little boy would come into the world, and that he would be afraid of his father because he loved his mother"*.[6]

It is from this intervention in the presence of the father and the son that something is situated differently for the boy concerning the function of the father. The value of the name that Freud gave him in the case, Little Hans, doesn't just point to a boy who is the little phallus for the mother, but it is also tied with the symbolic aspects of the father. We can see that Freud considered this intervention necessary for the boy and his parents, as a means of inscribing the law of prohibition of incest, directed primarily to the mother, but evoked through the father. It is at this turning point of identification between being and having the phallus that the paternal position is opened for the child. The intervention is what ties the threat of castration with a supposition in regard to the father. From the assumption of the father as "the one who always had the phallus" an identification on the basis of filial love is made possible[7]. As Little Hans states: *"How can the Professor say I am afraid of you father, when it is in fact you that I love?"*[8]

It is to the place of forgetting, the place of primary repression, that the father in the Freudian clinic owes its function as the law that regulates the prohibition of *jouissance* through the erection of a myth. Castration is the necessary threat which is enabled on the basis of an identification with the father as an ideal, as an image.

In the Lacanian clinic it is the function of the father beyond the myth, as a signifier, that is in question. It is from this question that Lacan clarifies the necessary distinction for psychoanalysis: to know the difference between "being a father and acceding to the paternal position".9

The paternal position is an exception, a position that is not ever fully attained by anyone, but which provides a necessary supposition for the progression of the Oedipus dialectic. To suppose that there is somewhere one who can fully respond as a father enables the function to work as a quest for each one.

For Lacan the paternal position is then inscribed for the child through lack. When he speaks of the "paternal lack" it is also related to the distinction made above, between the father in reality and the paternal position, hence: "to speak of paternal lack in the family, is not the same as to speak of his lack in the complex".10 So, it is not in terms of any dimension of reality, but only in terms of a third, as the way the real father intervenes as agent of castration, that we can speak of this paternal lack. The real father intervenes as law, the law of the prohibition of incest, which is enabled through the signifying function of the symbolic father, and this is what makes the imaginary father appear as privating.

In the R.S.I. seminar Lacan situates the function of the father in the Borromean knot.11 The Oedipus complex is this knot which is tied for the child in the form of the symbolic operation of primary repression that enables him to proceed as a sexual being in language. In this respect the paternal function is the father as name, the real Other, the exception that is only in the knot. This is the impossible supported by the symbolic which Lacan plays around with by stating that it ex-ists.12 It is the knotting of primary repression which supports the Other as lacking, as Lacan states:

> There is no Other, except in saying it, but it is impossible to say completely. There is an Urverdrängt, an irreducible unconscious, the saying of which is not only impossible, but introduces as such the category of the impossible.13

The paternal position then is made efficacious only through lack. This is the fundamental turning point in what Lacan terms the *"pere-version"*, the particular version which makes the Oedipus function as a knot for each subject. About this he says the following:

> It is enough that he be a model of a function. This is what the father must be, in that he can only be an exception. The only way for him to be a model of the function is by fulfilling its type. It matters little that he has symptoms provided that he adds to them that of paternal perversion [*père-version*], meaning that its cause should be a woman, secured to him, in order to bear him children, and that, of these children, whether he wishes to or not, he takes paternal care.[14]

The *"pere-version"* is what adds to the symptoms of a father, by marking a point of desire and allowing a supposition, an exception, to function for the child in regard to his role. As Lacan underlines, the father in reality cannot do other than to be a type, but in addition a limit needs to be marked in relation to his jouissance. For the child this limit marker, as symbolic castration, points to at least one *jouissance* that is prohibited, the one in relation to the mother, which makes the law efficacious for him and gives him access to desire as desire of the Other. The *"pere-version"*, then, is this point of opening the child to the real of the parental couple, that is, the sexual jouissance of the parents, situating the child as phallus in a discourse which is promulgated by desire.

It is in this discourse, which hereby situates the child as subject, that we may be able to discern whether the paternal position, as a model of a signifying function, as metaphor, has intervened for the child by opening a path out of the identification with the object of the *jouissance* of the primordial Other, the mother.

Designative naming as an intervention in the real of the parental couple

Freud's intervention in the session with Little Hans and his father served the purpose of inscribing a supposition in the child in relation to the paternal position, which made an exception function in regard to the father figure as such. It was an inscription which put the symbolic father to work, the one which had to some degree already functioned as an Other for Hans, his phobia being a proof of this call made to the father. However, Hans' search for a father, was marked by what Lacan calls a *"pere-equation"*, a comparison in which the father remained in an imaginary position of fraternal rivalry in regard to the mother.[15] But, through the writing of the father to Freud, this call to the Other was made effective as a proper demand of the child. Hans' symptom of phobia was the "present" to this Other, the one supposed of knowledge. It is in the "non-sense" sent to the Professor Freud, the one who speaks to God, one of the Names of the Father, that another sense was evoked.

Gustavo Etkin proposes that a specific intervention is required in the analysis of a child, which knots the function of the symbolic at the level of the irruption of the real; something he defines in terms of a "designative naming".[16] This intervention names something which is also at the same time already constituted in the act of naming, as a nomination. It is the symbolic in support of what has already been inscribed as Other for the subject, and as such it anticipates what is already functioning as Name of the Father for the child.[17] It is a support of castration in the sense that it names something with this operation of the signifier that evokes the real that at the same ex-sists since it can only be designated through a supposition. According to Etkin this designative naming is a pure signifier in act, which as such resonates the function of the Name of the Father.[18]

The naming knots the paternal position, by producing something that was there before, but which at the same time as it is supposed, is impossible to demonstrate, as it has never existed. As Etkin notes: "It is about an anteriority, which is posterior to the Act that designates it as an anterior existence".[19] This intervention knots something at the point where the real of the parental couple irrupts for the child, producing in effect the associations which Freud calls the child's first sexual theories and family romances. The intervention then functions as an enunciation of the impossible, as what makes the past a pre-historic period that ex-sists to the subject.

So, could we in the case of Little Hans determine Freud's intervention as such an act that effected a designative naming? In Hans' associations following this intervention, we see that the love of the father is evoked, as a veering towards the father at the moment of substituting the ambivalence with love of the father. The construction of a pre-historic period of childhood is similar to the construction of the father as totem, which situates him as an exception in the construction of a signifying myth. The law is enacted through this signifying function which masks the real of castration. According to Joel Dor Freud's intervention "realised a symbolic designation", through "a naming which signifies the idea that the child has of what mobilises the desire of the mother".[20]

But, could it also be that, in this intervention with the presence of both the father and the son in the room, something was heard of the prohibition of incest as spoken to the father? *Thou shall not reintegrate thy product by making him your object of observation and treatment.*

We are here not considering an analysis of the father, that is, an analysis of the man, Max Graff, which would be something completely different. Rather, it is this point of the real father as impossible which is supported through the name designated in the symbolic that also functions as a limit in regard to the father in reality. It is a marking of the symbolic in the repetition of what is transcribed from a father to a son, but in what emerges of the real through the accidental, the missed encounter, the *tuché*. In giving an account of the accidental irruption of the real, Lacan refers to Freud's reports of a father who encounters his dead son calling out to him in a dream:

> No one can say what the death of a child is, except the father qua father, that is to say no conscious being.[21]

So, for a father as well, the paternal position is the exception that marks a limit to his *jouissance* and functions as an addition to his symptoms. It is in a missed encounter that the failure in the sexual relation of the parents may be heard as what is repeated in the child's symptom. It is in regard to these "accidents" or the accidental factors of the ontogenesis of the subject, according to Freud, that we can determine the necessity of an intervention in regard to the real of the parental couple for the child.[22] Such an intervention may function as a designative naming which evokes the real through the symbolic of the law of the prohibition of incest that may signify the paternal function for the child in conjunction with the parents.

To conclude

To conclude we can draw a parallel to the case with which we began this paper. In this case of a 10 year old boy and his parents an intervention was considered necessary to support the place of the paternal position for the boy as well as for the mother. This position was lacking in regard to the father and was veiled in the discourse of the mother. The child's symptoms, the accidental factors and the burn marks on his body, which occurred when playing around with the welding tools of his father, were a call to this paternal position, to the "father" as law, at the point of a blurring of boundaries between the child's and the parents' fantasies. It is at this point of blurring of the child's and the parents' discourse that the symptom of the child is "hooked" onto the symptom of one or both of the parents.[23]

It is then, to the father we turn, the real one, the impossible, when the *tuché*, the accidents of his function appear as repetition in the child's symptom. But it is in the failure of the parental couple that we read this impossible real of the sexual relation for the child, and it is from this that we take direction in regard to any necessary interventions made to the parents and the child. Such interventions must be carried by the naming that designates the paternal position as an exception for the child, as well as for the parents, in order to support the writing that occurs for the child of his own symptom in an analysis.

Notes

1. Lacan, J. *Les complexes famileaux. Essai d'analyse d'une fonction en psychologie.* Navarin Éditeur.
2. Lacan, J. *Deux notes sur l'enfant* IN: *Ornicar? no. 37 (1986).*
3. Op. cit.
4. Mannoni, M. *L'enfant arriere et sa mere. Etude psychanalytique (1964).* Paris, Seuil, coll. Points, no. 132, 1981, note 1, p. 114, my translation.
5. Freud, S. *Analysis of a Phobia in a Five-year-Old-Boy (1909),* Collected Papers. Vol. 3. The International Psycho-Analytical Library No. 9. Ed. E. Jones. Basic Books. NY, 1959. Introduction, p. 149.
6. Op. cit. p. 186.
7. Lacan, J. *Le Séminaire, Livre IV. La Relation d'objet.* Éditions du Seuil. 1994. séminaire 06.03.1957.
8. Freud, S., *Analysis of a Phobia in a Five-year-Old-Boy (1909),* Collected Papers, Vol. 3, The International Psycho-Analytical Library No. 9, Ed. E. Jones. Basic books, NY, 1959.
9. Lacan, J., *Le Séminaire. Livre IV. La Relation d'objet.* Éditions du Seuil. 1994. séminaire 06.03.1957.
10. Lacan. J., *Les formations de l'inconscient. 1957–1958.* séminaire 15.01.1958
11. Lacan, J., *The Seminar of Jacques Lacan. R.S.I. 1974–1975,* unpublished translation.

12. Op. cit. Lesson 17.12.1974.
13. Op. cit. Lesson 17.12.1974.
14. Op. cit. Lesson 21.01.1975.
15. Lacan, J., *Le Seminaire, Livre IV. La Relation d'objet.* Éditions du Seuil. 1994séminaire 06.03.1957.
16. Etkin, G., *Nothing returns from the Real.* IN: Psychosis—Who Speaks? Papers of the Freudian School of Melbourne. Vol. 16. Lacanian Psychoanalytic Writings. Ed. D. Pereira. Melbourne. 1995, p. 73.
17. In this context the concept of "symbolic anticipation" developed by Jean Bergès and Gabriel Balbo in their book *"L'enfant et la psychanalyse"* is relevant, as it points to the manner by which the Name of the Father has intervened or not in the discourse of the mother with the child. See Bergès, J. & Balbo, G. *"L'enfant et la psychanalyse". Nouvelles perspectives.* Collection Bibliothèque de Clinique Psychanalytique. Masson. Paris. 1994.
18. Etkin, G., *Nothing returns from the Real.* IN: Psychosis—Who Speaks? Papers of the Freudian School of Melbourne, Vol. 16, Lacanian Psychoanalytic Writings. Ed. Pereira.Melbourne 1995, p. 72.
19. Op. cit. p. 69.
20. Dor, J. *Le Père et sa Fonction en Psychanalyse.* Editions Erès. 1998. p. 49, my translation.
21. Lacan, J. *The Seminar of Jaques Lacan. Book XI. The Four Fundamental Concepts of Psychoanalysis,* Ed. J. A. Miller, Translated by A. Sheridan. Penguin Books. 1979.
22. Freud, S. *Three Essays on the Theory of Sexuality* (1905), The Pelican Freud Library. Vol. 7. On Sexuality. *Introduction to the Third Edition* (1914).
23. In this context it is interesting to note that Robert Lévy in his book *L'infantile en psychanalyse* proposes that the child's symptom functions as the *sinthome* of one or both parents and from this he proposes that the analysis with a child and the parents is the enabling of a repression proper for the child. 131313 See Lévy, R., *L'infantile en psychanalyse. La construction du symptôme chez l'enfant.* Collection «Hypothèses». Éditions érès. Arcanes. 2008.

PART IV

ON LOVE AND KNOWLEDGE

CHAPTER FIFTEEN

The promise of love

Michael Plastow

> The approach to being, is it not there that the extreme of love, true love, resides? And true love—it was certainly not analytic experience that made this discovery, of which the eternal modulation of the themes on love adequately reflect—true love opens up onto hate.
>
> Jacques Lacan, *Encore*

An analysand, a young woman, began a session by speaking of the departure of a housemate. She said that she was glad he was moving out because she did not like him. Furthermore, in her eyes, he had been responsible for the loss of a glass of hers that had disappeared during the farewell party. "I hate him for it", she said, "the glass just disappeared and he's leaving anyway".

She had been referred following the break-up of a relationship. Even though *she* had precipitated the break-up, she refused to accept not having contact with her ex-boyfriend, pursuing him to the point that he had threatened legal action against her. Whilst retaining her love for the boyfriend, she reserved her hate for her rivals: the current girlfriend, his mother and his sister.

Later in this same session, she noted that she had been re-reading Ovid, specifically his *Remedies for Love*. She noted: "I wish I'd remembered that when I was feeling suicidal after I broke up" with the ex-boyfriend. This wish, formulated as a regret for something that had not happened, was also echoed by the regret for not being able to follow certain of Ovid's remedies, such as travelling which she felt was not currently an option for her.

We are presented with a difficulty in undoing the ties of love, a difficulty that manifests as hate. I would like to take up this reference to Ovid in respect of these questions of love and its undoing in relation to hate. We might then attempt to take this further in order to see where it might lead and to examine what might be done with this hate.

The *Remedies for Love*, or *Remedia Amores*, written as a guide for falling out of love, opens with the result of the failure to undo the bonds of love:

> Why has some lover cast the noose about his neck, and hung, a sad burden from a lofty beam? Why has one pierced his breast with the unyielding sword? He who, unless he gives o'er, will die of hapless love ...[1]

Ovid's project here is to propose how one might give over from love. But in articulating this melancholic position of the lover who cannot desist, he indicates how deadly the wager of love might be.

In its place he proposes that the object of love must be mourned:

> Who save a fool would forbid a mother to weep o'er the body of her son? Not then must she be counselled. When she has shed tears and fulfilled her mind's distress then may words set a limit to that grief.[2]

The *Remedies for Love* follows on from Ovid's work *Artis Amatoriae*, or *The Art of Love*. Here love is presented as an art or technique to be mastered, but only in so far as this constitutes a response to something to which one is subjected:

> ... to me Love shall yield, though he wound my breast with his bow, and whirl aloft his brandished torch. The more violently Love

has pierced and branded me, the better shall I avenge the wound he has made ...[3]

This avenging, the making good of this wound, Ovid tells us requires "work".[4] Thus there is sort of ethical act necessitated here. The object of love, Ovid proposes:

> ... will not come floating down to you through the tenuous air, she must be sought, the girl whom your glance approves.[5]

The path to love, though, is not a direct one: it passes via a deception. Thus Ovid proposes that "all love deceives and finds its sustenance in delaying".[6] And again he puts forward that in the game of love:

> You must *play* the lover, and *counterfeit* heartache with words: her belief in that you must win by any device.[7] [My italics]

That is, the subject can advance towards desire only via the deception of love, or via love as deception. And if the lover fools the beloved, in this game it is also he who is fooled. Thus, according to Ovid:

> Yet the pretender begins to love truly after all, and often becomes what he has feigned to be. Wherefore you women, be more compliant to pretenders; one day will the love be true which but now was false.[8]

In other words, the deception of love is precisely the path to truth, via the question of a becoming or being: the lover "becomes what he has feigned to be".

Moreover, one of the modalities of deceit that Ovid proposes as fundamental to love is that of the promise:

> See that you promise: what harm is there in promises? In promises anyone can be rich. Hope, once conceived, endures for long; ... Once you have given, you may be abandoned with good reason: your gift is gone, she will have taken it and lost nothing herself. But what you have *not given* you may seem always on the point of giving. ... lest what she has given be given for *nothing*, she will give yet more.[9] [My italics]

Here we are not so far from the manner in which Lacan much later defined love as "to give what one does not have to one who is not", at least in the first part of this formula, in this question of the "not given". What is specific to the function of the promise is that it has to remain unfulfilled. After all the promise, or *to promise*—here in the Latin *promittere*—is "to put forward" or "to put off". Love, as we noted before with Ovid, finds sustenance in delaying, that is, in putting off, in promoting precisely what is "not given".

We can say that it is precisely the promise that love offers that is able to sustain desire, keeping alive the "not given" to which Ovid refers. To be engaged to be married is to be "promised" to a loved one. But when the promise is put to the test of being fulfilled, it is inevitably found to be wanting in some way or other.

Once the honeymoon wanes and the promises not all fulfilled, then the promise that love held for the future, might turn to regret for what was not received in the past. Both cases attempt to make what is "not given" into a given, something that should be given, to make good what lacks. It is this point of realisation that something will remain "not given" in which the illusions of love are revealed that might mark the emergence of hate.

It is precisely hate that intrudes upon this deceit of love and threatens to disrupt its illusions. Accordingly, Ovid advises:

> ... approach your mistress' litter in dissembling fashion, and lest someone intrude hateful ears to your words, hide them, so far as you may, in cunning ambiguities.[10]

For Ovid, to hate is to participate as much in the passions as is to love:

> He who ends love by hating either loves still or will find it hard to end his misery.[11]

Freud also recognises that hate may follow on from love. He notes the following, however, in *Instincts and their Vicissitudes*:

> If a love relation with a given object is broken off, hate not infrequently emerges in its place, so that we get the impression of a transformation of love into hate.[12]

Nonetheless Freud points out that hate is frequently a forerunner of love. Thus:

> ... feelings of love that have not yet become manifest express themselves to begin with by hostility and aggressive tendencies ...[13]

Hence in a chronological sense hate may precede love. But Freud goes beyond this and in *The Ego and the Id* he proposes that:

> ... hate, as a relation to objects is older than love.[14]

Further, in the paper *The Disposition to Obsessional Neurosis*, he comes to the conclusion that hate is the precursor of love. There he refers to an assertion by Wilhelm Stekel, a psychologist who influenced Freud and was for a time a disciple of Freud's, to the effect that hate, and not love, is the primary emotional relation between men.[15]

What is put forward here is that hate not only precedes love in a chronological sense, whether in the individual case or in Freud's propositions of a developmental bent, particularly in *The Ego and the Id*, but that it also has logical priority to love.

Freud also notes that not only do love and hate appear to be transformed into one another, but that the two regularly accompany one another. He gives to this, of course, the term "ambivalence", a term that has been much overused to the degree that it has become an explain-all and therefore meaningless.

Lacan also notes that "there is no love without hate"[16] and proposes another term with the neologism *"hainamoration"*, translated as "hate-love" or perhaps we could render it as "falling in hate". Lacan had long linked the terms of love and hate to a third, that of ignorance, as the three passions of being, or "being or nothingness" he proposes in *Seminar I*.[17]

So if love and hate go hand in hand, if "there is no love without hate", nonetheless we can by no means say that they are simply two sides of the same coin, they are not equivalent. How then can we further differentiate love and hate beyond their affective concomitants?

Let us take a citation from James Joyce's *Ulysses*, from a scene in Bella Cohen's brothel:

Bloom: (Bitterly) Man and woman, *love*, what is it? A cork and a bottle?
Zoe: (In sudden sulks) I *hate* a rotter that's insincere. Give a bleeding whore a chance.[18] [My italics]

Now even if the cork fits the bottle, it does not fill it, a space remains. But this notion of love nonetheless promotes a certain oneness, even in such a physical metaphor. On the other hand, hate promotes a division, a disruption, a wound that is bleeding. Hate moves from insincerity towards the sincere, towards something of truth.

But how do we tease this cork and bottle apart? Now Lacan notes that Freud uses Empedocles, the pre-Socratic, like a corkscrew. Freud's principal reference to Empedocles is in *Analysis Terminable and Interminable* by which he draws support for the division of his two primal drives, Eros and destructiveness in the two fundamental principles of Empedocles, namely φιλια and νεικος, Friendship and Discord, or Love and Hate, the latter names drawn from a certain experience of human passions.[19] It was in particular in order to counter the lack of acceptance that the death drive had found, even amongst psychoanalysts, that Freud drew upon this ancient lineage.

In Empedocles, Love draws things together into a unity, a totality represented as a sphere that excludes all that it does not contain. Here difference is eradicated in favour of a Oneness, the many is eschewed in favour of the One. Hate, or Strife, on the other hand, favours the multiplicity of elements. "And these things", proposes Empedocles:

> ... never cease from constantly alternating
> at one time all coming together by love into one,
> at another time being borne apart separately by the hostility of strife.[20]

Love holds out the promise of a Oneness, that is, to draw upon Lacan, love promotes the possibility of a sexual relation. Hence it is hate that might be able to reveal the truth of the lack of a relation, of course, ineluctably, via this path of love.

But for Empedocles, only like can know like. And this applies not only to the two principles he proposes but also to the four elements that are the product of the division of the One:

> By earth we see earth, by water, water;
> by aither, shining aither; but by fire, blazing fire;
> love by love and strife by baneful strife.[21]

Thus the Oneness that love promotes can know nothing of strife or hate and the multiplicity sustained by it. Here we encounter Lacan's comment that Aristotle rightly draws out the consequences when he states that God, for Empedocles, in not knowing hate, was the most ignorant of all beings.[22] God as the Oneness or totality effected by love, can know nothing of what is outside of Him. He can then know nothing of hate and therefore of the many; God can know nothing of difference then. Here we return, albeit in a different way, to the illusion or deception that love promotes of which we spoke with Ovid.

Parmenides was not able to say more than that "Being is". Empedocles adds that Being is itself, a unity.[23] But if Being is here invested in Love, it is surely non-Being, or nothingness, towards which Hate moves in its annihilation of the One.

But whilst the existence and alternation of both principles of love and hate is incontrovertible, whilst both poles are necessary, Empedocles nonetheless makes his choice, placing himself on the side of hate or strife:

> I too am now one of these, an exile from the gods and a wanderer,
> Trusting in mad strife.[24]

Lacan also places his emphasis on discord, on the lack of a sexual relation, in reference to truth. This is the direction he takes in his reading of the pre-Socratics, particularly Empedocles and Heraclitus, in their radicalisation of discord and the primacy they give to it. The discord here refers to the principle of hate or strife as articulated by Empedocles, but also to the fundamental division indicated by the love/hate dichotomy. Lacan's, and Freud's, reference to the pre-Socratics, is necessary to overcome the bias in Western thought that was later introduced in the form of the Platonic Idea, as a type of apparent reconciliation of the radical divisions that the pre-Socratics were able to articulate.

Thus for Abel Jeannière:

> In Plato, beings are the reflections of the ideal unity of the One and
> of the Multiple; the primordial unity does not disappear where it
> is divided, it never completely breaks, each being is a reflection of
> the One and of the Multiple; in Empedocles, unity no longer exists,
> neither in the human world nor in man, it does not even exist in
> image ...[25]

Alain Badiou also proposes that:

> The Idea, in Plato's sense ... is like a cork plugging the hiatus
> between knowledge and truth. It brings a fallacious peace to the
> original discord.[26]

Once again this cork of love serves to obscure something, to perpetuate an ignorance. For Lacan it is precisely through hate that knowledge
can be de-supposed. He proposes that he be read in this way and that
he might read Aristotle in this way.[27] In relation to what we have been
putting forward, Lacan notes that:

> The relation of being to being is not this relation of harmony that
> has always, we don't quite know why, been given to us by a tradi-
> tion in which Aristotle, who sees nothing but supreme jouissance in
> it, converges with Christianity, for which it is a beatitude. This is to
> become bogged down in the grasping of a mirage.[28]

This mirage, this illusion we could say, is the promise that love holds
out to us, whether it is Christian love or a romantic love. This illusory
promise nonetheless allows love to continue. It is sustained by a "not
given", in other words this promise draws its power precisely from
remaining unfulfilled. This promise of love keeps desire alive precisely
by sustaining the "not given".

But if love is a cork and a bottle, to take up Joyce's ironical proposal,
it is hate then that comes to unplug this intimate relation to expose a
bleeding wound, the lack of a sexual relation. It is in this light that we
might consider Lacan's statement that "true love opens up onto hate".[29]
Hate, we could also say, opens up onto the truth of love.

Notes

1. Ovid. *The Remedies for Love*. Loeb Classical Library, Harvard University Press: Cambridge, Massachusetts, 1979, p. 179.
2. *Ibid.*, p. 187.
3. Ovid. *The Art of Love*. Loeb Classical Library, Harvard University Press: Cambridge, Massachusetts, 1979, p. 15.
4. *Ibid.*, p. 15. Here "work" translates the Latin *labor*.
5. *Ibid.*, p. 15.
6. Ovid. *The Remedies for Love. Op. cit.*, p. 185.
7. Ovid. *The Art of Love. Op. cit.*, p. 55.
8. Ovid. *The Art of Love. Op. cit.*, p. 55.
9. Ovid. *The Art of Love. Op. cit.*, pp. 43–45.
10. Ovid. *The Art of Love. Op. cit.*, p. 47.
11. Ovid. *The Remedies for Love. Op. cit.*, 223.
12. Freud, S. "Instincts and their Vicissitudes". *SE* XIV, p. 139.
13. Freud, S. "The Ego and the Id". *SE* XIX, p. 43.
14. Freud, S. "Instincts and their Vicissitudes". *SE* XIV, p. 139.
15. Freud, S. "The Disposition to Obsessional Neurosis". *SE* XII, p. 325.
16. Lacan, J. *Le Séminaire livre XX: Encore*. Seuil: Paris, 1975, p. 82.
17. Lacan, J. *Le Séminaire livre I: Les Écrits Techniques de Freud*. Seuil: Paris, p. 297.
18. Joyce, J. *Ulysses*. Penguin: London, 1992, p. 619.
19. Jeannière, A. *Les Présocratiques: L'Aurore de la Pensée Grecque*. Seuil: Paris, 1996, pp. 166–167.
20. Empedocles. *The Poem of Empedocles*. University of Toronto Press: Toronto, 2001, pp. 223–225.
21. *Ibid.*, p. 221.
22. Lacan, J. *Le Séminaire livre XX: Encore*. Seuil: Paris, 1975, p. 82.
23. Jeannière, A. *Op. Cit.*, p. 165.
24. Empedocles, *Op. Cit.*, p. 217.
25. Jeannière, A. *Op. Cit.*, p. 176.
26. Badiou, A. "Lacan and the Pre-Socratics". In: Žižek, S. (Ed.) *Lacan: the Silent Partners*. Verso: London, 2006, p. 12.
27. Lacan, J. *Le Séminaire de Jacques Lacan. Livre XX; Encore*. Éditions du Seuil: Paris, 1975, p. 164.
28. *Ibid.*, p. 133.
29. *Ibid.*, p. 133.

CHAPTER SIXTEEN

In the style of loving

Rodney Kleiman

"Love, it seems to some, I have downgraded." states Lacan in his 1964 seminar on the fundamentals of psychoanalysis.[1] Indeed one could be pardoned for perceiving a somewhat negative connotation attached to the phenomenon of love since "lacanism" reconceived it. Love is variously described as a deception, an illusion or a narcissistic construct. Given the available evidence who would argue with these views? Still worse, love is an imaginary formation; that terrible thing. Beware the imaginary formation, anathema to the poetic beauty of the symbolic and the sublime insubstantiality of the real.

Despite these unappealing characteristics, love continues to recur. It recurs not just in life but also in the course of every analysis. This recurrence is concurrent with the presence of analysis. The transference was and still remains, a manifestation of love. There can be no analysis without transference and therefore no analysis without love.

Freud must take some blame for the downgrading of love. He initially emphasizes the transference love in its production of a resistance to free association and the continuation of analytic work. A resistance that must be overcome so that the true work may continue. But it is clearly a necessary resistance and allows for the possibility of analysis and interpretation.

Lacan in his own time takes us to another field, when he bequeathed us his structure of language culminating in the privileging of the signifier. This he does by inverting the Sassurean algorithm, placing the signifier on top and dislocating it from an absolute connection with the signified.

The signifier represents the subject for another signifier. This radical reworking of the logic and structure of language and thus the unconscious demanded an associated reworking of the transference. The Sassurean structure by contrast, designated the sign as the unit of language. The sign defined as the composite of the signified over the signifier. It would seem we are much less enamoured of this original attempt at conceptualizing language and thus the status of the sign is at low ebb. The sign simply represents something for someone. The signifier represents the subject whereas the sign represents some thing. At times this sign can be construed as functioning outside of human discourse. For example in the mating rituals of the animal kingdom, the robin's red breast, or the complex dances of the bees in communicating to their co-workers the location of the nearest nectar. These signs certainly represent something, but are not representative of the order of the symbolic and the unconscious and thus the discourse of humanity.

What place then remains, if any, for the sign in human discourse? Why do I ask? I ask because of love, that most human of occupations. Love, it is said, is but a sign. Here is the final nail in the coffin. Love is but a sign. Thus love merely represents something for someone. Let us quickly dispense with its resistance and return to the purity of our signifiers and the desire they inscribe! Signs are not the real stuff of interpretation, so the only point to interpreting the love, which is transference, is to keep things moving and to overcome the resistance to speech evoked by love. But one might perhaps resistantly think otherwise. If these signs of love are the transference is not this transference itself still worthy of interpretation? Should we not perhaps reconsider the status of the sign?

Let us look at two clinical examples worth considering.

Firstly, here is a young man, intelligent and selectively organized in the manner of the obsessional. At the start of each analytic session there is a protracted ritual comprising the placement of various objects, the paraphernalia of modern life; phone, wallet, keys, sunglasses, coat, umbrella, book, etc. These things are placed, one by one, upon a chair before the descent onto the couch.

Actions, a ritual, a dance, performed in silence, without any speech or commentary. Why it's a sign! If it's a sign then is it love? Is this the sign of love, the love that transference invariably situates? These preparations are particular to this individual. What might be said about them? As a sign they must represent something to someone. What might be said to him or by him that returns the representation of this sign to the field of speech and the pertinence of the signifier? If this sign, a sign of love, is the elaboration of a mating ritual, could it be said of this dance: "Before I lie down with you, my love, my things need to be in place. They must be well secured in place, where I can keep an eye on them".

Prior to that anxiety-ridden jump into the impossibility of the sexual relation comes love. Love has a style. The signs are there. These signs are demanding to be spoken about, in order to carry the truth of the signifier.

The second example is a young woman. Upon exiting the waiting room in moving towards the consulting room, instead of leaving the door ajar and allowing me, as one might expect, to close it, she turns, grasps the handle in a slow almost pained but deliberate fashion and pulls the door shut behind her. It strikes me, this sign, because no-one else, no-one else out of quite a few, has maneuvered themselves into the position to make this action. Is it a sign? Is it a sign of love, a repetition within and of the transference? Is it a sign which represents who knows what, something particular?

Does it not at a certain moment possibly call forth the truth of the interpretation of some history? The moment of her past when she, somewhat amazingly, left her family behind in an instant. Amazing because of the undeniable intensity of that family in demanding that no one should ever leave it. Did she not attempt then to close the door on her past and on those figures constitutive of her love? Does she not now continue to close that door in order to keep someone out of the place where she loves?

Such signs, of course, could only come to be interpreted, at a moment where they are spoken in the treatment and in relation to the rewriting of history that occurs in an analysis. But are not these signs quite unlike the rituals of the animal kingdom, in that they carry not a simple meaning but a relationship to the signifier? If these were simply the signs of animal behavior they would otherwise be of no significance beyond the message that they communicate? Indeed then they would not even be recognized as worthy of either comment or consideration.

But within the transference such signs are not reducible to the mere representation of need, to stimulus and response. As action within transference and expressions of love they lead us beyond a simple sign towards interpretation.

This man does not need to secure his items. This woman does not need to close the door. Something of the style of their love and its expression demands these actions. These actions clearly occur without any recognition on behalf of the individual concerned that they are a sign of anything, let alone a sign of love. Would they even be aware that they have shown themselves in that moment in these actions? Would they even be able to recall what they had just done? Certainly neither has ever yet seemed close to commenting directly on these occurrences.

I want to take a step back now before returning to these considerations of the sign and the style of love and its possibility as interpretation. Lacan, as you are well aware, utilizes the writings of Plato and the character of Socrates presented therein, to approach a reworking of the concept of transference.

In the Transference Seminar, at least the version available to us, he states, as has oft been quoted,

> The secret of Socrates will be behind everything that we will say this year about transference. Socrates admitted this secret. But it is not because one has admitted a secret that a secret ceases to be a secret. Socrates claims to know nothing, except to be able to recognize what love is and he tells us (I come to a testimony of Plato, specifically in the Lysis) namely to recognize infallibly, wherever he encounters them, where the lover is and where the beloved.[2]

The *Lysis* tells the story of Socrates whilst out walking, as was his wont, meeting up with a number of Athenian youths. Lysis is one of these young men. What follows is the imposition of the Socratic method of questioning, directed at the enigma of the definition of friendship. Of course in the end the method does not arrive at knowledge of what friendship is but at recognition of ignorance. In spite of all knowing that this friendship exists between Socrates, Lysis, and the other youths, no one can define friendship.

Socrates greets Hippothales, the first youth he meets, near to the beginning of the Lysis. He asks Hippothales about his love object. "Whom is your prime beauty?" says Socrates. The boy blushes, take note of this sign, I add now, as Socrates did.

He answered only with a blush. So I added, said Socrates, "Hippothales, there is no longer any need for you to tell me whether you are in love or not, since I am sure you are not only in love, but pretty far gone in it too by this time. For though in most matters I am a poor useless creature, yet by some means or other I have received from heaven the gift of being able to detect at a glance both a lover and a beloved."

Socrates doesn't say that he knows what love is, as such. Who can know what love is? What he possesses is the ability to recognize the signs of love: to recognize the lover and the beloved. There is a world of difference between these two capacities. Whilst suggesting knowledge of love, there is no reduction to a knowing. Socrates has the capacity to interpret signs: the signs of love. Is this not Socrates and his interpretation of the transference? Just as in the *Symposium* his feat as an analyst is to recognize Agathon and Alcibiades; lover and beloved.

No one can know what love is. Yet it is possible to recognize love. It is because no one can know what love is that everyone wants to know what love is. Why not suppose that someone, Socrates, the analyst, knows? Why not hope that they know what no one knows?

As Socrates states, his capacity is not the possession of knowledge but the gift to recognize a sign. But more than that, he is able to speak of love via this recognition.

What is love? No one knows and yet it is the transference. What is the transference? No one knows yet it is love. The effects of transference as effects of love are recognizable.

What is gravity? No one knows yet we know of it and we name it. We know of it on the basis of its effects. Effects, which like love make the world, go round. Effects, which keep things in their place. Effects, which allow one to move through the doorways of opportunity.

If Lacan downgraded love it was to permanently remove it from the sphere of what could be knowable. This is the essential aspect of psychoanalysis. To work with the unknown, which can be named love and to give love its full weight and gravity.

The signs of love observed in an analysis are not confined to the behaviors I have mentioned as examples. There is many a manner in which love is expressed and a particular manner for each. These are the signs of the style of loving. Hear the speech, the pauses, the inflections, the actions, the affects, the hostilities, the demands, the way things evolve, the eagerness, the lassitude, the sleepiness, the boredom, the excitement, the clothing and the disrobing. All these signs add their weight to what is said because they can never stand on their own. They can only be recognized by their relationship to the signifiers of history as articulated in an analysis.

Thus I am, somewhat contentiously perhaps, disputing the over simplified dichotomy between the sign and the signifier which has allowed love to be downgraded in terms of its significance for the purpose of analysis. There is no natural sign in human discourse. The sign was left behind in the garden for the birds and the bees. The birds and the bees now take us quite somewhere else. Humanity is of a different order and cannot return to the world of the natural sign, anymore than to the free range of unimpeded sexuality.

Love still offers all the possibilities of interpretation.

It is the style of Dora's slap, the one she gives to Freud. It is the love within the inhibited vacillations of the Ratman. These are the styles and the manners that can be recognized. Why not come to recognize one's own style? It is not inconceivable that that is precisely what people do in concluding an analysis. The impact and effect such recognition might have in terms of what one could do with it should not be underestimated. To do something, not with the impossible knowledge of love, but with the recognition of one's own distinctive style of loving. It is a style replete with the anxieties, inhibitions and symptoms of the world of one's desire.

If there were a sexual relation there would be no love. Nature has no need of love. The origin of love, product of language, child of the symbolic, is the lack of the sexual relation. But it is still with love and its drama and demands with which we are drawn and entitled to work in psychoanalysis. Not in order ultimately to know the truth of love, but to recognize its style, its implications, its dependence on the signifier, and most of all to find in love its possibilities.

Notes

1. Lacan, J. *The Four Fundamental Concepts of Psychoanalysis,* Penguin Books [1987].
2. Lacan, J. *Transference The Seminar of Jacques Lacan Book VIII.* Translated by Cormac Gallagher.

CHAPTER SEVENTEEN

The conduct of love in psychoanalysis

Peter Gunn

As late as the Victorian era, behaviour, particularly the behaviour of women of the middle class, was prescribed by means of conduct manuals. Even today we have the manual of psychiatry, the *Diagnostic and Statistical Manual* (DSM), wherein conduct, when assessed as sufficiently at odds with "societal norms or rules", is assigned the status of a disorder.

To what then might we refer conduct in psychoanalysis? For enlightenment I would like to go back to two authors of the late eighteenth and early nineteenth centuries. In their writings each of these was, in their own way, at odds with the prescription of conduct.

Let us begin with the following passage:

> The truth, Juliette, is that, a certain undeniable progress notwith-
> standing, your conscience has yet to reach the stage I should desire;
> what I demand of it is that it become so warped as to be unable
> to reassume its former shape; to achieve this there are means to
> employ ... Those means, my dearest friend, are simple in them-
> selves: they consist in doing, immediately, in cold blood, that very
> thing which, done in the throes of passion, has been able to cause
> you remorse when later on you recover your wits. This way you

strike squarely and hard at the virtuous impulse the instant it bares itself. ... [E]mploy this secret, it never fails: directly a moment of calm favours the resurgence of virtue, announcing itself under the colours of remorse, for that is always the guise it wears in its endeavour to regain ascendancy over us—then, directly when you perceive it, commit forthwith the act you are wont to regret; by the fourth repetition of the trick you will hear the nagging voice of conscience no more, and then you shall be at peace for the rest of your days.

You might recognise this. It is from *Juliette*, the work of one The Marquis de Sade, also known as the Divine Marquis.[1] The words are put into the mouth of a woman, a woman to whom Sade gives the name Clairwil. This woman of clear will acts as a mentor for the novice Juliette.

Now on the face of it *Juliette* is also a conduct manual, albeit the reverse side of the medal. Here the sentiment of shame is to be taken by the young woman as a signal for conduct which runs counter to sentiment. But in Sade instruction has the force of an imperative, an imperative which calls not only for conduct which runs counter to sentiment, but which is to be obeyed without forethought and in cold blood. Indeed, it is to be obeyed with an indifference and a resolution which is deadly in its very execution.

It is by reference to this imperative that Clairwil chides Juliette for her lack of progress. And yet we know that just before she says this Juliette has joined her in an orgy of torture and murder. So it seems that here we have an imperative which goes beyond even the murderous. When it is subject to judgment even the murderous becomes inadequate, being thus reduced to the homicidal, and to sentiment. Indeed, according to Sade, to the extent that any act which this imperative incites remains subject to judgement that act is no more than conduct, conduct which is subject to the voice of conscience or its institutional manifestation, the court of law.

In its demand for yet more this then is an imperative which calls for something which goes beyond the realm of general, codified conduct itself. And, as Lacan shows us in "Kant With Sade", Sade here has something in common with another eighteenth century writer, Immanuel Kant.[2]

But rather than Kant let us now turn to an author who was very aware of conduct and conduct manuals, Jane Austen. You will remember that in Austen's novel *Emma* there is a scene in which our eponymous heroine finds herself alone with Mr. Elton in a carriage. She begins to talk on the subject of the weather but scarcely has she begun when, as Austen describes it, "she found her subject cut up—her hand seized—her attention demanded, and Mr. Elton actually making violent love to her".

Now, if I might be a little direct for a moment, there are many ways to speak about the fuck. All of them are circuitous. To make love is, in modern usage, one such way of speaking. This of course is not Austen's usage. The act she describes is itself a circumlocution: what Mr. Elton is doing is making a declaration of love.

If I shock you by mentioning the fuck and Austen's novel on love in the same breath I would ask you to consider that Lacan, when he speaks about love, is unsentimental, indeed, as unsentimental as Austen. Lacan tells us that that when one speaks of love, the love which relates to a man and a woman, one engages in an act of circumlocution around the fuck. That is, love, if it is spoken of, does no more, and also no less, than attempt to give articulation to that violent fleshly conjugation with the poetic indirectness of the word.[3] Thus, as Lacan tells us, for the speaking being, what makes up for the lack in the sexual relation is not the being of One but love.

Let us now consider conduct in another context, that of the psychoanalytic clinic.

A patient of mine, who I will call Tad, tells me that some time ago he had stopped praying to God. He gives as his reason his perception that he had been harshly dealt with by a judge in a court of law. This followed a charge of obscene exposure. He had appeared many times on similar charges but on this occasion the judge, who happened to be a woman, handed him a custodial sentence.

Now it would be easy to be seduced by this proffering of banishment from God. We might see it as suffering, the complaint of someone who we would categorise as neurotic. But if Tad ceased appealing to God he did not stop proffering himself in the eyes of women. If he was momentarily struck down by the possibility that his contentment in his pleasures might be thwarted by being put away this did not detain him for long.[4]

But, we neurotics cry, how does he, as it were, pull this off? It is true that, in speaking of this incident, Tad mentions that he thought the judge would favour the account of the woman to whom he exposed himself. But this does not take us very far. If we ourselves are unsentimental in the view we take of Tad's position we can, I suggest, see that he himself is rigorously unsentimental.

Tad is, in reality, no fool. Indeed, like the Marquis de Sade he shows himself to be something of a Kantian. There is, after all, a world of difference between who Tad is in those anonymous, clandestine encounters in the street or the carpark in which he presents himself for the eye of a passing woman, and who he is when, having apparently recovered his wits, he is named before a court of law.

What we can take Tad to have grasped at some level is that when he is exposed by his name in this way, that is, before a court of law, and in front of a woman to wit, she is likely to be as unsentimental as he. That is, he knows that, whereas a male judge might exercise some flexibility, judging him only on the witless exhibition of an appendage, a woman will undoubtedly apply the rules of conduct to which Tad finds himself attached by this appendage, conduct which, if the appendage is his, is judged to be that of a man. That being the case she will see through his artless appeals for love and be rigorous in acting to subject him to the law.

It is true that, by enlisting the efforts of another, in this case his lawyer, Tad did manage to successfully appeal. But this law, the one from which, faced by the woman judge, Tad pleads to be excused, is stiff in a more fundamental way. It is stiff not only in its indifference to sentiment but in the firmness with which it holds to the difference between the sexes.

We can surmise therefore that this is more than the law of the land. The woman judge would, Tad feared, act to subject him to the law of that one signifier, the phallus. It is this law which names men in their difference from those others who are called women. Under this law to be, in name, a man is to be excluded from the being of the woman. This law not only prescribes the conduct of men in order that they not cause offense to women but it itself exhibits that breach which is sexual difference.

For one such as Tad, though he appears as a man, he can only make himself present by what he presents for the gaze of a woman in the form of his penis. To be exposed by the law of the phallus as not-woman would be devastating.

But what Tad has over both us neurotics and also Immanuel Kant is that if, at bottom, he is unsentimental, his utilitarianism is of a different order of cold-bloodedness. A world in which this one woman judge can usurp God and get hold of the conduct manual has no need of his appendage. In that world God, the One he used to pray to, is now shown to be impotent and of no use to him. Those anonymous women, on the other hand, the ones whose eye his penis catches in the street or carpark, have him. If it appears to be he who catches their eye it is in fact they who have him, have him as object in their gaze. It is by way of this vicarious potency that he is transported to the Being of the (M)Other.

With Tad, as with Sade, there is more. But for Tad this more appears at the level of Being. It is manifested in the never-ending repetition of a scene in which, from a suitable distance, he makes a fixture of himself for the sight of the anonymous Woman. If for Tad the Woman is somewhat shadowy in her anonymity, it is precisely in this, in the universal obscurity of her countenance, that She, The Woman, exists for him and, in turn, designates him, albeit only by way of making him her appendage. As Lacan puts it, unlike the phantasy of neurosis the phantasy of perversion "can be named, it is in space, it suspends some essential relationship or other. It is not properly speaking atemporal, it is outside time."[5]

For both Tad and Sade it is at this place that all their resolute conduct comes to rest; here their Kantianism times-out. At the place where the subject of *jouissance* is put in question both of them, literally, keep Mum. It is by the *jouissance* of keeping this Mum-One who has the use of them that the very possibility of that question is held and kept outside.

But for the subject who would truly speak The Woman has a more radical obscurity: She does not exist, does not exist, that is, within the terms of speaking, and most particularly, those terms, man and woman, by which one speaks, and speaks most intimately, of the sexual relation.

Being in love we take the other as model for our conduct. But in an analysis the object of love is no more than a semblance, one which beckons beyond itself to something more which remains of value and which insists for the subject. The site of this more is the place of otherness and non-being which is posited by The Woman, that One who is singularly uncommon, being not-whole.

In the passage of an analysis therefore, where truth speaks in the transference, the fall of that object of love holds the possibility of an encounter with the Other, not as Being but as the locus of this value, the value of truth for the subject. If this necessitates letting go of Mum-One it holds to that love in which the subject is, by its ownmost name, at once implicated and impelled.

The first love we can, in retrospect, situate with the *jouissance* of the Other. The second love, to name it, is the Other *jouissance*. It is in the perversity of its radical otherness that this *jouissance* conduces to the love which is peculiar to psychoanalysis.

Notes

1. The Marquis de Sade (1968). *Juliette.* Austryn Wainwright (Trans.), New York: Grove Press, p. 450.
2. Lacan J. (2006). Kant with Sade. In Bruce Fink (Trans.), *Écrits: The First Complete Edition in English* (pp. 645–668). New York: W. W. Norton & Co.
3. See Lacan J. (1998). *Jacques Lacan: The Seminar, Book XX, Encore, On Feminine Sexuality: The Limits of Love and Knowledge (1972–1973).* Bruce Fink (Trans.), New York: W. W. Norton, p. 72.
4. On the subject's contentment in his pleasures see Lacan J., Kant with Sade, *op. cit.*, p. 647. Lacan cites Kant's *Critique of Practical Reason.* See Kant I. (1997). *Critique of Practical Reason.* Mary Gregor (Ed. & Trans.), Cambridge: Cambridge University Press, p. 63.
5. Lacan J. (1959). *Desire and Its Interpretation.* Seminar of 1958–59, lesson of 15th April 1959, unpublished English translation by Cormac Gallagher.

PART V

ANALYSIS, THE ARTS
AND THE WELL SPOKEN

CHAPTER EIGHTEEN

The Ob-scene

David Pereira

From time to time, the issue of what constitutes obscenity emerges as the subject of considerable debate, a debate to which psychoanalysis, in its concern with the field of erotics, is not indifferent. One of the most recent incarnations of this recurring controversy has taken as its subject a series of particular photographs in an exhibition of Bill Henson's work at *Roslyn Oxley9* gallery; photographs which came to the public's attention via a much publicized intervention of the law in the action of seizing and prohibiting those images.[1] Twelve pictures were confiscated from the exhibition and a further twenty from the gallery storeroom.

The Henson photographs therefore appear as the most recent catalyst for debate between the custodians of morality on the one hand, and the proponents of freedom of speech and expression on the other. The former found a champion in no less a figure than our Prime Minister who, in breathlessly pronouncing the words, "revolting, absolutely revolting", bequeathed to the debate a lascivious air embroidered with a salivatory glint. The demand from this side was for the swift action of the law; to lay and prosecute charges of obscenity. As it turns out, unsuccessfully, on account of the fact that definitions of obscenity are often not contained in the legislation and courts rely on traditional legal tests such as the capacity of the material to "deprave and corrupt" and/or to controvert "community standards".

On the other side of the debate, the Henson photographs galvanized in large part the support of the Arts community, championing the cause of freedom of speech and expression. What was notable here was the fact that amongst several commentators speaking for the freedom of speech and artistic expression, and against censorship, there was a persistent distancing from any hint that the images may be erotic. Statements of the type: "the images are not the least 'erotic'", with "erotic" suitably and comfortably caged within quotes, punctuated the assertions on this side of the debate. Artists and supporters of Henson were, for the most part, falling over each other to claim that whilst the work was of a nude, it was "not erotic".

Such a debate therefore finds itself contained within the comfortable counter references of obscenity on the one hand and freedom of speech and expression on the other, on the proviso that said freedom maintains its distance from the erotic.

A first question, then, is what position psychoanalysis occupies in this debate. Does the function and field of speech and language in psychoanalysis pertain to the freedom of speech, a noble end, or the more questionable end of obscenity?

Let me also observe that what I am addressing myself to as a topic or thematic is not *Psychoanalysis, the Arts and the Freedom of Speech* but *Psychoanalysis, the Arts and the Well-Spoken*. The "Well-Spoken" might not be found on the side of the freedom of speech, such freedom being the privilege, Lacan contends, of those at the Vatican. Psychoanalysis, rather, is bound to sticking as closely as possible to what is said and the weight of those words realized in their saying.

The question I will take up, then, is that of the relation between the obscene and the well-spoken. My particular interest in this question is addressed to the way in which the ethics of psychoanalysis as an ethics of the well-spoken, separates it from an ethics of decency through which psychoanalysis risks situating itself as a "more embracing moralism than any that has previously existed."[2]

Whilst the conception of the obscene remains loose within the legal statutes, we are obliged to try and specify a bit more what we are referring to when we speak of the obscene. What is the obscene to which we are referring here? Let us begin by returning to the incarnation of this debate concerning obscenity in reference to the Henson photographs.

In an interview he gave to Dominic Sidhu of *EGO* magazine, Henson noted the following:

> The reason I like working with teenagers is because they repre-
> sent a kind of **breach** between the dimensions that people cross
> through. ... I am fascinated with the interval, that sort of highly
> ambiguous and uncertain period where you have an exponential
> growth of experience and knowledge, but also a kind of tenuous
> grasp on the certainties of adult life.[3]

Judy Annear, senior curator for photography at the Art Gallery of NSW similarly notes that: "They are all vehicles for a whole set of feelings to do with what it means to be in transition."[4]

Annear's interpretation of the breach as "transition" is somewhat prone to an altogether too hasty elision; it somehow makes a more palatable or comforting reference of the radicality of this breach. This may be suggestive of the fact that there is something of the breach which is quite difficult to sustain. What is it which appears when this breach does not too quickly give way to transition, when one isn't just "passing through"? Might not this be exactly the space in which the obscene appears, in the very space of this breach?

This is clear for Georges Bataille for whom:

> Obscenity is our name for the uneasiness which upsets the physical
> state associated with self-possession, with the possession of a rec-
> ognized and stable individuality. Through the activity of organs in
> a flow of coalescence and renewal, like the ebb and flow of waves
> surging into one another, the self is dispossessed, and so completely
> that most creatures in a state of nakedness, for nakedness is sym-
> bolic of this dispossession and heralds it, will hide; particularly if
> the erotic act follows, consummating it.[5]

Thus, I am forcing Henson's reference to the nature of his work to join with Bataille's definition of the obscene in regard to this breach in self-possession, in order to assert that it is the obscene which appears in the space of this breach. With Bataille, what appears there is presented as clearly and carnally erotic; the involvement of the body as the scene of this dispossession is not shirked. The erotic does not envelop itself in the language of decency, rather, remaining redolent with the luxurious indecency of obscenity as characteristic of the power and function of the word itself in its capacity, not to communicate or to dialogue, but to dispossess, to discomfort or dis-ease.[6]

The fundamental property of obscenity is its capacity to produce a disruption in the subject's recognition of themselves. Bataille makes it clear that what he refers to as the "dispossession of the self" is a phenomenon of language, of the function and field of speech and language. In the text *Visions of Excess* and in the chapter titled "The Solar Anus" Bataille contends the following:

> Ever since sentences began to "circulate" in brains devoted to reflection, an effort at total identification has been made, because with the aid of the "copula" each sentence ties one thing to another; all things would be visibly connected if one could discover at a single glance and in its totality the tracings of Ariadne's thread leading thought into its own labyrinth.
>
> But the copula of terms is no less irritating that the "copulation" of bodies.[7]

In this, the function of speech within the field of language is not reduced to reference or to an unbroken chain of signification and meaning, anymore than the sexual is reduced to the comfortable domesticity of copulation. The obscene therefore, is the scene of the breakdown of the copula—a resistance in the function and field of speech and language in psychoanalysis to the identification of being—giving rise to a different function of speech within a field of language through which one might hear something other irrupting in the voice.

Consider the following, again from Bataille in relation to an "excremental phantasy" following an encounter with the image of the anus of an ape at the Zoological Gardens in London; an image of an "enormous anal fruit of radial and shit-smeared raw pink meat."

> For it is not self-evident that the noble parts of the human being (his dignity, the nobility that characterizes his face) instead of allowing only a sublime and measured flow of profound and tumultuous impulses, brusquely cease to set up the least barrier against a sudden, bursting irruption, as provocative and as dissolute as the one that inflates the anal protuberance of an ape ...[8]

The "bursting eruption" had earlier been described by Bataille as "a rattled grunt deep in my throat." In the broken chains of signification—in this breach—the obscene irrupts to announce that these are not simply chains of meaning which are at work in the function and field of speech and language in psychoanalysis, but chains of enjoyment, language carnalized by the imperative tone, the rattled grunt, the purring of *jouissance*.[9]

Such is the fruit of speech within a particular field of language which is typically that which moral authority will seek to exclude; to which it will bring the "affective charge of an obscene element whose obscenity derives only from the prohibition levelled against it."[10]

This statement "... an obscene element whose obscenity derives only from the prohibition levelled against it", encapsulates a relation between the obscene and the function of the superego which had not escaped Lacan, for whom the superego was the obscene and ferocious figure which forces us to enjoy. And further, an obscene and ferocious figure which arises as the imperative of *jouissance* "in the broken link of the symbolic chain, ..."[11,12]

Arising in that space of the breach which is the obscene, is a *jouissance* which distinguishes itself from the comfort of that insipid pleasure which Bataille tells us in *The Story of the Eye*, ensures that decent people "are never frightened by the crowing of a rooster, or when strolling under a starry heaven."[13]

For Bataille:

> In the violence of overcoming, in the disorder of my laughter and my sobbing, in the excess of raptures which shatter me, I seize on the similarity between a horror and a voluptuousness that goes beyond me, between an ultimate pain and an unbearable joy.[14]

This joy, this *jouissance*, arises in a breach situated within an experience which "goes beyond me". Within the breach, the breach in which the obscene appears in the broken chains of the symbolic, we encounter the possibility of hearing a *jouissance* which gives the voice of the superego its imperative tone. For the superego, "in its intimate imperative", Lacan tells us, "is the voice of conscience, that is a voice first and foremost, a vocal one at that, and without any authority other than that of being a loud voice ...".[15] It is a voice which demands to be heard.

The *jouissance* embodied in the imperative quality of the voice, is to be heard. It is not any longer the instrument of understanding or meaning. "Indeed", writes Lacan, "were the law to give the order '*Jouis!*' [Enjoy], the subject could only reply '*J'ouis*' [I hear]."[16] The emphasis is on the hearing; not on the meaning or the understanding, but on the imperative tone and its hearing, its being heard.

The voice hollows out a space between speech and language and becomes the support of a *jouissance* which is other to the scene of meaning—the ob-scene of the function and field of speech and language oriented to meaning; a breach in the field of meaning.

What does this imperative tone have to do with the "Well-Spoken" and the voice which is privileged by it? The "Well-Spoken" finds a very precise reference in the essay of Raymond Queneau titled *What is Art* penned in 1938. Queneau asserts there that:

> It is not enough to say, nor to say well; the thing must be worth saying. But what is worth saying? There's no getting around it: that which is useful.[17]

Now, in what sense useful?

In a conversation with Georges Ribemont-Dessaignes in 1950, Queneau said that:

> You can't eat the word "bread", you can't drink the word "wine" but they have their importance when they are said well. I don't believe in a language that takes itself for something it isn't ... There's a force to language, but you have to know how to apply it.[18]

There's a force to language, but you have to know how to apply it; you have to know how to use it, not instrumentally, but via a certain suspension of meaning. Such a suspension creates a breach through which arises the ob-scene of meaning, carried by the function of voice when it is free to be something other than substance.

The voice presenting itself in the well-spoken, as the embodiment of *jouissance*, is no longer the representational, no longer the illustrative; it no longer speaks "about", no longer found within chains of signifiers tying one thing to another, nor standing for any object outside itself. Such a voice becomes that which hollows out a function of speech within the field of language specified as *lalangue*, in which can be heard a certain force of language, a certain power of the word. It touches on the experience of psychoanalysis in which the experience of language is not simply instrumental—a means of communication or dialogue. It is testament to the fact that what we know how to do with *lalangue*—how we use it—"goes well beyond what we can account for under the heading of language."[19]

"*Lalangue* serves purposes", Lacan reminds us, "that are altogether different from that of communication."[20, 21] The voice, between speech and language, resonates with the warm, fresh words of *lalangue*, embodied with a *jouissance* whose obscenity is found in its surplus to the domesticating fiction of the copula of being, and the copulation of the sexual relation.

In the breach, the voice gears into the body and the body resonates with the voice. The words which emerge—warm fresh words, used before they have cooled in the light of day—retain the heat of the body. Such a relation between voice and body was already recognized by Leonardo Da Vinci for whom: "The spirit has no voice, because where there is voice there is body."[22]

Let us return, then, to my question of the relation between the obscene and the Well-Spoken.

Alain Badiou, in regard to the function of the word in poetry, contends that "Against the obscenity of 'all seeing' and 'all saying'—of showing, sounding out and commenting everything—the poem is the guardian of the decency of speech."[23] For Badiou, this was Lacan's ethics of the Well-Spoken, aligned by him with the decency of speech. His decency perhaps leaves him fearless in relation to the crowing of roosters.

Similarly, Jean-Michel Rabaté calls for psychoanalysis, like literature, to "invite the reader to experience language not just as an instrumental means of communication, but as an active medium, a site of cultural interaction that enables critical thought and a new sense of political or ethical agency ..."[24,25] Therefore, for both Badiou and for Rabaté an ethics of decency or political agency arises in the breach hollowed out by the voice between speech and language. Despite Badiou's confident assertion of such, we are nonetheless left with the question as to whether this is the ethics of the Well-Spoken for Lacan.

My argument has been that for Lacan, within this breach one encounters the ob-scene of an ethics of decency or political agency. One encounters the word, not as caretaker of decency, but as the imperative sound of the embodiment of a *jouissance* which opens up the space for the opulence of the obscenely well-spoken as an erotics; an erotics whose rattled grunt fails to find refuge in the safe confines of quotation marks. Rather, leaving us capable of being fearful of the crowing of roosters.[26]

Notes

1. Bill Henson is a contemporary Australian artist working in the photographic medium. His work is held in major public and private collections within Australia and internationally.
2. Lacan, Jacques. *The Ethics of Psychoanalysis 1959–1960. The Seminar of Jacques Lacan Book VII).* Translated by Dennis Porter. Jacques-Alain Miller (Ed.). Norton, New York, 1992. Lesson of 18th November 1959.
3. Sidhu, Dominic. "Nocturne: The Photographs of Bill Henson" in *EGO* (www.egothemag.com) 29th August 2005.
4. Annear, Judy. *International Herald Tribune.* May 28th 2008.
5. Bataille, Georges. *Erotism: Death and Sensuality.* City Lights, San Francisco, 1986, p. 18.
6. In this sense the obscene is to be differentiated from the pornographic. Cf. Beckett (*Damned to Fame*, p. 269) regarding his translation of "120 Days of Sodom" where he notes that: "I have just read the 1st and 3rd Volumes of the French edition. The obscenity of surface is indescribable. Nothing could be less pornographical. It fills me with a kind of metaphysical ecstatsy."
7. Bataille, Georges. *Visions of Excess: Selected Writings, 1927–1939.* Allan Stoekl (Ed.). Theory and History of Literature, Vol. 14. Univ. of Minnesota Press, Minneapolis, 1985.
8. Bataille, Georges. "The Jesuve", in *Visions of Excess.* Op. cit., p. 78.
9. Lacan, Jacques. *Television: A Challenge to the Psychoanalytic Establishment.* Joan Copjec (Ed.), Norton, NY, 1990. "For these chains are not of meaning but of enjoy-meant (jouis-sens) ..."
10. Bataille, Georges. "The Pineal Eye", in *Visions of Excess.* Op. cit., p. 81.
11. Lacan, Jacques. "The Freudian Thing", in *Ecrits.* Translated by Bruce Fink. Norton, NY, 2006, p. 361.
12. Lacan, Jacques. *Encore: The Seminar of Jacques Lacan, Book XX.* Norton, NY, 1998. Lesson of 21st November 1972. "Nothing forces anyone to enjoy except the superego. The superego is the imperative of *jouissance*—Enjoy."
13. Bataille, Georges. *The Story of the Eye.* City Lights, San Francisco, 1987, p. 49.
14. Bataille, Georges. *The Tears of Eros.* City Lights Books, San Francisco, 1989. p. 20.

15. Lacan, Jacques. "Remarks on Daniel Lagache's Presentation: 'Psychoanalysis and Personality Structure" in *Ecrits*. Op. cit., pp. 572–573.

16. Lacan, Jacques. "The subversion of the subject and the Dialectic of Desire in the Freudian Unconscious", in *Ecrits*. Op. cit., p. 696.

17. Queneau, Raymond. *Letters, Numbers, Forms: Essays, 1928–1970.* Translated by Jordan Stump, Univ. of Illinois Press, Chicago, 2007.

18. *Ibid*, p. 179.

19. Lacan, Jacques. *Encore*. Op. cit., p. 139. "The unconscious is knowledge, a knowing how to do things with *lalangue*. And what we know how to do with *lalangue* goes well beyond what we can account for under the heading of language."

20. Lacan, Jacques. *Encore*. Op. cit., p. 138.

21. *Ibid*, p. 3. "*Usufruct*—that's a legal notion, isn't it?—brings together in one word what I already mentioned in my seminar on ethics, namely the difference between utility and *jouissance*."

22. Leonardo Da Vinci, cited in, Agamben, Giorgio. *Infancy and History: On the Destruction of Experience*. Translated by Liz Heron. Verso, London 2007, p. 13. "The spirit has no voice, because where there is voice there is body."

23. Badiou, Alain. *Theoretical Writings*. Continuum, New York, 2004, p. 235.

24. Rabaté, Jean-Michel. *Jacques Lacan: Psychoanalysis and the Subject of Literature*. PALGRAVE, NY, 2001, p. 9.

25. Giorgio Agamben recognizes the very same possibility of an ethics arising in this space of the voice, this "moat", as he calls Henson's breach, between the speech and language.

26. Bataille, Georges. *The Story of the Eye*. Op.cit., pp. 48–49. "To others the universe seems decent because decent people have gelded eyes. That is why they fear lewdness. They are never frightened by the crowing of a rooster or when strolling under a starry heaven. In general people savour the 'pleasures of the flesh' only on condition that they be insipid."

CHAPTER NINETEEN

The *jouissance* of *The Gambler*

Linda Clifton

Lacan writes:

> You mark the six sides of a dice, you roll the dice—from this rolling … emerges desire. I am not saying human desire, for after all the man who plays with the dice is captive to the desire thus put into play. He doesn't know the origin of his desire, as it rolls with the symbol written on its six sides.
>
> Why is it only man who plays dice?[1]
>
> What is a dice if not an instrument designed to give rise to pure chance?[2]
>
> What is chance? Chance is attached essentially to the conception of the real qua impossible …
>
> … impossible to question because it answers at random.[3]

It is certainly not by chance that what has been referred to as an epidemic of problem gambling is evident in our polis. It is not by chance because it could be said that this epidemic has in fact been sponsored by the state. As Lacan put it the essence of the law is to "divide up, distribute, or reattribute everything that counts as jouissance."[4] A liberalisation of gaming laws which has brought great financial benefit to two successive governments has effectively resulted in a state sanctioned promotion of gambling in its many forms.[5] This promotion has been so successful that an unexpected excess has been produced. The citizenry has enjoyed too much and the problem gambler has emerged as a social problem. The problem of an unfettered and at times lethal *jouissance*. We are reminded of Lacan's "Nothing forces anyone to enjoy [*jouir*] except the superego. The superego is the imperative of *jouissance*—Enjoy!"[6]

Lacan speaks of *jouissance* as the "jar of the Danaides".[7] The Danaides were daughters of Danaus, a mythical Greek king. Forced to marry their cousins, these brides, with one exception, stabbed their husbands to death on their wedding night, with daggers their father had provided; the murderers were punished in the Underworld by having to fill leaky jars with water.

"Once you have started you never know where it will end. It begins with a tickle and ends with a blaze of petrol. That's always what jouissance is."[8] Lethal indeed.

The social problem thus created in our time as an unwanted dividend of the state's gamble has prompted an attempted assuagement of the guilt so central to the phenomenon of gambling. In a redirection of some of the profits from gambling the state now sponsors an agency where those who identify themselves as gamblers can speak. Whereas they usually pay a high price to risk and often lose everything gamblers are now invited to speak "for free". In fact they have already paid for the privilege many times over with their losses—a redistribution of *jouissance* could we say? A supposed social good to cure the social problem which the state has created—the problem of a surplus *jouissance*.

It was also perhaps not entirely by chance that I was invited to consult with this agency as it was thought that a psychoanalyst might have something to offer to those working with problem gamblers. A subject of knowledge about gambling was supposed in psychoanalysis.

This paper arises out of my encounter with the impasses of those who work directly with problem gamblers and with what a perusal of the psychoanalytic literature on pathological gambling indicates as a certain deficit in the knowledge of gambling supposed to psychoanalysis, a deficit that is evident from Freud's opening hand. I will indicate the nature of this deficit and while still following Freud in privileging Dostoevsky's literary text I will propose that a different reading is possible with Lacan that leads to a posing of the question of the *jouissance* of the gambler, a question as to the nature of his enjoyment.

In 1863 Dostoyevsky recorded his idea for a story about a "certain type of Russian abroad."[9]

> I take a straightforward nature, a man ... highly educated, but in all respects immature, who has lost his faith and does not dare to *believe*, who revolts against the authorities and fears them ... the main thing about him is that his living juices, forces, impetuosity, daring have gone into roulette. He is a gambler, and not a mere gambler ... He is a poet in his own way, but the point is that he himself is ashamed of this poetry because he deeply feels its baseness, although the need for risk also ennobles him in his own eyes ... The whole story is ... how he gambles for three years at roulette in the gambling houses.[10]

The novella which resulted was to be called Roulettenburg but was published in 1866 as *The Gambler*. Roulettenburg, the fictional city of the story is as the Dostoyevsky scholar Jackson puts it "nowhere or anywhere in Europe."[11]

> The mixed French and German components of the name suggest the illegitimate and rootless character of the place. This is the land of Babel, a place without a national language or culture. The gambling salon—the heart of Roulettenburg— ... is in continuous movement. Everything is in flux in this city: people, languages, currencies, values.
>
> Roulettenburg is the classical city of capitalism: the market is supreme and everyone is engaged in accumulation. Everyone risks money to make money, and what he wins or loses wipes out what he has staked; ... Even people, like stakes at the table, move upward or downward in the eyes of other people according to the value judgement of the roulette wheel.[12]

There are many gamblers in Roulettenburg but the narrator and central character of *The Gambler* is Alexis who has no aim in life but is in thrall to the enigmatic Polina who treats him with contempt. He compares her to an empress who would undress in front of a slave, not considering that the slave was a person. He writes in his diary of her inaccessibility and the impossibility of the fulfilment of his fantasies. At the very moment however when Polina finally gives a sign of love to Alexis, her slave, the spell of this courtly love is broken and what can only be designated as a true mania for gambling ensues. Ostensibly in the casino to win for his lady, Alexis forgets his love as he is gripped by the passion for gambling.

It was of course far from being by chance that Dostoyevsky wrote about a Russian gambler abroad as his own period of reckless gambling is well documented. However, I do not seek in my reading of *The Gambler* to elucidate something of Dostoyevsky as a subject on the basis of his fiction. My interest is not in Dostoevsky's pathology read through the brilliance of his writing. Nor is it his biography that is of interest here but Dostoevsky's art which I believe allows a fictional truth to emerge from his writing, a writing of the *jouissance* of *The Gambler* and the failure of his love.

To give you a taste of the gambler's "shameful poetics", Alexis, Dostoevsky's gambler, records the following as he gambles more and more recklessly:

> *In horror I sensed …*
>   *My whole life rested on a bet!*
>   *There was … a single moment of waiting, similar, perhaps in its impression, to the impression experienced by Mme. Blanchard in Paris when she was hurtling from her air balloon to the ground.*
>   *I felt only some sort of dreadful enjoyment of success, violence, power …*[13]

What is this dreadful enjoyment?
  Jackson writes that,

> Few subjects provide such a remarkable point of conjunction for so many areas of thought and human experience as does the phenomenon of gambling. Here … "all shores meet" … social, psychosexual, economic, philosophical, religious.[14]

One of these conjunctions occurs between literature and psychoanalysis when the writings of Freud and Dostoyevsky intersect in Freud's 1928 paper *Dostoyevsky and Parricide*.[15] In 1926 Freud was invited to write an introduction to a new edition of *The Brothers Karamazov*. It was suggested that he write about the book and its author. Such invitations are not without their dangers and Freud's *Dostoevsky and Parricide* qualifies for Lacan's opprobrium and the critical epithet of psychobiographical. Freud draws on both Dostoevsky's literary output and on biographical material, including his letters to produce an analysis of two aspects of his troubled life—his epilepsy and a period of unrestrained and destructive gambling. Despite the weakness inherent in its psychobiographical method the importance of *Dostoevsky and Parricide* lies in its being Freud's only analysis of gambling as a neurotic symptom.

Although Freud drew on Dostoevsky's novels as a source for his analysis he did not mention *The Gambler* despite it being regarded as one of Dostoevsky's most transparently autobiographical novels, based not only on the author's addiction to gambling, but also on his love affair with the young beauty Polina Suslova. Passages from his letters sound identical to passages from the novel.

Instead of exploiting *The Gambler*, Freud, by an odd sleight of hand, interpolates an account of another novel about gambling, *Twenty four hours in the life of a woman*—written by his friend Stefan Zweig—into his analysis of Dostoevsky.

Freud writes of the period in Dostoevsky's life when he was "obsessed by a mania for gambling."

> As often happens with neurotics Dostoevsky's sense of guilt had taken a tangible shape as a burden of debt, and he was able to take refuge behind the pretext that he was trying by his winnings at the tables to make it possible for him to return to Russia without being arrested by his creditors.[16]

But despite this pretext Dostoevsky knew "that the chief thing was gambling for its own sake"—*le jeu pour le jeu*. He "never rested until he had lost everything." He broke promises to his wife and reduced them to poverty. "When his sense of guilt was satisfied by the punishments he had inflicted on himself, the inhibition on his work became less severe—Dostoevsky's literary production never went better than when they had lost everything."[17]

Freud asks "what part of a gamblers long—buried chidhood is it that forces its way to repetition in his obsession for play?"[18] His answer to this question recalls a letter he had written to Fliess in 1897.

> It has dawned on me that masturbation is the one major habit, the one "primal addiction" and that it is only as a substitute and

replacement for it that these other addictions—alcohol, morphine, tobacco etc. come into existence.[19]

For Freud gambling was all about the hands. The hands that feverishly gathered up the gold and coins from the roulette table were the hands that had engaged in other play, infantile play, hands that had found their way to the forbidden rhythms, the forbidden *jouissance* of masturbation

Freud supported his contention that masturbation is the primary addiction at play in gambling with his interpretation of Zweig's aforementioned novel which centres on the attempt by a older woman to rescue a young man from gambling. She is drawn to him at the roulette table by the sight of his beautiful hands. Freud interprets this novel as having as its unconscious underpinning a common wishful phantasy from puberty in the form of a boy's wish that his mother should herself initiate him into sexual life in order to save him from the dreaded injuries caused by masturbation.

> The vice of masturbation is replaced by the addiction to gambling and the emphasis laid on the passionate activity of the hands [in Zweig's novel] betrays this derivation ... the passion for play is an equivalent of the old compulsion to masturbate; playing is the actual word used in the nursery to describe the activity of the hands upon the genitals. The irresistible nature of the temptation, the solemn resolutions, which are nevertheless invariably broken, never to do it again, the stupefying pleasure and the bad conscience which tells the subject that he is ruining himself ... all these elements remain unaltered in the process of substitution.[20]

The Freudian conception of gambling as a substitute for infantile masturbatory conflicts suggests that the satisfaction, the pleasure, the thrill of gambling is a sexual satisfaction in disguise. It can be located in a kind of cul de sac, a deviation from the path which leads to the attainment of normal adult sexuality. Gambling as an activity is thus part of a sexual series involving the body and its *jouissance*, the multiple significations of the word play and the paternal prohibition "Don't play with yourself." This would seem to imply that gambling like masturbation is a sexual satisfaction that attempts to do without the other. In Lacanian terms then it is a phallic *jouissance*, the *jouissance* of the idiot.[21]

But we can also remember that Freud points to Dostoevsky's admission that he gambled "for gambling's sake." "The main thing is the play itself ... I swear that greed for money has nothing to do with it although Heaven knows I am sorely in need of the money."[22]

What is this *le jeu pour le jeu*?

Does it not suggest an intrinsic motivation in gambling, a particular enjoyment, beyond or in addition to its theorization as substitute for infantile masturbatory activities and conflicts? Forrester asks a similar question about "gambling in its specificity, not as a derivative of something else—play, masturbation, or whatever. How are we to characterize this specificity?"[23]

Before we leave Freud's analysis and pursue this question of enjoyment further it is interesting to note that in a letter to Theodore Reik Freud makes clear his negative transference to Dostoevsky as a neurotic and as a gambler when he acknowledges that he lost interest in the paper *Dostoevsky and Parricide* halfway through and that despite his admiration for Dostoevsky as a creative artist he had little patience for pathological natures in "art and life", having "exhausted" it "in analysis".[24] He reveals to Reik his objection that Dostoevsky's insight was so much restricted to abnormal mental life. "Consider his astonishing helplessness in the face of the phenomena of love. All he really knew were crude, instinctual desire, masochistic subjection and loving out of pity."[25] It is my impression from the psychoanalytic literature that beginning with Freud the gambler often leaves the analyst somewhat cold.

After Freud there continues to be a deficit both quantitative and qualitative in the analysis of gambling. With a couple of exceptions few analysts have written extensively on gambling. One of the exceptions is Edmund Bergler, whose writings on gambling over three decades from the 1930s culminated in a book *The Psychology of Gambling*. Bergler comments that "the analytic literature on gambling is none too enlightening." There is a "lack of clinical material and a more or less schematic application of experiences gained by the treatment of non-gambling neurotics." Thus the "disease entity neurotic gambling has been explained by means of analogy, which ... did not fit."[26]

In terms of the question of an enjoyment intrinsic to gambling Bergler acknowledges that the gambler seeks and enjoys "an enigmatic thrill which cannot be logically explained since it is compounded of as much pain as pleasure."[27] In a chapter entitled *The Mysterious Thrill of Gambling* Bergler elaborates on his tightly constructed theory of the gambler's unconscious.

> In approaching the gambler's unconscious, the first salient fact that we discover is his fanatical belief in infantile megalomania. ... Just like a child, he expects that he will win because he wants to win. When a gambler places his stake on a card or a color or a number, he is not acting like a person who has adapted himself to reality; he is "ordering" the next card to win for him, in the complete illusion that he is omnipotent.
>
> Mentally he has regressed to the earlier period in which he was omnipotent, that is to infancy, when all his desires were automatically fulfilled. His present megalomaniacal attitude is an act of aggression against his parents and other educators who forced him into the awareness that he was not omnipotent. ... there can be no neurotic aggression without guilt. The guilt is expiated by self punishment. In the case of the gambler this takes the form of an unconscious desire to lose and a wish to be rejected by the outer world.[28]

In relation to the self punishing aspect of gambling Bergler asserts that it is clear that the "adversary [the poker partner, the roulette wheel, the stock exchange] is always unconsciously identified with the fantasy of the refusing mother, and later, father. Only one thing can be expected from this "monster"—refusal, denial and defeat."[29]

The enigmatic thrill referred to by Bergler is linked to what he designates as the psychic masochism of the gambler. In relation to love Bergler asserts that the real gambler is as masochistic in love as he is at the roulette wheel. "Fundamentally he is not interested in normal love, although he often goes through the motions. But this is only a defence against his basic passivity."[30]

Thus, this post Freudian conception of gambling writes gambling—like Freud—as a kind of scenario that allows a re-enacting of unresolved conflicts from infancy. Unlike Freud, for whom the Oedipal father figured in this unconscious scenario, Bergler points to the pre Oedipal mother. The activity of gambling itself—the games of chance that are played—are regarded as infantile and thereby ideally suited to such a re-enactment. This analysis of gambling thus infantilizes the gambler who is considered to be childlike, even childish. In this context it is not surprising that a certain moralism and a derogatory tone in relation to this so- called childishness are not far below the surface in analytic writings on gambling before Lacan.

Bergler presents a typology of gamblers: the "classical" gambler, the "passive feminine" male gambler, the "defensive pseudosuperior" gambler, the gambler "motivated by unconscious guilt", the "unexcited" gambler and the female gambler.[31] This characterization of the gambler as a type, a type who fails numerous implied standards of cultural, social, psychological and sexual health is not uncommon in the post Freudian American analytic literature. While Bergler undoubtedly had extensive clinical experience with a wide range of gamblers it is striking that in reading his case studies all sound as though they came out of the same mould. All failed characters they in fact come out of Bergler's mould. Bergler adopts a combative approach to his patients, needing to break down their defences and prove to them the truth of his analysis of their gambling, their adherence to one of his six types of gambler. As the gambler is a type the knowledge of each one is pre-given—there are no surprises nor interest in how the signifying elements of language have structured the desire of each one or how the dominant discourses of the time—pre and post World War 2 America traversed these subjects.

These deficits in the psychoanalytic literature lead me to privilege Dostoevsky's literary portrait of the 19th century Russian gambler—a writing about gambling which achieves Dostoevsky's stated aim for it "to attract attention as a vivid and detailed depiction of the game of roulette".[32] There is a kind of poetry about his fictional nineteenth century gambler light years away from the prosaic social and psychological failure that is the gambler as written by psychoanalysis mid to late twentieth century America.

Lacan, while writing on Pascal's wager and concepts such as chance, probability, certainty and destiny does not address the pathology of gambling beyond a few cogent reflections. However, I find in the passion of the gambler which resonates in Dostoevsky's novel a certain rapport with Lacan's formulations on *jouissance* and the relation of *jouissance* to desire and to love. The writing of *jouissance*, the *jouissance* of the gambler as fictional subject in Dostoevsky invites the question of the particularity of that *jouissance*. In reading *The Gambler* with Lacan we can come closer to being able to address the question of whether there is an enjoyment intrinsic to gambling, perhaps Dostoevsky's dreadful enjoyment.

At different points in his gambling trajectory over the three year time span of the novel Alexis gives his testimony about his enjoyment. Here he reflects on how he began to gamble:

> Yes, sometimes the wildest idea ... the most impossible idea, becomes so firmly fixed in your head that finally you take it for something that can be realized ... that is not all: if the idea is united with a strong passionate desire, you will quite likely at some time finally take it for something fateful, essential, predestined, for something that just cannot fail to be and to happen.[33]

This "something fateful, essential, predestined" is the decision to gamble and to continue to gamble of Dostoevsky's gambler. Whereas each one, child or adult, gambler or nongambler is subjected to the structuring effects of the signifier and to the operations of chance it is the gambler who insists repetitively on bringing about, on forcing an encounter with destiny. It is this insistence on staging and restaging this encounter, that marks the gambler.

For Lacan, "The gambler's passion is no other than the question asked of the signifier which is figured by the *automaton* of chance."[34] "In the game of chance no doubt he is going to read his destiny in it. He has the idea that something is revealed there that belongs to him all the more so given there is no one confronting him."[35]

As cited earlier, for Lacan chance is attached essentially to the conception of the "real as impossible ... impossible to question because it answers at random."[36] The gambler invests these random answers with a meaning particular to him. We can hear this in Dostoevsky's fictional account as well as in a more contemporary and nonfictional testimony given by Francis Bacon, artist and sometime roulette player. His reflections on his relationship with luck or chance, terms which he seems to use interchangeably, resonate with both Dostoevsky's fictional account and Lacan's theoretical account.

> Luck's a funny thing; it runs in long patches, and sometimes one runs into a long patch of very good luck ....
>
> ... I used to think that I heard the croupier calling out the winning number at roulette before the ball had fallen into the socket ... And I remember one afternoon I went in there, and I was playing on three different tables, and I heard these echoes. And I was playing

rather small stakes, but at the end of that afternoon chance had been very much on my side and I ended up with about sixteen hundred pounds, which was a lot of money for me then.

Those apparently most impersonal of signifiers, numbers, are invested with luck which attaches itself to Bacon for delirious periods of time during which he hallucinates the croupier's calls. Bacon reads something personal in these chance outcomes, these random answers of the real. "But now I seem to have run out of that patch. ... I feel that now my luck has completely deserted me as a gambler, for the present time."[37]

Luck deserts Bacon like an unfaithful lover. Alexis, Dostoevsky's gambler becomes an unfaithful lover when he enters the casino.

> The whole casino crowded around. I do not remember whether I thought of Polina even once during that time. I was then experiencing a kind of insurmountable enjoyment in seizing and raking in the banknotes, accumulating in a pile in front of me.[38]

> ... from the very minute I touched the gaming table ... it was as if my love had retreated into the background ... Am I really in actual fact a gambler, did I really in actual fact ... love Polina so strangely ...[39]

From the aura of Polina his lady, in whose radiance he had wanted to be for the rest of his life, Alexis throws himself into the passionate freefall of gambling. Ideas of fate, predestination and death not only enter the gambler's calculations but sweep him along. He is undeterred when his very survival is in the balance abdicating to the time and judgement of the roulette wheel, propelled by that dreadful enjoyment beyond the pleasure principle. As Forrester puts it the world of the gambler is a life "withdrawn from life, a world of timeless crisis time ... "the 'final moments of consciousness before execution or suicide.' "[40]

But what about love? The love of Alexis for Polina had been sustained as the unfulfilled desire of courtly love. But then gambling intervened. Lacan proposes a very particular relationship between desire and jouissance which may indicate why love failed.

> Far from desire being desire for jouissance it is precisely the barrier that keeps you at the distance that is more or less correctly calculated from this burning hearth, from what is precisely to be avoided by the thinking subject and which is called *jouissance*.[41]

In the following testimony of Alexis this "burning hearth of jouissance" which is the gambler's destiny is evoked. It exhausts life and forgets love.

> *I really was possessed by a dreadful sense of risk. Perhaps having gone through so many sensations one's soul is not sated but only inflamed by them, and demands more sensations more and more powerfully, too, up until final exhaustion.*[42]

Freud in *Dostoevsky and Parricide* writes of fate, the fate that the gambler invokes, as the projection of the father. However he also writes in the *Theme of the Three Caskets*[43] of the three fateful women in the life of a man—mother, lover and death. Alexis cannot sustain himself as a lover when Polina shows by her sign of love that she is not an empress but a woman. Her offering of herself to him "in her entirety", as she puts it, sets in motion Alexis' descent into a vortex of gambling. Like the spinning of the roulette wheel Alexis now spins in front of that other empress, Lady Luck being one of her names. Unable to sustain a love for an other in the form of a woman he invokes the Other to whom he now plights his troth, the Other as chance, fate, destiny.

Alexis retreats from the other in the form of a mortal, thereby castrated woman but offers himself as slave, as object of *jouissance* to that Other who will finally offer in return only destruction and death. *Jouissance* of the Other.

> *The point is that one turn of the wheel and everything changes ... What am I now? Zero! What might I be tomorrow? Tomorrow I might rise from the dead and begin to live once more! I might find the man within myself while he is not yet lost!*[44]

Notes

1. Lacan, J. *The seminar of Jacques Lacan Book 11 The Ego in Freud's Theory and in the Technique of Psychoanalysis 1954–1955* Ed. Jacques—Alain Miller Cambridge University Press 1988 p. 234.
2. Lacan, J. *The Seminar of Jacques Lacan Book X111 The Object of Psychoanalysis 1965–66* Trans. Cormac Gallagher. 2.2.66
3. *ibid.*
4. Lacan, J. *The Seminar of Jacques Lacan Book XX Encore 1972–3* Ed. Jacques—Alain Miller. W. W. Norton & Company p. 3.

5. In the state of Victoria, Australia
6. Lacan, J. op. cit. p. 3.
7. Lacan, J. *The Seminar of Jacques Lacan BookXVII The Other Side of Psychoanalysis 1969–70* Ed. Jacques—Alain Miller W. W. Norton & Co. p. 72.
8. *ibid.*
9. Jackson, L. J. *The Art of Dostoevsky Deliriums and Nocturnes* Princeton University Press 1981 p. 208.
10. *ibid.*
11. *ibid.,* p. 210.
12. *Ibid.,* p. 211.
13. Dostoevsky, F. *The Gambler* Hesperus Press 2006 pp. 113–116.
14. Jackson, R.L. op. cit p. 14.
15. Freud, S. *Dostoevsky and Parricide* St. Ed. Vol. XXI p. 190.
16. Freud, S. *ibid* p. 191.
17. Freud, S. *ibid.*
18. Freud, S. *ibid.*
19. Freud, S. *Extracts from the Fliess Papers Letter 79* St. Ed. 1 p. 272.
20. Freud, S. *Dostoevsky and Parricide* St. Ed. Vol. XXI p. 193.
21. Lacan, J. *The Seminar of Jacques Lacan Book XX Encore 1972–73* Ed. Jacques—Alain Miller W. W. Norton & Co. 1998 p. 81.
22. Freud, S. op. cit p. 190 note 1.
23. Forrester, J. *Transference and the Stenographer: on Dostoevsky's The Gambler* in *The Seductions of Psychoanalysis Freud Lacan and Derrida* Cambridge French Studies No. 26 Cambridge University Press *1991* p. 275.
24. Freud, S. op. cit Appendix p. 196.
25. Freud, S. *ibid.*
26. Bergler, E. *The Psychology of Gambling* International Universities Press, Inc. 1970 p. 79.
27. Bergler, E. *ibid.,* p. 7.
28. Bergler, E. *ibid.,* pp. 23–24.
29. Bergler, E. *ibid.,* p. 27.
30. Bergler E. *ibid.,* p. 89.
31. Bergler, E. *ibid.,* pp. 78–100.
32. Dostoevsky, F. in Jackson, R. L op. cit. p. 208.
33. Dostoevsky, F. *The Gambler* Hesperus Press 2006 p. 111.
34. Lacan, J. *Seminar on The Purloined Letter* in *Ecrits The First Complete Edition in English* W. W. Norton & Company 2006 p. 28.
35. Lacan, J. *The Seminar of Jacques Lacan Book 11 The Ego in Freud's Theory and in the Technique of Psychoanalysis 1954–55* Ed. Jacques—Alain Miller Cambridge University Press 1988 p. 300.
36. See note iii.

37. Bacon, F. in Sylvester, D. *Interviews with Francis Bacon The Brutality of Fact* 1987 Thames & Hudson p. 51.
38. Dostoevsky, F. op. cit. p. 115.
39. Dostoevsky, F. *ibid.*, pp. 123–124
40. Forrester, op. cit. p. 281.
41. Lacan, J. *The Seminar of Jacques Lacan Book XII The Object of Psychoanalysis 1965–66.* 23.3.66.
42. Dostoevsky, F. op. cit. p. 116.
43. Freud, S. *The Theme of the Three Caskets* St. Ed. Vol. XII.
44. Dostoevsky, F. op. cit. pp. 136–7.

CHAPTER TWENTY

Freud and Faust

Michael Plastow

> *Now fills the air so many a haunting shape, That no one knows how best to escape.* **Goethe: *Faust*, Part II** (cited as epigraph to Freud's *The Psychopathology of Everyday Life*)

In response to a hypothetical request to name the most magnificent works of world literature, Freud responds by citing:

> ... Homer, the tragedies of Sophocles, Goethe's *Faust*, Shakespeare's *Hamlet* [and] *Macbeth* ...[1]

But unlike other works that Freud holds in high regard, such as Shakespeare's *Hamlet* and Sophocles' *Oedipus Rex* in which there is a specific theoretical elaboration upon a text, references to *Faust* are extensive and scattered throughout Freud's opus. Let us see if we can discern a thread to Freud's references to *Faust* in view of the high opinion in which he holds Goethe's great work. And we can further examine Freud's esteem for this text in regard to his own psychoanalytic itinerary in order to attempt to say more about the particular place that Freud holds for *Faust*.

Freud makes reference to *Faust* in regard to his own formation. He notes:

> I was compelled during my first years at the University, to make the discovery that the peculiarities and limitations of my gifts denied me all success in many of the departments of science into which my youthful eagerness had plunged me. Thus I learned the truth of Mephistopheles' warning:
>
> *It is in vain that you range around from science to science:*
> *each man learns only what he can learn.*[2]

An expression of Freud's modesty, no doubt, but a recognition of his limits. From there Freud was able to recognise what *was* possible and then work to realise this. Such a truth it would seem initially evades Faust when we first encounter him. Faust declares:

> *Philosophy have I digested*
> *The whole of Law and Medicine*
> *From each its secrets have I wrested,*
> *Theology, alas, thrown in.*
> *Poor fool with all this sweated lore,*
> *I stand no wiser than before.*
> *...*
> *And round we go, on crooked ways or straight,*
> *And well I know that ignorance is our fate,*
> *And this I hate.* [43][3]

Faust is not ignorant of the sterile disembodied nature of the knowledge he has accumulated, stating that:

> *... in return am destitute of pleasure,*
> *Knowing that knowledge tricks us beyond measure* [45]

It is in this desperate state that he invokes the spirits, attempting to be their equal, proposing:

> *The hour is come, as master of my fate*
> *To prove in man the stature of a god* [54]

Faust has as a master his deceased father, a father in whose footsteps he follows but to whose legacy he has a complex relation:

> My father's stuff, bequeathed to be my prison,
> With scrolls of vellum, blackened and besmutched,
> Where still the desk-lamp's dismal smoke has risen.
> Better have spent what little was my own,
> Than sweat for petty gains by midnight oil.
> The things that men inherit come alone
> To true possession by the spirit's toil.
> What can't be used is trash; what can, a prize [53]

Freud utilises part of this citation in *Totem and Taboo*[4] and elsewhere, in order to discuss the relation of what is inherited to the way in which it is put to use.

To be able to accede to something other than the barren knowledge he has accumulated, Faust must not only forgo his mastery, but also submit to another master, *the* Master, one of the names of Mephistopheles, the name that lends itself to the title of Mikail Bulgakow's wonderful version of the Faust legend, *The Master and Margarita*.

Thus at the moment of the making of his pact, Faust declares:

> What I propose, I do not lightly dare:
> While I abide, I live in servitude,
> And whether yours or whose, why should I care? [88]

But if the devil goes by the name of Mephistopheles or the Master, he goes by many other names. Thus in *Faust* he is referred to as snake, Satan, Destroyer, Prince of Flies, Prince of Lies, Lord of Hell, Old Nick, Squire Satan, the Evil One, Lord Marquis, Lord Mammon, Squire Urianus, Squire Voland and Mephisto, amongst others. In his *General History of the Devil*, Gerald Messadié proposes that the devil is "polynomial, *par excellence*".[5] We might go a step further and say that the devil is metonymic in his function as agent of desire.

In the more ancient texts of the Old Testament, we find Satan as one of the sons of God acting as His agent, doing God's will, testing the faith of His followers. By contrast, in the later texts of the Old Testament, and in those of the New Testament, Satan had now become the polar opposite of God as a capricious agent of evil,[6] as Freud testifies in citing Faust's Mephistopheles:

> Destruction,—aught with Evil blent,—
> That is my proper element.[7]

This change came about under the influence of the Babylonian captors of the Jews who transmitted their Mesopotamian mythology to them, including indirectly via the Essenes. It is also from the Essenes that woman became associated with the devil, through her flesh she is the very ally of the devil.[8]

The fathers of the church in the fourth century, in order to endeavour to explain these conflicting presentations of the devil, in their attempt to establish a coherent doctrine, invented the mythology of the fall of Satan. However there was little agreement as to what the cause of this fall from grace might have been and hence there are many versions. Again, according to Messadié:

> In the fourth century, Lactanius, counsellor of the emperor Con-
> stantine, tried once again to get around the problem by attributing
> Satan's fall to the jealousy aroused in him, not by man, but by the
> Son, the Logos.[9]

As with Adam and Eve and their encounter with the snake and introduction to the Tree of Knowledge, it is the introduction of the Word, the word made flesh, that becomes implicated in the fall and therefore in the possibility of desire.

Whatever the cause of the fall, the devil, having fallen from God's grace, is incomplete. Mephistopheles is quite clear about this. He states that:

> ... a God alone
> Can hold this sense of oneness. [90]

And when Faust charges him with being all-knowing, he responds:

> Omniscient? No, not I; but well-informed. [83]

And it is through his encounter with the devil that Faust is able to come to recognise the limits of his endeavours:

> *... In vain I gathered human treasure,*
> *And all that mortal spirit could digest:*
> *I come at last to recognise my measure,*
> *And know the sterile desert in my breast.*
> *I have not raised myself one poor degree,*
> *Nor stand I nearer to infinity. [91]*

But what is the nature of this bond that Faust signs with the Devil? Freud asks:

> Why does anyone sign a bond with the devil? Faust, it is true, asked contemptuously: ... "What hast thou to give, poor Devil?" But he was wrong. In return for an immortal soul, the Devil has many things to offer which are highly prized by men: wealth, security from danger, power over mankind and the forces of nature, even magical arts, and, above all else, enjoyment—the enjoyment of beautiful women.[10]

Thus a bond with the devil leads directly to a carnal enjoyment of the body. Perhaps then it is not surprising that to seal such a bond mere words or ink cannot suffice: the bond must be signed with a drop of blood, a little loss or sacrifice of a piece of the body. To accede to this, a submission to the Devil is required. So then Faust is able to move from his disembodied world of ideas, to an enjoyment of the body.

Following the signing of the bond, Mephistopheles is able to pronounce:

> *Wealth shall be yours, beyond all fear or favour,*
> *Be pleased to take your pleasures on the wing,*
> *Voluptuous beauty taste in everything,*
> *And may you flourish on the joys you savour. [89]*

Similarly, in Freud's paper *A Seventeenth-Century Demonological Neurosis*, the Devil had asked the painter who also made a bond with him, to:

> ... turn to enjoyment and entertainment, and the painter remarks that "this indeed came to pass at his desire ..."[11]

Freud remarks in a footnote that in the original manuscript there is some indication that this enjoyment and entertainment has a specifically sexual meaning.

Like Freud proposes with the painter, what is represented in the
bond is a demand for the Devil to release him from his self-enclosed
suffering, his soul not specifically demanded by the devil but offered
by Faust.

After signing the bond Faust declares:

> Bring now the fruits of pain or pleasure forth,
> Sweet triumph's lure, or disappointment's wrath,
> A man's dynamic needs this restless urge. [89]

In *The Interpretation of Dreams*, Freud cites a passage from Faust as an
association of a patient to a dream. This is from the Walpurgis Night
section, towards the end of *Faust Part I*:

> FAUST (dancing with the Young Witch):
> A lovely dream once came to me,
> And I beheld an apple-tree,
> On which two lovely apples shone;
> They charmed me so, I climbed thereon.
>
> THE LOVELY WITCH:
> Apples have been desired by you,
> Since first in Paradise they grew;
> And I am so moved with joy to know
> That such within my garden grow.[12]

Freud notes that there cannot be the faintest doubt what the apple-tree
and the apples stood for and moreover, lovely breasts had been among
the charms which had attracted the patient to the woman associated
with the dream. Here the Tree of Knowledge reveals itself to be the Tree
of Carnal Knowledge.

In his paper on Leonardo Da Vinci, Freud notes that:

> because of his insatiable and indefatigable thirst for knowledge,
> Leonardo has been called the Italian Faust.[13]

In this context Freud here refers to the change that takes place in Faust
in Goethe's play. He speaks of this as a:

> ... transformation of the instinct to investigate back into an enjoy-
> ment of life—a transformation which we must take as fundamental
> in the tragedy of Faust ...[14]

So here Faust's drive to investigate, his erudite search for knowledge, is in Freud's opinion transformed into an enjoyment of life.

We are accustomed to hear asserted that Freud said that the aim of analysis is to love and to work.[15] To this, Winnicottians like to add "and to play". This formula "lieben und arbeiten" was cited by Erik Erikson[16] as Freud's answer to the question of what he thought a normal person should be able to do. Nonetheless this phrase is nowhere to be found in Freud's works.

If something comes close to this assertion it is in his paper "Analytic Therapy" from the *Introductory Lectures* in which he wrote that:

> … a neurotic is incapable of enjoyment and efficiency …[17]

… from which we might conclude that an analysis might have a bearing upon enjoyment and efficiency. Interestingly, Freud notes the painter, in his account of his pact with the devil, stated that he had lost:

> … most of the possibilities of enjoyment in life. Perhaps he himself was only a poor devil who simply had no luck; perhaps he was too ineffective …[18]

Here the painter's lack of enjoyment and effectiveness echo that which Freud attributes to the neurotic. Freud himself aspired to enjoyment and efficiency, writing to Martha Bernays:

> Couldn't I for once have you and the work at the same time?[19]

In his *Address in the Goethe House*, read by his daughter Anna on the occasion of receiving the Goethe Prize, Freud nonetheless warns about the efforts of biographers. He writes:

> But what can these biographies achieve for us? Even the best and fullest of them could not answer the two questions which alone seem worth knowing about. It would not throw any light on the riddle of the miraculous gift that makes an artist, and it could not help us to comprehend any better the value and the effect of his works.[20]

History then has a limit at the point of an unknowable. What is emphasised is the value Freud places on the *effect* of Goethe's work.

This unknowable in some way touches upon the body and its enjoyment of which we have spoken. In *The Interpretation of Dreams* Freud writes of a dream that:

> ... related to a dissection of the lower part of my own body, my pelvis and my legs.[21]

In relation to the dream he speaks about a loss:

> I thought about how much it was costing me to give to the public just this book upon dreams—I should have to give away so much of my most intimate being.[22]

At this point Freud cites Goethe from *Faust*, the very same citation with which he finishes his *Address in the Goethe House*, perhaps the line most often cited by Freud, attributing to Mephistopheles:

> After all, the best of what you know may not be told to boys.

Freud immediately goes on to say that:

> The task which was imposed on me in the dream of carrying out a dissection *of my own body* was thus my *self-analysis* ...[23]

In his correspondence with Fliess in the same context, he refers to what is given away in the same book:

> No other work of mine has been so completely my own, my own dung heap, my own seedling ...[24]

Here this work is something quite physical, quite carnal, which falls from the body.

We have traced Freud's reading of Faust's itinerary and of his own history from the question of the limits of knowledge and the place of love, through the notions of debt and desire, to the enjoyments of body and its losses, connoting the place of the object. We could then put forward the hypothesis that Freud, by virtue of an encounter with *Faust*, is able to elaborate something of his own self-analysis and psychoanalytical theory. We might even propose that Freud's self-analysis occurs, in part, through a transference to the text of Goethe's *Faust*.

Notes

1. Freud, S. "Contribution to a questionnaire on reading". *SE* IX, p. 145.
2. Freud, S. "An autobiographical study". *SE* XX, p. 9.
3. Goethe, J. W. von. *Faust: part one.* Penguin: London, 1949, p. 43. Page numbers from this text are placed in square brackets at the end of citations.
4. Freud, S. "Totem and Taboo". *SE* XIII, p. 158.
5. Messadié, G. *Histoire Générale du Diable.* Robert Laffont: Paris, 1993, p. 337.
6. *Ibid.*, pp. 340–342.
7. Freud, S. "Civilisation and its Discontents". *SE* XXI, p. 121.
8. Messadié, G. *Op. Cit.* p. 338.
9. *Ibid.*, pp. 357–358.
10. Freud, S. "A Seventeenth-Century Demonological Neurosis". *SE* XIX, p. 79.
11. *Ibid.*, p. 80.
12. Freud, S. "The Interpretation of Dreams". *SE* IV, p. 287.
13. Freud, S. "Leonardo Da Vinci and a Memory of his Childhood". *SE* XI, p. 75.
14. *Ibid.*, p. 75.
15. Harari, R. *Les Noms de Joyce.* L'Harmattan: Paris, 1999, p. 91.
16. Erikson, E. *Childhood and Society.* Norton: New York, 1950, p. 229.
17. Freud, S. "Analytic Therapy". In: Introductory Lectures on Psychoanalysis, *SE* XVI, p. 452.
18. Freud, S. "A Seventeenth-Century Demonological Neurosis". SE XIX, p. 104.
19. Freud, E. L. "Letter from Sigmund Freud to Martha Bernays, October 21, 1885". In: *Letters of Sigmund Freud 1873–1939,* pp. 175–177.
20. Freud, S. "Address Delivered in the Goethe House at Frankfurt". *SE* XXI, p. 211.
21. Freud, S. "The Interpretation of Dreams". *SE* IV, p. 451.
22. Cited in: Porge, E. *Freud Fließ: Mythe et chimère de l'auto-analyse.* Anthropos: Paris, 1996, p. 27. I have utilized this citation from the French rather than the *Standard Edition* version as it best conveys the intimate loss that Freud is describing here.
23. Freud, S. "The Interpretation of Dreams". *SE* V, p. 452–453.
24. Masson, J. *The Complete Letters of Sigmund Freud to Wilhelm Fliess, 1887–1904.* Belknap Press: Cambridge, Mass., 1985, p. 352.

CHAPTER TWENTY ONE

The Invention of Solitude—the invention of a style

Tine Norregaard Arroyo

All the unhappiness of man stems from the fact that he is incapable
of staying quietly in his room.

—Pascal

He who is willing to work gives birth to his own father.

—Kierkegaard

Memory: the space in which a thing happens for a second time.

—P. Auster

These three quotes are all taken from Paul Auster's novel,
The Invention of Solitude.[1] It is his first novel, as he has before this
only written and translated poetry, which he notes that his father
somehow did not think much of. It is a novel in which he is concerned
with "a search for the father" in a style of writing that makes references
to autobiographical elements from Auster's own life, as well as involving quotes from a multitude of other authors. The story evolves from
different points of loss that evoke a solitude in Auster's life; starting

with the death of his father, the fear of losing his son due to a serious illness and the family mystery he encounters in the search for the absent paternal grandfather, to a tackling of the question of the solitude of writing. The story is woven around the relationship between a father and a son which in different ways poses a question of how the paternal functions in Auster's own family history and what it means to become a writer in one's own name.

When Lacan speaks about style in regard to the literary field it is the author Marguerite Duras he pays homage to.[2] He acknowledges her style of writing as a practice of the letter which crosses paths with the practice of psychoanalysis. It is a style which takes writing to the point where it does away with any meaning of the said by rather playing with language to make way for the unconscious.[3]

In this paper I wish to present Auster's novel which in its style invents the solitude of writing itself, to discuss how it is possible to recognize in his style a practice of writing that also crosses paths with psychoanalysis.

The author and style

In *What is an Author?* M. Foucault makes a necessary distinction between the writer and the author, stating that the author is the function by which we recognise style as something of the writing rather than of the writer.[4]

> Everyone knows that, in a novel offered as a narrator's account, neither the first person pronoun nor the present indicative refers exactly to the writer or to the moment in which he writes but, rather, to an alter ego whose distance from the author varies, often changing in the course of the work. It would be just as wrong to equate the author with real writer as to equate him with the fictitious speaker; the author function is carried out and operates in the scission itself, in this division and this distance.[5]

It is from this author function that the ethical principle in contemporary writing is sustained in terms of what Beckett states: "What does it matter who is speaking, someone said, what does it matter who is speaking".[6] It is an ethics which puts writing forward as a practice that works with the signifier rather than with the signified, and it is in this manner that author function operates in the distance and effacement of the writing subject. The style at play in the author function then, is one that marks a relationship between writing and death: the writer assumes "the role of the dead man in the game of writing", and it is in this game that the narration of the story comes to life.[7]

In the introduction to the French version of *Écrits*, Lacan poses that style is man himself.[8] This is a reference to Buffon, who proclaimed style as the "well spoken". However, in posing this, Lacan does not expect anything other than to be taken by surprise (buffonant) by this style that visits man.[9] It is not style as an expression, nor as a sign; it is not what expresses or reveals the man in the content of his writing, but rather it is the address of man as what returns of his discourse in an inverted form. Style, then as the "well spoken" is writing in support of desire, as desire of the Other. At the end of this introduction Lacan invites the reader to recognise the style of the collection of writings as the following:

> From the journey of which these writings are milestones, and from the style which their address commands, we want to take the reader to a consequence where he must put in something of himself (mettre du sein).[10]

We know that Lacan named this collection of *Écrits* "open letters" as they are spoken rather than written presentations.[11] It is through these letters, which always return to their destination, the address they command, that he as the author "avows" them: in the way that their style may evoke a question to the subject. As Michael Plastow notes it is "as a subject able to be revealed through style" that these writings invite the reader to engage in a transference to the text.[12] But this subject revealed as style evoked in transference engages with the writing itself, where the subject operates as Foucault states in scission, as divided by the object that falls from "the man". So, in consequence it is, as Lacan points out, rather the object cause of desire which answers to the question of style.[13] It is at the point of the letter in resistance, held up, "en souffrance", in suffering, that the transference of the writing leaves a trace of the fundamental discordance between knowledge and being in the subject.[14] It is transference invoked at the point where the letter in the reading, like in speaking, shows its failure; where in this sense the writing subject is also a reader and the address of the writing is to the Other, an Other who is lacking.

Lacan begins his *Écrits* with the seminar on Poe's novel *The Purloined Letter*, and he affirms Poe as a writer who is able to form a message on this letter, to put it to work, to circulate it and make of it a story, with the enigma left in suspense.[15] The enigma is what promotes a writing from transference by leaving the letter in "suspense", and what carries the mark of a particular style is this working and reworking of this transference at the place of a "third" in the writing.

A portrait of the author and his father

The first part of Auster's novel is titled Portrait of an Invisible man and it is introduced with a photograph of the Auster's paternal family with a tear marking the place where the grandfather should have been. This loss in the picture echos another loss from which the story begins, the death of Auster's own father, a loss which the writing attempts to bridge, but, which at the same time only increases the distance between thinking and writing:

> I am so aware of the rift between thinking and writing. For the past few days, in fact I have begun to feel that the story I am trying to tell is somehow incompatible with language, that the degree to which it resists language is an exact measure of how closely I have come to saying something important, and that when the moment arrives for me to say the only true important thing (assuming it exists), I will not be able to say it. There has been a wound, and I realize now that it is very deep. Instead of healing me as I thought it would, the act of writing has kept this wound open.[16]

The story then, takes on its own form with the absence that this loss introduces.

This is an absence associated with a father, whom, as Auster states: "even before his death [..] had been absent".[17] While looking through the father's personal artifacts Auster uncovers the truth of his father and his family history. These emblems of the father reveal the mark of an absence in a man, not only around his position in the family and to his son, but also in relation to himself as such. It is a description of a person, whose image of himself is basically the sole reflection of a pattern of familiar habits:

Always a man of habit, he would leave for work early in the morning, work hard all day, and then, when he came home (on those days he did not work late), take a short nap before dinner. Sometime during our first week in the new house, before we had properly moved in, he made a curious kind of mistake. Instead of driving home to the new house after work, he went directly to the old one, as he had done for years, parked his car in the driveway, walked into the house through the back door, climbed the stairs, entered the bedroom, lay down on the bed, and went to sleep.[18]

Many other situations display a similar absence and invisibility in his life, like the empty pages of the album entitled the "Auster Family", and the lies and stories he invented about himself to women he had relationships with during his later years after the parents' divorce. No vices or pleasures had a place in his life. The father's position is a solitary one, but not a solitude chosen, as Auster writes, in order to discover himself, rather it is solitude in the sense of a withdrawal, a retreat from himself: "In the sense of not having to see himself, of not having to see himself being seen by anyone else".[19]

It is this absence in the father which also makes Auster state that he in his early years lived in the "orbit of his mother". He was sick with cramps and his mother was filled with loneliness. It is from this small orbit that he determines the first search for his father, resulting in an intense longing for any sign of appreciation from him.

You could not trust him to know what you wanted, to anticipate what you might have been feeling. The fact that you had to tell him yourself vitiated the pleasure in advance, disrupted a dreamed of harmony before a note could be played. And then, even if you did tell him, it was not at all sure that he would understand what you meant.[20]

Like the construction in an analysis Auster writes a story which reveals an absence carried on the side of the father through the lack of the paternal grandfather, who due to infidelity and mistreatment of the family responsibilities, died at the hands of the grandmother herself.

There are many descriptions of the disappointments occurring from a missed encounter with the father, and, yet, in the midst of all this there is suddenly a recounting of an episode which leaves a different kind of inscription in relation to the father. It is a situation where the father on demand starts telling an adventurous story to his son about "his prospecting days in South America". Whether the story is true or not does not matter much to the boy at this moment, it is only the telling of it that is relevant; it is the signifiers of what is carried from a father to a son.

> His language was flowery and convoluted, probably an echo of the books he himself had read as a boy. But it was precisely this literary style that enchanted me. Not only was he telling me new things about himself, unveiling to me the world of his distant past, but he was telling it with new and strange words. This language was just as important as the story itself. It belonged to it, and in some sense was indistinguish-able from it. Its very strangeness was proof of authenticity.[21]

This father marked by absence becomes present in the stories told to his son, and it is in the strange language of the storytelling that he becomes authentic for the son. In this search for the father something of his solitude is heard in the style of the strangeness that marks the language in which these stories are told. A similar strangeness of language in a story that crosses paths with many other stories marks the style of Auster's own literary writing. Could this be the "invention of solitude", as a re-invention, a metaphorisation that ties something in resonance with the metonomy of the father's speech? The invention of solitude would then be the equivocation of the "paternal mystery" necessary to write in one's own name. As Lacan notes:

> ... it is between the signifier in the form of the proper name of a man and the signifier that metaphorically abolishes him that the poetic spark is produced, and it is in this case all the more effective in realizing the signification of paternity in that it reproduces the mythical event in terms of which Freud reconstructed the progress, in the unconscious of all men, of paternal mystery.[22]

The style of writing of his story can be traced in the chance occurrence whereby as Auster notes: "a young man 20 years later winds up in the same room where his father faced the horror of solitude".[23]

Writing in the room of the father

Like in the myth of the murder of the father of the primal horde, the father appears in a second time as law, as memory. Auster's story passes from autobiographical elements relating to a mourning of the loss of the father in the first part to the evoking of his presence in memory in the second part titled "The Book of Memory", where the protagonist is no longer I, Paul Auster, but "A" or "he". The second part is introduced in the following manner:

> He lays out a piece of blank paper on the table before him and writes these words with a pen. It was. It will never be again.[24]

Auster himself comments on the nature of chance that appears as the particular mark of his style by evoking the effects that a memory of a story told by a friend has on him. It is a story about M, whose father had hidden in a room in Paris during the war, a chambre de bonne, which by chance twenty years later M unknowingly came to stay in, and which his father discovers, through the address on the letter he sent him, is the same room. About this Auster says the following:

> It begins therefore with this room. And then it begins with that room. And beyond that there is the father, there is the son, and there is the war. To speak of fear, and to remember that the man who hid in that little room was a Jew. To note as well: that the city was Paris, a place A. had just returned from (...), and that for a whole year he once lived in a Paris chambre de bonne—where he wrote his first book of poems, and where his own father, on his trip to Europe, once came to see him. To remember his father's death. And beyond that, to understand—this most important of all—that M's story has no meaning.[25]

In the story remembered it is the letter that returns something, an address to the sender, and it is the circulation of this letter which effects a writing. It is in this way that Auster as a writer makes a claim to the letter which by chance returns to the same address, the same room as the room of his father.

It is the letter as an element of chance that evokes a point of the Real in Auster's writing, the tuché, which opens the door to "the most cruel part of the object":[26]

> The first word appears only at a moment when nothing can be explained anymore, at some instant of experience that defies all sense. To be reduced to saying nothing.
>   Or else, to say to himself: this is what haunts me. And then to realize, almost in the same breath, that this is what he haunts.[27]

This manner whereby writing evokes the letter as a failure in knowledge as the point of an encounter with the Real, is what sustains Auster's writing as particular. Lacan also refers to this "solitude" in the writing of a particular style, as that which arises out of an acknowledgement that the "I" is not the subject's being, but only something presumed in "that which speaks".[28] He says the following:

> That solitude, as a break in knowledge, not only can be written, but is that which is writing par excellence, for it is that which leaves a trace of a break in being.[29]

Could this exile, this solitude, be what echoes an invention necessary to writing; what the title of Auster's novel alludes to: *The Invention of Solitude*?

The invention of solitude as the invention of a style

In his seminar *The Sinthome* Lacan proposes that the father is a symptom or a sinthome and that it is the ex-sistence of the symptom which supposes the knotting of the imaginary with the real and the symbolic "enigmatically".[30] Here Lacan gives an example of Joyce's *A Portrait of the Artist as a Young Man* as a writing in the "singular", which enacts this sinthome, that is a writing of a style which refers us to Joyce the author. Joyce's' style of writing may speak of the man Joyce, but it is as a portrait painted of the artist Joyce, and not as an all of Joyce the man.[31]

The first chapter in Auster's book, "Portrait of an Invisible Man" echoes this tittle of Joyce's book as he plays with the autobiographical references to the man Auster, but at the same time constantly refers to quotes from everyone else. It is a style of writing in which the subject is drowned, always slipping away in all the references to an elsewhere. J. P. Lebrun terms this as a writing in the intransitive form; a writing produced from the "absence of the absence".[32] In a reference to Duras, who states that it is only "writing that is stronger than the mother" the paternal principle of writing is, according to Lebrun, the enactment of castration in the subject's relationship with *jouissance* and writing. At least one *jouissance* is prohibited, the one in which the subject returns to the All of the mother. It is writing as a dit-mension, a "lying" about what is said; writing as including something of the not-said. It is an enunciation, an equivocation, which as such moves from the personal to the particular. In this sense writing is a rewriting through the equivocal of the signifier which resonates with the letter.[33] It is hereby that the writing of a singular style evokes the object cause of desire, which opens the door to a room, where as Lacan states in reference to Aristotle, "man thinks with his object".[34]

It is in this room of the solitude of the father where by chance Auster finds himself as a writer. His particular style of writing is something that evokes the strangeness of language of his father's stories: at the moment it touches on the real of his own life and death, it turns towards a multitude of associations which resonate in similarity through words, names of places or events in time. It is then a lying, a "dit-mension", which in its proliferation of language still produces a truth.

David Pereira poses that the litura, evolved from Lacan's play on words regarding the relationship between, literature, littoral and psychoanalysis, is the element that knots the letter in a writing which returns something to the address of the sender between "inscription and erasure":

> It addresses the problem of how to transmit a knowledge which is not cut off from truth but rather, in being cut, is able to produce truth.[35]

Auster's writing as a search for the father is not a return to the father, not a claim made to an inheritance. Rather it is a writing in a second time; the "Book of Memory"; a writing founded on an unlawful illegitimate act, the murder of the paternal grandfather, that is the evocation of something which "haunts" and itself sustains a continuous "haunting". The paternal principle which founds this writing of the particular is therefore neither a submission nor foreclosure of the law, but a "torsion"of this law, turning it towards itself in forging something new from this point; the invention of a style.[36] It is in the resi-due of a debt to the father that is constantly worked and re-worked that the lituraic element points to style from the transference that is evoked in the writing, and it is this practice of writing that crosses paths with psychoanalysis.[37]

Lacan outlined the "pass" as the testimony whereby an analyst authorises himself, with some others, through the particular style that is able to be heard, to be written, from what he has come to know about the "horror", the outcast, the solitude of the experience with the unconscious in the transference.[38] Perhaps, we can also say that Auster through the writing of this first novel with the transference that the writing evokes, that is with some others, the readers, authorises himself as an "author" through the particular signature of his style of writing: the invention of solitude.

Notes

1. Auster, P. *The Invention of Solitude*. Faber and Faber. London. 1982.
2. Lacan, J. *Homage to Marguerite Duras on Le ravissement de Lol V. Stein*. Translated by P. Connor. San Francisco City Lights Books. 1987.
3. Op. cit. p. 124.
4. Foucault, M. *What is an Author?* IN: (Ed) J. Faubion *Aesthetics, Method and Epistemology*. Vol. Two. Penguin Books. The New Press 1998, p. 215.
5. Op. cit. p. 215.
6. Op. cit. p. 205.
7. Op. cit. p. 207.
8. Lacan, J. *Écrits*. Éditions du Seuil, Paris. 1966. Introduction.
9. Op. cit.
10. Op. cit. Unpublished translation.
11. Lacan, J., *Lituratèrre*. Extract from *Lacan's Seminar A discourse which does not make a semblance*. 1971. Unpublished translation.
12. Plastow, M. *On the Subject of Style*. IN: D. Pereira (Ed) *Papers of the Freudian School of Melbourne*. *Vol. 18*. Melbourne. 1997. p. 22.
13. Lacan, J. *Écrits*. Éditions du Seuil, Paris. 1966. Introduction.
14. Lacan, J., *Lituratèrre*. Extract from *Lacan's Seminar A discourse which does not make a semblance*. 1971. Unpublished translation.
15. Lacan, J., *Lituratèrre*. Extract from *Lacan's Seminar A discourse which does not make a semblance*. 1971. Unpublished translation.

16. Auster, P. *The Invention of Solitude*. Faber and Faber. London. 1982. p. 32.
17. Op. cit. p. 6.
18. Op. cit. p. 8.
19. Op. cit. pp. 16–17.
20. Op. cit. pp. 21–22.
21. Op. cit. p. 23.
22. Lacan, J. *The Agency of the Letter in the Unconscious*. IN *Écrits: A Selection*. Translated by A.Sheridan, W.W.Norton & Company. New York. 1977. p. 158.
23. Auster, P. *The Invention of Solitude*. Faber and Faber. London. 1982.
24. Op. cit. p. 75.
25. Op. cit. p. 80.
26. Lacan, J. *The Four Fundamental Concepts of Psychoanalysis*. Translated by A.Sheridan. Penguin Books. 1977. p. 59.
27. Auster, P. *The Invention of Solitude*. Faber and Faber. London. 1982. p. 81.
28. Lacan, J. *On Feminine Sexuality, The Limits of Love and Knowledge. 1972–1973. Encore.The seminar of Jacques Lacan. Book XX*. Translated by B. Fink. W. W. Norton & Company. New York. 1998. p. 120.
29. Op. cit. p. 120.
30. Lacan, J. *Le sinthome. Séminaire 1975–1976*. Éditions de l'Association Freudienne Internationale, p. 18.
31. Op. cit. p. 15.
32. Lebrun, J. P. *Écrire comme symptôme*. IN: Bulletin de l'Association freudienne internationale, *N 77, Mars 1998*. p. 5.
33. Lacan, J. *Le sinthome. Séminaire 1975–1976*. Éditions de l'Association Freudienne Internationale, p. 16.
34. Lacan, J. *The Four Fundamental Concepts of Psychoanalysis*. Translated by A. Sheridan. Penguin Books. 1977. p. 59, p. 62.
35. Pereira, D. *Writing, Inheritance, Transmission: The Freudian Legacy and the Lacanian Litura*. IN: O. Zentner (Ed) *Papers of The Freudian School of Psychoanalysis: Crucial Question of Psychoanalyis*. Melbourne 1990. p. 54.
36. Op. cit. p. 58.
37. Op. cit. p. 58.
38. Lacan, J. *Note to the Italian Group*. 1973. Unpublished translation pp. 5–6.

CHAPTER TWENTY TWO

The enigma of Rrose Selavy

Madeline Andrews

The first man to compare the cheeks of a young woman to a rose was obviously a poet; the first to repeat it was possibly an idiot.

—Salvador Dali[1]

Rrose's identity poses a question: name, first name, sex and habitus ...

—Marc Decimo[2]

The work of art connects up to those rare moments that are the only really creative ones, those moments when the work revulses subjective causality—the pulsional destiny ... of its author.

—Thierry de Duve[3]

Dali opens a brief dedication to the artist Marcel Duchamp in the preface to a collection of interviews conducted by Pierre Cabanne, with an ironic quip on poetic licence. Those familiar with Duchamp's work will recognise in Dali's comment a reference to Rrose Selavy, a feminine nom de plume that Duchamp adopted in

1920. In 1921, masquerading as a woman, Duchamp posed as Rrose for a series of photographic portraits produced by Man Ray. The additional letter (r) in the name, if not pronounced silently, reads in the French vernacular as "Er-Rose", which is suggestive of an error.[4] The sound of "Eros" is also unmistakable, the letters of which are an anagram of the word Rose. In 1967, on the rare occasion of allowing himself to be interviewed, Duchamp stated that he believed in eros, not as an "ism" (ideology) but rather, as "a truly rather widespread thing" that had replaced the literary schools of Symbolism and Romanticism, allowing him to think beyond the constraints of existing theories. Duchamp described the place of erotics in his work as "enormous". Hidden but not disguised, he said, erotics was a way, "to bring out the daylight things that are constantly hidden".[5]

According to the art critic, Francis Naumann, "like Athena, who sprang forth fully formed from the head of Zeus", Rrose was born from Duchamp's fertile mind when the idea of changing his identity and name to a Jewish one, was displaced by the thought, "why not one's sex?"[6] Naumann proposes that Rrose's appearance was possibly styled on Charlie Chaplin's protagonist in the film, *A Woman*. However, beyond a play of appearances, Duchamp's approach to the feminine sex was taken up far more seriously, and I would suggest, encountered at the level of an impossible relation, the *impossible to represent*, in a work entitled, *The Bride Stripped Bare by Her Bachelors, Even* (also known as *The Large Glass*). Notably, after more than ten years of application to this work, Duchamp ultimately abandoned it, leaving it unfinished. Whereas the identity of Rrose Selavy initiated a type of masquerade, her conception can also be read as an act of nomination that was deadly serious. Anticipated in the spirit of eros as an error, and distinguished by the repetition of the letter, her name can be understood as carrying the mark of a desire, which shows itself in the work of Duchamp in a series of returns.

In the post Homeric Greek myth known to us through Apulieus, Eros (aka Cupid) falls victim to his own villainy, by accidentally piercing himself with his own dart and becoming infatuated with a mortal (Psyche).[7] Now on this rare occasion, the affair between a god and a mortal was permitted but under the provision of a single rule; that Psyche abstain from casting eyes upon her lover. Beset by doubt, Psyche eventually wavers in her resolve and far from a sight for sore eyes, Cupid is revealed to her as resplendently beautiful. Yet this can only occur through a conjugal error that has Psyche banished by the gods into the realm of the underworld. Thus the woman behind the artist, Er-rose, formed part of Duchamp's critique of "the retinal", that is, his resistance to a painterly, bourgeois, aesthetic that privileged art as a visual delectation.[8]

Notably, more than a hundred years later, Duchamp's art has been recognised as having retained something of its original force:

> Today, we can only observe that Duchamp has stood the test of time remarkably well, or should I say the test of familiarity (Duchamp's *bête noire*), which ultimately and inexorably invades our minds.[9]

In the city from which Duchamp took exile, some forty years after his leaving, Jacques Lacan was tackling an eros/error conjunction of a different order. Having distanced himself from the rites and rituals of the neo-Freudians, Lacan was questioning the privileged position of the imaginary in the practices of the American psychoanalytic institutes. In the early seminars, Lacan took to dismantling ego-centred interpretations of the Freudian unconscious, satirically dressing down the codified ethics of the I.P.A., and critiquing the myth of the subject in the history of Western thought. According to Lacan, in the grip of the ego psychologists, the disclosure of an erotics essential to psychoanalysis had been reduced to a deaf epistemology, habituated to the terms of a fixed lexicon and theory of psychic defence mechanisms. This critique was similar in structure and effect to Duchamp's critique of the retinal.

Now if I am to proceed with examining the work of an artist alongside that of a psychoanalyst, this must be understood as a very tenuous juxtaposition to be making. I take the liberty here, only for the purpose of pursuing a question, which I think inevitably arises whenever we look to art to tell us something about psychoanalysis. It is a question that inquires as to where, and it what way, the visual, written and performing arts might penetrate or intersect with, the discourse of psychoanalysis, if at all. In this paper, the question will be pursued through a consideration of the art (art-ifice) of Duchamp and of Lacan, with due respect to the fact that the function of an artist, and a psychoanalyst, are very different. The articulations of artists and psychoanalysts nevertheless have discursive effects in their respective fields. Both Duchamp and Lacan declared that no metalanguage or master existed to dictate the terms of their work, and in each case, intervened in an imaginary-symbolic tie that was dominant in the prevailing discourse of the times.

In the early seminars, Lacan addressed himself to a fundamental error in elaborations of the subject in the humanities and sciences. This error, or *méconnaissance* (misrecognition), had grafted the subject as "man" onto a concept of being, limited to the field of the specular relation. According to Lacan, in the discourse of psychoanalysis, it was this same error that had reduced Freud's theory of the unconscious, to a theory of the imaginary subject (a theory of the ego). Thus the subject of desire, as subject to the effects of the signifier, had been left in abeyance by the second generation of analysts. In seminar eleven, Lacan noted that the psychoanalyst lured by the illusion of the specular relation, was responsible for a type of fatal error in the direction of the treatment. This was to demystify the object of the transference by identifying it with the person of the analyst. Lacan insisted that the subject was situated elsewhere, repeatedly deferred as missing in the chain of representation and thus never reducible to a relation:

> Transference may lead us to the heart of repetition ... that is why it is necessary to ground this repetition first of all in the very split that occurs in the subject in relation to the encounter. This split constitutes the characteristic dimension of analytic discovery and experience; it enables us to apprehend the Real, in its dialectic effects, as *originally unwelcome*.[10]

In seminar two, Lacan refers to this split in terms of a division between the look and the gaze, evidenced by a "stain" - a remnant of discourse elusive to the subject's imaginary identifications with the Other. Lacan nominated this remainder as the litter, or letter, of the subject's entry into discourse - something in excess of meaning and resistant to representation. In Lacan's development of the psychoanalytic seminars and Duchamp's approaches to art, something of this order, excessive and insistent, demanded a form of nomination, which in each case, was seriously taken up. Duchamp's artistic devices forced the spectator into a position, in which aesthetic interpretations couched in habituated terms of reference collapsed. Similarly, Lacan's theory of the desire of the analyst intervened in the specular dimension of psychoanalytic transference, emphasising the ethic of the well spoken over and above interpretations of meaning. In each case, this privileging of the letter was not received lightly by members of the establishment. In their respective times, Duchamp and Lacan were subject to personal attack, threat of censorship, group effects, mimicry, and distortion of their ideas.

Before proceeding, I want to briefly consider a text described as seminal in the history of art critique, Walter Benjamin's *The Work of Art in the Age of Mechanical Reproduction*.[11] In 1936, Benjamin wrote of the implications of a radical transformation in art that corresponded with the advent of new technologies. With the invention of the camera, moving pictures, the lithograph and the printing press, the art replica and mass production of artworks were made possible. According to Benjamin, the dissemination of the multiple copy precipitated a shift, in which the aura (or ineffable presence) of the classical object was dislodged. The status of the artwork, no longer traceable to time, place, or the hand of the artisan, was emancipated from a *"parasitical dependence on ritual"* and the constraints of a stable referent.[12] The mechanics of reproduction thus shifted the status of the art, from the culturally prescribed rites of the sacred object, to the economy of the openly readable, commodity of exchange. From cult value to exhibition value, this shift opened new possibilities that were immediately embraced by the emerging avant-garde.

The situation was thus perfectly primed for artists to begin experimenting with the effects of replication, the erasure of the identity of the artist, and artworks as objects of unmediated signification.[13] Duchamp embraced the new technology: photography, lithography, printing, and the use of synthetic materials and found objects. Replicas were signed off as originals, genuine works under pseudonyms. Copies of iconic works were comically desecrated (the most famous example being Duchamp's bearded and moustached version of the Mona Lisa). A retrospective exhibition, which Duchamp packaged as a limited edition deluxe box set of miniatures, was released before he had held his first solo exhibition. These gestures, which ruptured established codes of artistic decorum, also marked a point of discontinuity in the relation between artist and artwork, object and spectator, form and function, representation and present-ation.

According to De Duve, Duchamp's position as an artist, in response to an impasse encountered in the "infra-thin" space of a choice between painting/non-painting, was founded by an act of nomination. It was an act of naming (the death of painting) that registered these two positions as one, marking the site of an irreversible passage that Duchamp was later to refer to as: "a kind of pictorial nomination". Of circumstances surrounding this event, De Duve writes:

> In Neuilly, between March and May 1912, a series of four drawings prepare the way for the painting *The Kings and Queen Surrounded by Swift Nudes (Le roi et la reine entourés de nus vites)* ... that image and name have lost their references in entering a poetic dimension that refers the effects of language to its own laws. In short, it is the law of Cubism, its "retinal" legality, as well as its familial over-determination, that Duchamp declares he wanted to move beyond as quickly as possible.[14]

In 1912 upon his arrival to New York, Duchamp declared that for him, painting was entirely washed up. Earlier that year, his now celebrated work, *Nude Descending A Staircase* (a mechanistic rendition of a naked woman depicted in perpetual motion), had been rejected by the Paris Exhibition of Independents. Leaders of the group (which included his brother), discrediting the work as "an obscenity", requested he remove it from the gallery. Duchamp later noted, that although this rejection prompted his decision to leave Paris, it was principally in response to an impasse he perceived in painting as an art form generally, which led to his decision to abandon the canvas altogether.[15] Duchamp later referred to his rejection from the PEI as a fortuitous event, which prefaced a period of disengagement from all art movements and fashions. At the end of this period Duchamp announced a decision to abandon the artisanal pleasure of "olfactory masturbation" in order to pursue something where the eye and the hand would count for nothing.[16] The works that followed took a radical turn.

Duchamp turned a gloved hand to the use of mixed mediums and found objects, made readily accessible through new developments in manufacturing. Queer mechanical inventions based on strange-logic formulas and installation works accompanied by instruction manuals for the viewer, followed. Montages of borrowed images were inscribed with mysterious, ambiguous text. More and more, Duchamp's art was performed as a deliberately collapsible spectacle outside the conventional space of the gallery.[17] Duchamp's elusiveness as a public figure heightened the effect. The Scarlet Pimpernel of the art scene, he frustrated the critics by rarely appearing in public and failing to arrive where expected. Duchamp's slipperiness deliberately confounded those intent on cataloguing his ideas as a cohesive oeuvre, according to a personal style. Public response, from a group still anticipating artists as emissaries of beauty, perspective, simulated realities and technical proficiency, was fiercely hostile: shock, outrage, disgust. Irrespective of the fact that Duchamp played the part of a provocateur, often deploying his work as an incitement, the critics nevertheless falsely interpreted his work as singularly perverse in intention and incomprehensible by design.

In 1954 Lacan, in an acknowledgement of the ideas contributed by artists, stated that: *"Poets, as is well known, don't know what they're saying, yet they still manage to say things before anyone else"*.[18] This tribute was also specifically directed to the poet Rimbaud, whom Lacan suggested, had nailed the essence of the Copernican discovery—(the decentred subject of the enlightenment) with four words: *"I is an Other"*.[19] This "I is an Other" points to the foreign dimension of desire (alien to the ego and undercutting the specular) that Lacan demonstrated as an effect of language and signification, which the subject comes to embody. Lacan introduced a cut, pointing to a rupture in the image and representation of "man" as an effect of discourse, which inevitably speaks from another place:

> The unconscious completely eludes the circle of certainties, by which man recognises himself as ego. There is something outside this field which has every right to speak as I ...[20]

Thus, if Rimbaud effectively nailed it, perhaps we can say that Duchamp effectively performed it, through a series of installations and experimental works that elicited the strangeness of the familiar in the surreal language of ordinary objects.

Parallels could be easily drawn between the gestures of Duchamp and Lacan: a predilection for language games, irony, poetics, and experimentations with logic and science. However rather than indulge these imaginary points of comparison, I refer to something else, namely, a necessity for invention to which Duchamp and Lacan responded, each in singular style, beyond any concern for authorisation from a sanctioning Other. Reflective of an adherence to neither modernist nor nihilist movements, Duchamp's art can no more be considered a form of art for art's sake, anti-art or Dadaism, than Lacan's psychoanalysis as structuralist, a return to Freud, or an extension of the anti-psychiatry movement. On the contrary, both these artists stepped into the very

breach that their work opened out, in order to test the implications further.[21] In the Proposition of October 1967, Lacan formulated, as one of
the principles of the psychoanalytic method, the *pure intention* of the
psychoanalyst, claiming that the "psychoanalyst derives authorisation
only from himself".[22] Notably, this "himself" had nothing to do with
a "self" and everything to do with the status of the subject's desire at
the end of his analysis. In this way, Lacan wrested the responsibility for
the transference from the codified rules of an insurance pact, placing it
squarely within the structure of a language pact, and in the mouth of
the analyst capable of testifying to his desire. It is precisely this desire,
which is carried by the insistence of the letter.

In 1963 the formulation of the *objet petit a* came to pass: Lacan's most
radical invention to date. It was the result of over 20 years' intensive
intellectual labour and its development would be the catalyst for many
more. According to Allouch, this little object emerged from the angst of
a theoretical crisis in which Lacan's formulation of the Other across the
three registers (the Symbolic, Imaginary and Real) reached an impasse.[23]
The object *petit a* (letter *a* and surplus of the *autre*) was born of this crisis and in the seventies, emerged like a phoenix from the centre of the
Borromean Knot, which Lacan had used to demonstrate the interlacing
of the registers. Thus the invention of the object *a* was an act of nomination, which designated the letter as litter of the impossible to theorise.
Lacan formulated this good for nothing object as something that the
analyst resembles, that is, as the dissimulating semblant of cause, which
as Real, poses a limit to sense. From that point onwards, the intervention
of the psychoanalyst would be formulated as the cutting of sense and a
knotting of non-sense, as opposed to an interpretation of meaning. It is
at the point of that encounter, in which the subject's conventional bear-
ings are lost that the angst of castration may be felt in the form of dread,
horror, or repulsion. Notably, these were precisely the types of reactions
that Duchamp's readymades elicited at the time of their release.[24]

In 1913 Duchamp invented what was to become known as "the readymades". These found objects were mass-produced items of manufacture
specifically chosen by Duchamp for lack of any historical or aesthetic
value. *Bottle Rack* for example, was an ordinary piece of merchandise
that Duchamp picked up at a local jumble sale and brought back into
the studio. But it was Duchamp's ingenuity alone that inspired him to
baptise each of these objects with a new name, authorising each one
with his proper signature. Through an act of nomination, these good for

nothing readymades were designated as art, through a singular process of selection and nomination. The titles given to them were paradoxical, emphasising a point of functional or semantic disjuncture (e.g. *Bicycle Wheel*, *Trap*). Thus, the only point of recognition a readymade elicited in the viewer was a missing value, emerging in the gap between function and form, referent and name. Further to the abandonment of painting, Duchamp declared himself an "anartist", but I would argue, only insofar as he was able to make of this impasse, an act of creation.

According to De Duve, Duchamp's invention of the readymades was the other side of a declaration concerning the death of painting and Enlightenment aesthetics. Perhaps we can consider Rrose Selavy as one of the readymades, a readymade woman, in which the "r" of her *erros* returns. This letter runs like a loose thread, or *roter faden*, through many of Duchamp's works, some of which were signed by Rrose.[25] It returns in Duchamp's *Rotoreliefs* and in his 1951 work, *Objet Dard* (obviously a play on the *objet d'art*) in the form of a sculpted wooden handle in the shape of a flaccid penis. That same year, Rrose Selavy was signatory to a commissioned work entitled, *Why not sneeze R(r)ose Selavy?*, in which the weight of the letter and release of the sneeze were ironically placed in parenthesis.

Towards the end of his career Duchamp disclosed that his most profound influence had in fact been a writer, Raymond Roussel (R.R.).[26] Duchamp's attention to language, as reflected in his love of jokes, puns, double entendres, alliterations, anagrams and neologisms, was a critical aspect of his work.[27] In this way, he appeared to be unstoppably drawn to the elliptical, equivocal, and paradoxical. But if we rule out as explanation whim or fashion on Duchamp's part, why then, the insistence of so much non-sense? A certain para-doxa, as exemplified in Duchamp's adoption of the name Er-Rose, may direct us toward an answer. There, a condensed play of the signifier reminiscent of the logic of dreams, and which Freud demonstrates in his workings of the *Traumdeutung* is evidently at play. In the dream of Irma's injection, Freud encounters a point of saturation in the associations and it is at the limit of a proliferating non-sense (a formula of letters), to the extent that no more signifiers can be produced, that a point of excess eclipses the dreamer. As with the dream, at the borders of the "retinal", the aesthetic code, and the limits of the sexual, Duchamp forced the terms of the representational to the threshold of the non-interpretable. An encounter with this real, it must be emphasised, is not in keeping with a "reality" as such. Jean Baudrillard's description of the surreal indicates this aspect of the experience:

> Miracles never result from a surplus of reality but, on the contrary, from a sudden break in reality and the giddiness of feeling oneself fall. It is this loss of reality that the *surreal* familiarity of objects translates. With the disintegration of this hierarchical organisation of space that privileges the eye and vision, of this perspectival simulation—for it is merely a simulacrum—something emerges that, for want of something better, we express in terms of *touch*, a tactile hyperpresence of things, "as though one could hold them". But this tactile fantasy has nothing to do with our sense of touch; it is a metaphor for the "seizure" resulting from the annihilation of the scene and space of representation.[28]

According to De Duve, with Duchamp's invention of the readymades he effectively created the *real* painting. It is this annihilation of the scene and space of representation that demonstrates the function of the name:

> Duchamp chooses an industrial product, displaces it, puts it to another purpose, whereby it loses all its utilitarian value, as well as all ergonomic adjustment of its form to its function, but, by the same token, gains a function as pure symbol.[29]

Freud claimed that psychoanalysis was one of three impossible professions, however in 1913, Rrose Selavy produced a formula for the function of the anartist perhaps suggestive of a fourth:

$$\frac{arrhe}{art} = \frac{merdre}{merde}[30]$$

In 1917, the most controversial of Duchamp's readymades, *Fountain*, had its debut at the first exhibition of the American Society of Independent Artists in New York. The work consisted of a standard urinal, which Duchamp turned on its head, had mounted and signed under the pseudonym: *R. Mutt*. The policy of the Society of Independents (of which Duchamp was a founding member) was no jury, no prizes & unrestricted entry. Scandal erupted when contrary to the agreement, certain members of the committee made a collective decision to remove the work, having appraised it as vulgar, plagiaristic, and a plain piece of plumbing. Without disclosing the identity of the artist, Duchamp's immediate response was to publicly resign from the group. Evidently, taking the piss out of the urinal, and the artist out of the "show of independence" was a deadly serious matter. The release of a new independent newspaper followed, entitled *The Blind Man,* in which Duchamp critiqued the scandal under a different alias.

Duchamp was in his 70's before he was taken seriously as an artist in New York, and if the Society of Independents rejected a mechanical nude now internationally acclaimed for its ingenuity, the International Psychoanalytic Association's response to Lacan's work in the 1950s and 1960s was comparably naïve in its hostility. When Lacan introduced the variable length session, one of the most crucial innovations of the psychoanalytic method to date, the IPA placed a ban on his teachings. No less today, Lacan's work continues to be misconstrued as inscrutable, doctrinal and ethically suspicious, alongside a flurry of misguided texts on "how to read" the seminars. In 1971, Dali made the following observation regarding the reception of Duchamp's work:

In Paris in the early days, there were 17 persons who understood the "readymades"—the very rare readymades by Marcel Duchamp. Nowadays there are 17 million who understand them, and one day, when all objects that exist are considered readymades, there will be no readymades at all.[31]

Likewise, when all we are left of Lacan's teaching is a "how to" manual, and the apprehension of the Real is as welcoming as a front doormat, there will be no psychoanalysis at all.

Juxtaposing the work of an artist and a psychoanalyst is a little like trying to put together cabbages and kings. Lacan, when he was trying to put some French and English together at Baltimore, suggested that it was perfectly feasible to count cabbages and kings in the series of the integer. However as speaking beings, it is as signifiers not integers, that the effects of our erasure must be singularly counted. The conjurer of cabbages and kings, Lewis Carroll, performed the erasure of the subject in literary art form, revealing it as a nonsense with the logic of a dream. But unlike psychoanalysis, neither the visual arts nor literature is a praxis of speech, even though, as we have seen, it may experiment with the text. Although the Real does not speak, what distinguishes a psychoanalysis is the presence of the analyst, which supports the possibility of a testimony of desire, carried by the letter.

In juxtaposing the work of a psychoanalyst and an artist, a certain logic emerged in the artistry of a non-sense-ability. This logic, such as encountered in the dream at the limits of recognition (and if we resist waking in fright), demands that the dreamer invent something. It was in the spirit of the type of non-sense that counts cabbages with kings to the point of a necessity of naming, that the readymade and the theory of the *objet a* came to pass, marking a shift in discourse from representation to signification.[32] From Freud to Lacan, a work of transmission altered the discourse of psychoanalysis irreversibly.

In a way, your analyst is readymade. But your analyst is not readymade as an analyst. He doesn't represent an analyst for an analysand, but a signifier, for another, and another until the point of encounter, which his presence supports. Indeed he has a name and this was readymade like yours, when he was shunted into the world of language. This is not to suggest that an analysis is a matter of adopting new names. Rather, it is a question of knowing what to do with the readymade one.

Notes

1. Carbanne, P. *Dialogues with Marcel Duchamp*. Trans. R. Padgett. Da Capo Inc, New York, 1987, p. 13.
2. Decimo, M. *Marcel Duchamp and Eroticism*. Ed. M. Decimo. Cambridge Scholars Publishing, U.K., 2007, p. 4.
3. De Duve, T. *Pictorial Nominalism: On Marcel Duchamp's Passage from Painting to the Readymade*. University of Minnesota Press, Oxford, 1991, p. 60.
4. Fifty years later, when interviewed by Carbanne, Duchamp stated that: "The double "r" comes from Picabia's painting, you know, the "Oeil Cacodulate" ... the one Picabia asked all his friends to sign ... the word "arrose" demands two R's, so I was attracted to the second R—"Pi Qu'habilla Rose Selavy". *Ibid.*, p. 64.
5. Carbanne, P. *Ibid.*, p. 88.
6. Naumann, F. Marcel Duchamp: A Reconciliation of Opposites. In *Marcel Duchamp: Artist of the Century*. Eds. R. Kuenzli & F. Naumann, MIT Press, U.S.A. 1989, p. 21.
7. Graves, R. *Greek Myths II*, London, Folio Society, 2002, p. 545.

8. In a letter to Alfred Stieglitz in 1922, Duchamp writes: "You know exactly what I think about photography. I would like to see it make people despise painting until something else will make photography unbearable." In Naumann, F. & Obalk, H. Op. Cit. p. 109.

9. Decimo, M. *Marcel Duchamp and Eroticism.* Ed. M. Decimo, Cambridge Scholars Publishing, U.K., 2007, p. 2.

10. Lacan, J. The Seminar of Jacques Lacan, Book XI: *Four Fundamental Concepts of Psychoanalysis.* Ed. J-A. Miller, Trans. A. Sheridan, Norton & Co., New York, 1981, p. 69. Italics added by the author.

11. Benjamin, W. The work of art in the age of mechanical production. In *Illuminations.* Ed. H. Arendt Trans. H. Zohn, Fontana, London, 1992.

12. Benjamin, W. *Illuminations. Ibid.,* p. 218.

13. "Art is taking more the form of a sign, if you wish; it is no longer reduced to a decorative role. This is the feeling that has directed me all my life". Duchamp in Cabanne, P. Op. Cit. p. 93.

14. De Duve, T. *Pictorial Nominalism: On Marcel Duchamp's Passage from Painting to the Readymade.* 1991, p. 14.

15. Referring to the incident in the interview with Carbanne, Duchamp stated that: "I was really defrocked, in the religious sense of the word". Carbanne, P. Op. Cit. p. 66.

16. De Duve, T. Resonances of Duchamp's visit to Munich. In *Marcel Duchamp: Artist of the Century.* Op. Cit. p. 43.

17. The following is one of numerous examples; whilst living as 11 rue Larrey Duchamp invented a door that could be both open and closed at the same time. The door was later removed to become a gallery exhibit.

18. Lacan, J. The Seminar of Jacques Lacan, Book II, *The Ego in Freud's Theory and in the Technique of Psychoanalysis.* Ed. J-A. Miller. Trans. S. Tomaselli, Cambridge University Press, 1988, p. 7.

19. Lacan, J. *Ibid.,* p. 7.

20. Lacan, J. *Ibid.,* p. 8.

21. Carbanne: "One has the impression that every time you commit yourself to a position, you attenuate it by irony or sarcasm". Duchamp: "I always do. Because I don't believe in positions". Carbanne: "But what do you believe in?" Duchamp: "Nothing of course! The word belief is an error ... I don't believe in the word 'being'". In Carbanne, P. Op. Cit, p. 89.

22. Lacan, J. Proposition of 9 October 1967 on the Psychoanalyst of the School. Unpublished translation.

23. Allouch, J. How Lacan invented the Object (a). In *Papers of the Freudian School of Melbourne, Vol. 19, The Lacanian Discourse,* 1998, FSM, Melbourne.

24. "A painting that doesn't shock isn't worth painting". Carbanne quoting Duchamp in Carbanne, P. Op. Cit. p. 69.

25. In a footnote in his book on jokes, Freud, referring to the analogy of the "roter faden" used by Goethe quotes him as follows: "We hear of a peculiar practice in the English Navy. Every rope in the king's fleet, from the strongest to the weakest, is woven in such a way that a *roter faden* (scarlet thread) runs through its whole length. It cannot be extracted without undoing the whole rope, and it proves that even the smallest piece is crown property." In Freud, S. *Jokes and Their Relation to the Unconscious.* Penguin, London, 1962, p. 55.

26. "It was fundamentally Roussel who was responsible for my glass, *The Bride Stripped Bare By Her Bachelors, Even* ... I felt that as a painter it was much better to be influenced by a writer than by another painter. And Roussel showed me the way." Duchamp, 1946, in an interview with James Johnson Sweeney. In *The Bulletin of the Museum of Modern Art, Vol. XIII*, no. 4–5, p. 21.

27. Duchamp: "I like words in a poetic sense ... words are not merely a means of communication ... for me, this is an infinite field of joy- and it's always right at hand". Kuenzli, R. In *Marcel Duchamp: Artist of the Century.* Op. Cit. p. 6.

28. Baudrillard, J. *Seduction.* MacMillan, London, 1990, p. 62.

29. De Duve, T. *Pictorial Nominalism: On Marcel Duchamp's Passage from Painting to the Readymade.* 1991.

30. "Arrhes" translates from the French to English as a "deposit" or "downpayment". The term "merdre" appears in the opening address of King Ubu in the play by Alfred Jarry, *Ubu Roi.* Duchamp's formula can be found in *The Essential Writings of Marcel Duchamp.* Eds. M. Sanouillet & E. Peterson, Thames & Hudson, London, 1975.

31. Carbanne, P. Op. Cit. p. 14.

32. X: "What else is there?"
    D: "There's *it*."
    X: "*It*?"
    D: "*It*. Whatever has no name."
    Excerpt from an interview by with Duchamp, in De Duve, T. Op. Cit. p. 191.

CHAPTER TWENTY THREE

The art of interpretation—drawing a line[1]

David Pereira

I will in fact confess to a significant discomfort in speaking here today. Over the years, I have drawn a somewhat rigid line between what could be called my work life and my private or personal life as they have come to occupy divided geographies; divided landscapes. The place from which I speak today produces a shift in that line, a disruption or permeability to that line, which is not without anxiety and discomfort. In effect therefore, in speaking today in Queenscliff, I am introducing the idea of drawing this line differently. As you will hear as we proceed this afternoon, this line and how it is drawn is of fundamental importance to the question of the art of interpretation; of fundamental importance to the act of painting and to the psychoanalytic act of interpretation. The drawing of his line is of fundamental importance in anyone's life, most commonly dividing one's private practices from those which are available to the public. In this context consider the risk, the anguish, of the artist whose most private practices are shown, made available to the public. The artist is always engaged by the question of how to draw this line.

Now, the place from which one speaks will always have an impact on what is to be said. With reference to the place where we are today I want to quote you something from an historical work titled *The Enduring Rip* by poet and author, Barry Hill.

> To grasp the genesis of Queenscliff stand on the rock shelf at low tide at the Heads of Port Phillip. Put the Point Lonsdale Light-house ... behind you and look across the water to Point Nepean. Between these points—only three kilometres—is a stretch of water called the Rip, the significance of which is inseparable from the endeavour of white settlement in the Bay.
>
> The Rip is the momentous meeting place of two domains of water. One mass of water comes in and out of the bay as a tide. The other is the heave and swell, the fetch that has come all the way up from the Antarctic. The two seas in the act of meeting and exchange create a turbulence as dangerous as anywhere in the world. For the force from the outside, with the Southern Ocean behind it, is coun-tered by the lunar propulsion of the Bay—a huge bay, as we know, that must find its way out through the narrow Heads.
>
> From this vantage point the outcome of the conflict is not at all clear. On the one hand, the heave and indigo weight of ocean waters must surely dominate. Yet the tide from the great bay, its greener, faster waters, rushes at the swell at twelve knots ...
>
> Much of this takes place in the force-field of the water's sur-face. Far below—further than most people realize—there is the tur-bulence you get around mountain peaks ... to come through the Heads, to cross the Rip, is to negotiate a passage where the immeas-urable forces below must constantly complicate any of the weather on top.[2]

This shifting line of force, drawn between the tide of the bay and the force of the Southern Ocean, is not indifferent to the question I want to address this afternoon on the art of interpretation. In this, I do not intend to interpret works of art—which runs the risk of lapsing into cli-ché's and generalizations about the state of modern man and the world he lives in. Nor is it my intention to analyze the artist, degenerating into the worst kind of psychobiography. Rather, to make a proposal con-cerning art *as* interpretation; a proposal concerning the ways in which art enters our lives and affects us, moves us.

In order to support this proposal I will refer to the work of David Beaumont, a selection of whose paintings hang on the walls around you. Beaumont's work takes up this shifting line of force in a manner which first drew me to his paintings by way of disturbance; not unlike the disturbance I feel today.

I want to begin by asking how modern art works? What does it do? What function does it serve? Let's begin with the proposition that art, in some way, makes sense of our experience. In which way?

Firstly, it makes sense of our experience in perhaps sustaining a dialogue with the viewer at the level of understanding and narrative. In this regard art tells us about a world and a reality which we already know and seek to comfort ourselves in relation to by locating it within a certain optical space—pinning it down. The painting presumes to represent and offer a story about the world we live in and recognize; the world which our eye has grown accustomed to. It speaks "about" this world, representing it to us in an illustrative, descriptive optical organization which allows the eye to grasp the object it contemplates; to trap it, catalogue it, and return to it at leisure for pleasure.

At this level painting perpetuates a series of clichés contributing to a *malerisch* quality of pictureliness and quaintness. These are the cli-chés which populate the canvas of any painter which is far from being a virginal white surface. A whole category of things which could be termed clichés already fills the canvas before the painter begins. Now, this category of things exists precisely as categorical; this is to say, as able to be catalogued and categorized, fixed to a canvas like insects in a collection—inert.

Painting these clichés, allowing them to prevail, places the painting within the domain of narrative and meaning; they allow the painting to comfort the eye of the viewer in allowing that eye to take hold of the painting through the construction of a narrative. The painting will tell a story, it will offer a meaning. The line is drawn as a narrative thread so as to delimit and circumscribe its object and ensure the coherence and consistency of the work. Such painting, whilst offering itself as repre-sentational, lacks a certain presence, we could say.

This kind of proposition—that painting makes sense of our experi-ence in sustaining meaning and narrative—prompts the following from the painter Francis Bacon, in an interview given in 1975:

> Nine-tenths of the nation, ninety percent of people, ninety-five per-cent of people, are absolute fools, and they're bigger fools about painting than anything else. Because it's a terribly rare thing for

people to feel anything about painting. They can feel, oddly enough, about music, they can feel even about the theatre. But hardly any-one really feels about painting; they read things into it—even the most intelligent people—they think they understand it, but very, very few people are aesthetically touched by painting.[3]

Can we count ourselves amongst the five percent who are not absolute fools? Perhaps only insofar as we are able to further interrogate this proposition that art, in some way, makes sense of our experience. What more can we expect from painting? How is painting to escape the dead weight of this cliché driven, sense making, story-telling enterprise? Again, labouring the point somewhat no doubt, this is equally a question for psychoanalysis.

Abstraction is one response to this question in its attempt to show us—not represent, but present to us—something of our experience of the world, and ourselves caught up in the forces which prevail in it. Abstraction proceeds by attempting to codify, to submit these forces to a symbolic binarism. Through this, it proposes to reduce the chaos, the real forces, to a minimum, thereby offering a certain asceticism through which it raises itself above the figurative and narrative cliché's. The forces at play in the rip are turned into a minimalist stream which we can cross in order to discover the abstract and symbolic forms. The line is drawn so as to assert the rule of symbolic order over real force.[4]

What abstract painting elaborates is a symbolic code formed on the basis of categorical oppositions. It draws the line sharply and categori-cally. From this derives a conception of binary choice which attempts to order the chaos through the imposition of categories. According to Deleuze, "It restores to man a pure and internal optical space, which will perhaps be made up exclusively of the horizontal and the vertical."[5]

Whilst Kandinsky defined abstract painting by "tension", it is a tension which is ultimately codified and resolved within the work. Nothing spills out; there is no real surplus to the symbolic codifica-tion resulting in the characteristic cleanliness and dryness of the work. The tension therefore remains one of categorically distinct elements.

Consider now this first picture of Beaumont's, an untitled work from 1997.

Note the dominance of categorical divisions. Relative to the later work, it presents itself as clean and tonally defined. The lines divide, catalogue and categorize. The cleanliness of the picture, its resolution, arises

Untitled (97 cm × 81 cm).

through drawing the lines in order to present tension as neutralized. I made a slip here in initially writing "neuralized", pertaining to the nervous system, the neurons. And yet this is exactly what abstraction falls short of—in neutralizing tension within the picture, it fails to directly impact, as Bacon, says, on the nervous system of the viewer.

We are not yet, therefore, at that place which Bacon speaks of as being aesthetically touched; we are missing something of the body. In order to be amongst the five percent who are not fools, we have to find the body. Now, this body made its appearance some two weeks ago when the title of the lecture was mistakenly published in a local publication as *The Art of Impersonation*. In psychoanalysis one is required to do something with one's mistakes, even perhaps those which one inherits—to make work what does not work. In this, I make of "The Art of Impersonation" the "Art of Embodiment"; to give body, materiality, flesh. The body slips in.

Consider this second picture of Beaumont's which I think demonstrates a movement away from abstraction through the accident, we could say, of the body.

We find in this second painting a movement away from the dryness of abstraction with the introduction of disjunctions of pure tones and broken tones. The genesis of the line which interests us is to be seen however in this seeping, this bit of spillage, which draws the eye into the painting. It exists as a surplus which creates a breach, a rift, a rent

Night Field (112 cm × 87 cm).

in the purity of tone and categories of the codified system. Something of the contemplative is disturbed as the body seeps into the picture. Colour structure gives way to colour force, as the broken tone indicates the immediate exercise of a force within a yet clearly delimited space. The line looks almost accidental—an accident in the purity of being which marks the entry of the body.

Such embodiment refers to another way in which art makes sense; referring to what in the history of art has acquired the term "sensation." Sensation refers to an effect on the real of the body which is not hijacked by understanding. In making sense of our experience we therefore now touch on sensation rather than the sense of meaning.

When asked in an interview why he wanted to avoid telling a story, Francis Bacon answered:

> I don't want to avoid telling a story, but I want very, very much to do the thing that Valery said—to give the sensation without the boredom of its conveyance. And the moment the story enters, the boredom comes upon you.[6]

Sensation is what is painted. What is painted on the canvas is a body, not insofar as it is represented as an object, but—Deleuze tells us—insofar as it is experienced as "sustaining this sensation."[7] It is the body therefore, not as represented, but as scene of the presentation of the turbulence of forces. When sensation is linked to the body in this way, it "ceases to be representative and becomes real."[8]

Consider this third painting. We see the beginnings of the manual, not technical line. It is given by the operation of the violence of the hand. The contour of the line circumscribes nothing other than the eye which it draws into that space.

In the next three paintings I want you to consider we find a dismantling and dislodging of the narrative of coast, of the relation of land to sea to effect a disturbance through the insistence of this line which renders presents this tension, this rip, the force of an undercurrent; an undercurrent of sustained sensation. The line, as it appears in these paintings, does not exist to differentiate land from sea, or sea from sky. Rather than a categorical division, it operates as a line of tension, a shifting line of force as the point where the eye is seized by the picture. It renders visible forces which do violence to the clichéd images associated with the coastal narrative. The rip, the rent, in the figurative—the

Lavender Shard (101 cm × 86 cm).

Dry Stack (112 cm × 86 cm).

Cove (137 cm × 244 cm).

Outward (85 cm × 100 cm).

representations and clichés—gives rise to the something which exerts greater presence in the picture.

The shadowy hulls and pier, for example, gain this status of presence which is a consequence of the violence done to their conventional representations. Their status as images fades as they acquire real presence.

The barely submerged—hidden but revealed—elements of the picture, finding expression in the hulls, for example, are juxtaposed with the thickening of paint in this play of the viscerality and yet shadowy presence of the real body. In escaping the boredom of the narrative, sensation is able to act immediately upon the body. It becomes the foundation for an erotics of painting which renders the eye not the possessor of the painted object, but possessed.

Bacon described this project as "attempting to remake the violence of reality itself;"[9] to render visible the action of invisible forces upon the body. Now, what was necessary to fund such a project? Bacon was left to fund his project from the reservoir, or better perhaps, the cesspool of what he called his "exhilarated despair". This was what his painting was concerned with, what animated it, his exhilarated despair; the fragment of that curious amalgam of enjoyment and anguish to which the artist owes his existence and which finds a way, called painting, of being transmitted through the operation of his hand.

The artist brings to bear the violence of this fragment of exhilarated despair which has coursed through his existence, to be embodied—impersonated—in each work which finds itself worthy of the designation "art". The *work* of art is exactly this embodiment of *jouissance*, the embodiment of exhilarated despair.

The importance of sensation, therefore, concerns the manner in which the picture transmits a certain *jouissance*, an enjoyment, which is not able to be resolved at the level of a representation or symbolic codification through which the object is apprehended. Rather, it is the eye which is seized in such a manner as to produce apprehension in the viewer. The painting seeps with a surplus, an excess which is funded from the artist's exhilarated despair. It is in this way that the painter breaks with the clichés of his own work, the way in which he does violence to the clichés and representations which inhabit the canvas as he approaches it.

Beyond the figurative, narrative, sense making function of art then, we find an art which joins with the notion of interpretation in psychoanalysis in that it does not try to reproduce reality, but to confront, to encounter, the real; a real which is more real than reality; a real which is inhabited by the twisting force, the power, the invisible forces of the rip, the tear, the rent in being. It is everything in reality which eludes us and yet impacts upon us in ways which we find incapable of representing. We encounter it there where experience fails us. This is what is at stake in the function of interpretation in psychoanalysis as it is in art which does not simply represent or narrate a story.

At this point in the painting where the line is drawn such that it does not represent, it acts along the lines of a rip, a rift in the structure of representation and narrative which opens onto the force of sensation. It is this capacity to exceed representation at this point of exhilarated despair which might be argued to be the defining characteristic of art and of interpretation in psychoanalysis. This is the point of tension in the painting where it strains and rips as it exceeds itself; where it exceeds the dryness of an architectural abstraction; the paint thickens and ejaculates with the wetness of sensation.

Now, I will conclude with a reference to this painting with the rip, the tear, the rent in the fabric of its being. It reveals to us the way in which a hole or a tear defines a real body. This, to me is the defining work. I could tell you a story about this work. Well, I will tell you a story.

It was late on Christmas Eve last year, when an unseen unknown body picked up a piece of blue stone from some distance from here and hurled it through the front window of the gallery at this picture, passing through the window and dislodging its frame. A rigid boundary was rendered permeable.

I remember speaking with the understandably distressed artist in the aftermath about the encounter of forces of creation and destruction. The narrative maintained a clear and distinct categorical division, in placing the forces of creation on the side of the painting and the forces of destruction on the side of the unseen, unknown, shadowy figure, the trace of whose presence becomes unmistakable.

Albeit violent, it is a nice story—neat.

Is however the projectile the cause of the rip in this painting? No more than throwing a rock into the ocean off Point Lonsdale would be the cause of the Rip, the twisting and dangerous force of water between the Heads. To claim that the tear, the rip, is a violence done to the painting, as plausible, as verifiable, as factual as that might be, is nonetheless not true. The argument I have tried to develop today says that this painting is not ripped because of the piece of rock thrown at it. What is

Beyond the Slipway (150 cm × 200 cm).

true, and this is what interpretation in psychoanalysis concerns, is that the painting rips along the line of a tearing, twisting force there where something separates itself from the story, the narrative, to be present as a real force. This is the point in the painting where the violence of the hand swallows up the eye in possessing it in an exhilarated despair.

Notes

1. The Public Lecture series of The Freudian School of Melbourne has been a way of opening the work of the School with a view to promoting discussion and debate around important topics in psychoanalysis and related fields. They have been held for many years at the Monash

Medical School at the Alfred Hospital. This lecture in Queenscliff is the first held outside of Melbourne. My gratitude is extended to Fiona Kelly and *Salt Contemporary Art* for hosting this lecture as part of their arts program, an initiative of this gallery which importantly promotes discussion in the field of arts within the region. All reproductions of paintings contained within this paper appear with the express consent of the artist David Beaumont, and Salt Contemporary Art.

2. Hill, Barry. *The enduring rip: a history of Queenscliffe*. Melbourne University Press, Melbourne 2004, p. 1.

3. Sylvester, David. *Looking Back at Francis Bacon*. Thames & Hudson, New York, 2000, p. 249.

4. Deleuze, Gilles. *Francis Bacon: The Logic of Sensation*. Translated by Daniel Smith. Continuum, London, 2003, p. 73. "Abstract optical space has no need of the tactile connections that classical representation was still organizing".

5. *Ibid.*, p. 73.

6. Sylvester, David. Op. cit., p. 65.

7. Deleuze, Gilles. Op. cit., p. 25.

8. *Ibid.*, p. 33.

9. Sylvester, David. Op. cit., p. 81.

PART VI

DEATH AND PSYCHOANALYSIS

CHAPTER TWENTY FOUR

An architecture of death from Tanizaki to Mishima

Oscar Zentner

Homo sapiens arrives at consciousness through his erect sex[1]

Bataille, G

Shikibu enjoins a man not to think that he must separate his life into two ways
　He should be a samurai, regardless of his love life[2]

Yamamoto, T

Initiation {…} is something that strictly concerns jouissance[3]

Lacan, J

We all know since Freud, that no one can be analysed *in effigy or in absentia*. For the matter I attempt to discuss this is only the first obstacle that we face. The second one, no less insurmountable, is that commenting on the works of two Japanese writers I have to take yet another precaution to avoid the fascination that the encounter with a very different kind of culture often provokes in us.

It is Marguerite Yourcenar,[4] who explicitly calls the attention on this point, although such declaration of intent is not always possible to attain.

Tanizaki was born in Tokyo in 1886.[5] He was above all else a writer deeply engaged with the aesthetical possibilities of the articulation of style, jouissance, eroticism and death. His profoundly erotic novels together with a fascination with the West would be intermingled with the traditional Japanese way. *In Praise of Shadows*, written in 1933,[6] can very well be considered a short treatise on aesthetics, and it is revealing of what according to him constitutes the distance that separates the East from the West.

The characters of his novels undergo ordeals, in which their doomed future is foretold, but there is nothing unconvincing either about them, or their desires being often subverted by jouissance. Needless to say that Tanizaki did not wait for Lacan, or for that matter for any psychoanalytic discovery, in order to convey the dissimilarity and articulation of desire to jouissance.

In one of his novels *The Key (Kagi)*, diaries written by husband and wife are supposed to be secret, however they know in different ways that each of them cheats the other by reading them so that the diary of each becomes an enticing command for the other to follow. It is as if Tanizaki's fiction masterly repeats Borges repeating Carlyle's words: "The universal history is an infinite sacred book, in which all men write and read and try to understand while they write in it."[7]

Tanizaki's explicit interest in untrue facts could have easily subscribed to Lacan's statement that "the best moment in love is that in which one is swindled."[8] Lacan will go even further saying that "Psychoanalysis is a swindle, it is a swindle in the sense that poetry is."[9]

Much as his themes of life and death, desire and jouissance are empowered, they remain confined, embodied, so to speak, on paper. Apparently this is to state the obvious, since art by psychoanalytic definition is always destined to be a question of sublimation. Yet I will run the risk of a psychoanalytic heresy here because things are perhaps less simple, as Mishima, another of the modern masters of Japanese literature, will corroborate.

Junichiro Tanizaki and Yukio Mishima exposed from different angles an exotic tradition; the Orient, that appears to us like the utter Other of the West. Indeed, this is corroborated by the words of Junichiro Tanizaki who, looking at its own culture with what he supposes to be our gaze remarked that "the mysterious Orient of which Westerners speak probably refers to the uncanny silence of these dark places."[10]

His writings are a perfect example of harmonic aesthetics corroded with a mortal edge that he expresses within an erotic of Eros. I understand by this an erotic in which desire by keeping its objects outside the reach of exhaustion, always unfulfilled, overruns jouissance. As you know, from the perspective of Eros, all acts are under the sway of desire; imperfect and therefore condemned to be repeated, they all are true parapraxis,[11] except one, which for being perfect cannot be repeated: suicide.

Yukio Mishima on the other hand is our exponent of an erotic of death; and I understand by this an erotic of *jouissance*.[12] Such erotic consists in exhausting one by one each of the objects of desire. In contrast to Tanizaki, it is not an erotic of incompletion. Lacan's invention of the cause of desire as object (a), presents itself under the semblances of; the gaze, the voice, the breast, the faeces and the phallus. The object (a) as *a loss* is within the domain of Eros, reassures both repetition and postponed jouissance through the prevalence of desire; yet the object (a) as *plus* within the domain of *jouissance* is beyond repetition, completes desire and annihilates it by the pure prevalence of *jouissance*.

The whole Opera Magna of Mishima went into the direction of perfecting a single deed, as he said; "I want to make a poem of my life."[13] Mishima's erotic of death,[14] with his Seppuku is the act that affords neither failure nor repetition; it abolishes mourning, if mourning is attached to whoever is the guarantor of his castration.[15] Following Lacan's rigour and finesse, we are distinguishing for the pre-condition of the object relations the object (a) as lost, whilst for narcissism the object (a) as *plus* results in a *jouissance* of the body. Our distinction between erotics of desire and erotic of death is reinforced by the explicit promotion of narcissism *of the object of the body*[16] made by Mishima together with his criticism of Tanizaki for expressing a non-narcissistic masochism.

Not long before his death Mishima wrote for an exhibition devoted to his life,

> Just when I was about to complete my tetralogy, *The Sea of Fertility* {...} A writer, once he begins looking back on his past works, drives himself into a dead end, but what is wrong with letting others arrange his past?[17] {...} I made only one suggestion: that was to divide my forty-five years of life—a life so full of

contradictions—into *Four Rivers; "Writing", "Theatre", "Body", and "Action", all finally flowing into The Sea of Fertility.*[18]

One thinks at once of that other immense homage paid to Λήθη (Lethe) in *Finnegans Wake,* in its final flowing of forgetfulness, the Liffey River.[19]

Literature has taught me, in my work as an analyst, that psychoanalytic practice is akin a practice of fiction. Fiction allows as well having a workable definition of the notion of cause, which, as Lacan elucidates, implies that there is cause only where something does not work.[20] This is the very thing that Freud implicitly stated describing those phenomena that do not work when he wrote about the cause of dreams, lapsus linguae, symptoms, parapraxis and the like in *The Psychopathology of Everyday Life.*

Yet regarding Mishima, he is rather the opposite, isn't he? It is because something does work, and very successfully,[21] that he will disprove many psychoanalytic misconceptions. Mishima confronts us with *Tyche* (encounter, chance) and not with *Automaton* (repetition) and psychoanalysis qua psychoanalysis is only viable when there is *Automaton.* This might be perhaps one of the reasons why Lacan felt obliged to say (though exaggerating a bit too much) though for different reasons; that both a Roman Catholic and a Japanese are not analyzable. Not every Roman Catholic is James Joyce[22] and not every Japanese is Mishima, assuming that the latter was what Lacan had in mind.

This *kamikaze of aesthetics* will tell,

> According to my definition of tragedy, the tragic pathos is born when the perfectly average sensibility momentarily takes unto itself a privileged nobility that keeps others at a distance, and not when a special type of sensibility vaunts its own special claims. It follows that he who dabbles in words can create tragedy, "but cannot participate in it". It is necessary moreover, that the "privileged nobility" finds its basis strictly in a kind of physical courage.[23]

From this aspect nothing can both more alien to Mishima than art as sublimation.[24]

Were the shadows so venerated by Tanizaki a necessary condition for what takes place at the end? I do not think so. He did it with the only card he possessed. "We have much in common but I have a card they do not have: The Emperor." He stated as much to an acquaintance after the debate with left-wing students at the university of Tokyo. He acted according to the most sacred of the samurai codes, that card is the submission to the lord, in this case the Emperor. We found in the *Hagakure*, that *concerning martial courage, merit lies more in dying for one's master than in striking down the enemy;* and as such Seppuku becomes the most glorious act, since death is the ultimate Lord[25] to which life submits itself.

The articulation of both Japanese writers is antithetical—Tanizaki's aesthetics is an aesthetics of desire whilst Mishima's, whose aim was, "to revive the soul of the samurai within myself"[26] is of *jouissance*. His seminal work *The Sea of fertility,* was finished and ready with a note for his publisher the very same day in which only a few hours later after the failed attempt to revive the Samurai past of Japan,[27] he would, like a samurai of old,[28] commit Seppuku.

Mishima's reference to Tanizaki in *Confessions of a Mask* [see n 14] is telling,

> "What are you reading these days?" I asked ... "Novels you mean? Well I have read Tanizaki's 'Some Prefer Nettles'" ... [p. 234]

> Even during our conversation my mind had been filled with an endless swarm of doubts. I swore by God that my mood of wanting to meet Sonoko was a genuine one. But in it there was clearly not the slightest sexual desire ... [pp. 239–240]

For Mishima desire, sexual desire lies outside heterosexual love.

Let me quote in full the way the *Hagakure* deals with homosexual love,

> When one is young, he can often bring upon himself shame for a lifetime of homosexual acts. To have no understanding of this is dangerous. As there is no one to inform young men of this matter, I can give its general outline.
>
> One should understand that a woman is faithful to one husband. Our feelings go to one person for one lifetime. If this is not so, it is the same as sodomy or prostitution {...} A young man should test an older man for at least five years, and if he is assured of that person's intentions, then he too should request the relationship. A fickle person will not enter deeply into a relationship and later will abandon his lover. If they can assist and devote their lives to each other, then their nature can be ascertained. But if one partner

is crooked, the other should say that there are hindrances to the relationship and sever it with firmness. If the first should ask what those hindrances are, then one should respond that he will never in his life say. If he should continue to push the matter, one should get angry; if he continues to push even further, cut him down.

Furthermore, the older man should ascertain the younger's real motives in the aforementioned way. If the younger man can devote himself and get into the situation for five or six years, then it would not be unsuitable.

Above all, one should not divide one's way into two. One should strive in the way of the Samurai.[29]

Mishima, knew this well, he strove without dividing his way into two.

Do we need a further proof of the way some psychoanalysis comforts itself lagging behind the most pedestrian prejudices? Let us remember that homosexuality was born, so to speak, as psychopathology in 1869 and died, so to speak, only three years after Mishima's Seppuku, that is, in 1973, when the (North) American Association of Psychiatry no longer considered it to be psychopathological. Heterosexuality in contrast, was born later, in 1890.

It might be timely finishing here, to rescue, as might be expected from an analysis, Lacan's dictum, *One is only responsible for what one knows.* This finds an startling echo in Mishima's *Runaway Horses* in which the character Isao read (repeating the teachings of Neo-Confucian school), *To know and not to act is yet not to know,*[30] thus anticipating according to his own sense of Tragedy, the lonely sojourn, without return that he was training himself to embark on by taking off his mask.

Notes

1. Bataille, G. *The tears of Eros*, p. 3.
2. Yamamoto, T. *Hagakure (In the Shadows of Leaves)* 1659–1719.
3. Lacan, J. Seminar *Les non dupes errant.* Session of 20.11.1973. Unpublished Seminar. My translation.
4. Yourcenar, M. *Mishima ou La vision du vide.* Edition Gallimard, Paris, 1981.
5. Only twenty years after the Meiji restoration.
6. This is roughly the years of the Ni Ni Roku failed *coup d'état.* The Japanese army was divided between those whose political thought was to strike North, that is, the Soviet Union, and those whose strategy was to attack South, that is, the British Empire. After the failed *coup d'état* the

Emperor Hirohito gave the order to crush the rebellion thus favouring the other faction of the Japanese Army.

7. Zentner, O. *Borges and the Fantasm of Reality*. Paper read at The National Library of Canberra for the Centenary of the birth of Jorge Luis Borges in November 1999. Published in Papers of The Freudian School of Melbourne, Vol. 21.

8. Allouch, J. The Sex of the Master, p. 79. My translation.

9. Zentner, O. *Unconscious and Interpretation*. Revista de Psychoanalysis,published by Asociacion Psicoanalitica Argentina, Vol. LXI, No 3 September 2004, p. 687, Buenos Aires.

10. He is describing the importance of the darkness in the Japanese abode, and the way he does it reminds us of the way Goddard, the film director, did it in the Heideggerian-Lacanian dialogue of his film *Masculine-Feminine*, in which a child asks his Mother: *Mum, what is language?* He receives as an answer Heidegger's/Lacan's: *Language is the house that man inhabits.*

11. This was clearly intended in the title Freud gave to one of his important books, *The Psychopathology of Everyday Life,* a book often quoted, seldom read and very often misunderstood.

12. Allouch, J. In *The Sex of the Master*, quotes Ovid and Foucault, *Amorous experience is a forgetfulness of the self, a loss of identity ... Epicure said long before Freud that a man who does not enjoy fabricates the illness that consumes him ... Justly so, Foucault denounces the mistake of believing that one has only a relationship to desire, neglecting the interplays of jouissance ... Beyond any shadow of doubt, we could have avoided sidestepping this question, had we considered the problematic of jouissance. Problematic that from 1971 occupied Lacan in his seminars. It would have been a way of taking Lacan a L'envers (!) from the path opened by him since the Seminar L'angoisse in which the vector desire → jouissance ordered the whole process of subjectivity.* pp. 92–93. My translation.

13. Scott Stokes, H. *The Life and Death of Yukio Mishima.* p. 109, Penguin Books, 1986.

14. Mishima for instance is stimulated by an eroticism which I think is Occidental, Roman-Catholic in fact, rather than Oriental. This he narrates himself in [Confessions of a Mask trans.by Meredith Wetherby, Tuttle Publ. 2000] regarding his encounter with those European books brought home by his father, where the encounter with the reproduction of the painting of St Sebastian by Guido Reni culminates in his ejaculation. Notwithstanding the fact that his final erotic act is clearly inscribed in an Oriental ethic, it is not an Oriental or Japanese ethic because he commits suicide, but rather for the proper ritual and etiquette for which his thoughts and body were being trained.

15. See Allouch, J. *Érotique du deuil au temps de la mort sèche.* E.P.E.L, Paris, 1995.
16. Lacan, J. *L'envers de la psychanalyse,* session of 14.01.1970, p 55. Edition du Seuil. *In the erotic practice that I evoked, thus of flagellation, to call it by its name, just in case you are really deaf, the jouissance takes up the ambiguity {...} of the equivalence of the gesture that marks the body, object of jouissance; but jouissance of whom? Jouissance of the Other? True it is one of the ways of entrance of the Other {...} But the affinity of the mark with the jouissance of the body itself is where it is indicated that only by means of jouissance the establishment of the division by which the distinction between narcissism and object relation takes place.* My translation.
17. Zentner, O. The similarity of this statement with that of Masud Khan is striking. See *Winnicott avec Khan,* paper read at the *Lacanoamerican reunion of psychoanalysis,* Recife, Brazil, 2001.
18. Scott Stokes, H. *The Life and Death of Yukio Mishima,* p108.
19. Zentner, O. *Joyce—après le mot le deluge, The Letter—Lacanian Perspectives in Psychoanalysis,* Vol. 31/32, 2004, Dublin, Ireland.
20. This should suffice for us to be cautious and to re-consider each time that sublimation is put forward like a *deus ex machina* to explain creativity.
21. Lacan, J. *The only perfect act is suicide, because it cannot be repeated (Automaton).*
22. Lacan, J. Seminar *le sinthome.* Unpublished.
23. Mishima, Y. *Sun and Steel,* p. 14 My underlining.
24. In fact as it is obvious with Mishima's work, the identification between art, creativity and sublimation or reparation calls for an urgent revision.
25. Freud, S. *The Psychopathology of Everyday Life,* Standard Edition.
26. Scott Stokes, H. Idem, p. 161.
27. On 25.11.1970, Mishima, together with his aides from the Tatenokai (his private army), took hostage the commanding General of the Eastern Army (Jieitai), General Mashita. He ordered the general to assemble the soldiers and he addressed them. Without any hope whatsoever of producing the rising of the army, before leaving the parapet he saluted the Emperor with the traditional shouting *Tenno Heika Banzai* (long live the Emperor). Minutes afterwards he committed Seppuku.
28. Yamamoto, T. Hagakure—*The book of the samurai,* Kodansha International Ltd, Japan, 1983.
29. Yamamoto, T. *Hagakure—The Book of the Samurai,* p. 58, 1983. Kodanshka International, Tokyo.
30. From this viewpoint, Joyce as well as Mishima, in their own ways knew *how to make do with their symptoms.* See the testimony of Phillip Sollers regarding the interest of Lacan to know how *he did it* without ever having had an analysis in *Lacan meme,* L'infini, p. 11, V. 78, 2002, Edition Gallimard, Paris, France.

CHAPTER TWENTY FIVE

Erotics of mourning in the time of dry death

Jean Allouch

Introduction to the translation of fragments of « Erotique du Deuil au Temps de la Mort Sèche » (Erotics of Mourning in the Time of Dry Death) *by Jean Allouch*

We have translated the first pages of the book which has more than 350 pages. The book alternates chapters called *Etudes* (Studies) addressing psychoanalytic theory with chapters Allouch calls *Littérature Grise* (Grey Literature).

Following in Freud's footsteps, Allouch in the *Littérature Grise* starts with very personal material, including his dreams and his interpretation of them. We had to include the latter in order to give the reader an idea of how the book came to be. However, this gives a wrong impression of the proportion of *Littérature Grise* which represents in fact a relatively small part of the book.

* * *

Erotics of Mourning in the Time of Dry Death

This unknowing knowledge	*El saber no sabiendo*
Is of such high power	*es de tan alto poder*
That scholars debating	*que los sabios arguendo*
Can never overcome it	*jamás le pueden vencer;*
As their knowledge does not extend	*que no llega su saber*
To hear not hearing	*a no entender entendiendo,*
All science transcending	*Toda sciencia trascendiendo.*

(John of the Cross)

!Que te sirva de vela!
  Address (*Envoi*)

> [...] *nothing could be said "seriously"*
> *(be it to form a limited series)*
> *if not taking its sense from the comical order.*

(Jacques Lacan, "L'Etourdit", Scilicet 4,
Paris, Seuil, 1973, p. 44.)

Poets, yet again, will have led the way.

Let mourning be carried to its status as "act". Psychoanalysis tends to reduce mourning to "a work"; but there is an abyss between work and the subjectivation of a loss. The act is likely to effect in the subject a loss with no compensation at all, a dry loss. Since the First World War[1], Death expects no less. We no longer clamour together against it; it no longer gives its place to the sublime and romantic encounter of lovers, by it transfigured. Indeed. Nevertheless, in the absence of rites in regard to it, its current savagery has as its counterpart the fact that death pushes mourning to an act. A dry death, a dry loss. From now on only such a dry loss, only such an act, manages to leave the dead to his or her death, to Death.

Kenzaburo Ôe[2] characterizes this act (which indeed may demand a certain work) as a "gracious sacrifice of mourning". Through this, the grief-stricken one effects his or her loss by supplementing it with what we will call "a little bit of oneself"; here is, strictly speaking, the object of this sacrifice of mourning, this little bit not of you, nor of me, but of oneself; therefore both of you and of me, in as much as "you" and "me" remain in "self", not distinguished from each other.

Eroticised (otherwise it is not clear about what the pure loss would be), this little eroticised bit of oneself calls for an erotics of mourning. Through these stakes, through this phallic stake ("the little"), the notion of "work of mourning" was unfurling a veil of obscurantism rather than of decency. Discard this veil (a different gesture to lifting it), and nothing will be lost from modesty. Whoever finds it offensive to see the function of the phallus thus emerge at the very heart of the horrendous suffering of mourning may relinquish this book right here …

"My heart is in the coffin there with Caesar" publicly proclaims Shakespeare's Antony[3]. The version of mourning proposed here is situated between two possible readings of this sentence. First reading: "I am suffering because my heart is in this casket, it is not in its right place as it has been ripped out of me by death", such is the person in mourning. Second reading: "Yes, indeed, that is where it is, and I leave it in this place where, I now acknowledge it, it belongs", here is the gracious sacrifice of mourning, here is the end of mourning. Since mourning, like in psychoanalysis, in essence has an end.

The mystic pushes the passage to the act of this vow of renunciation to its extreme limit. It is not just the stolen object that would be given up, but the theft itself, the act to which mourning responds, act for act. So proposes John of the Cross:

Why, since you have wounded	Por qué, pues has llagado
This heart, have you not healed it?	aqueste corazon, no le sanaste?
And having stolen it from me,	Y pues me le has robado,
Why did you leave it thus	por qué asì le dejaste
And not take the theft that you stole?	y no tomas el robo que robaste?

And again, Shakespeare: discovering that their father's death would have made Ophelia go mad, Laërtes, shattered, declares[4]:

Oh Heavens, is't possible, a yong maid wits
Should be as mortall as an old man life?
Nature is fine in Love, and where'tis fine
It sends some precious instance of it selfe
After the thing it loves

Naming this *precious instance of it selfe* "little bit of oneself" should help us to express its function in mourning.

For death alone to be able to grant this status of lost object is something for which we have immediate proof through a little story, all the more exemplary as it takes place between children, with the implacable lack of pity evident in certain events in school yards. This takes place in

Mexico, where it is still known, for instance, that giving children their dead relatives or even their own death mask to eat (both made of sugar, with the identity of the person written in a frame) does not make them sick, far from it.

At recess, a child, taller and more solid than another child, forcibly takes an object deemed precious held by a smaller one. Following this, how does the problem present itself for the latter? Surely, he cannot tell on him [*cafarder*], as this is contrary to children's ethics. But neither can he purely and simply submit to the law of the jungle and accept a loss to which he does not consent—otherwise he would become depressed [*cafarderait*], in another meaning of the same word, he would get the blues [*avoir le cafard*][5]. What then? What will he do? What resolution will it give him?

Yet there is a Mexican solution, as if prefabricated, and directly originating from this well-known close relationship with death that is so characteristic of this country. Thus the child from whom a stronger one has taken the object (raised to the function of desirable object, of *agalma*, through the theft itself), the one who is therefore violently transformed into a lover [*désirant*], into *eraste*[6], while he was serenely strolling in so far as carrier of the marvellous object, as the *eromen* that perhaps he did not know himself to be[7], he might say to the usurper:

> – May this be your veil!
> – *¡Que te sirva de vela!*

Implying … (but it is so obvious that it does not need to be said):

> – May this be your veil … for your burial!
> – *¡Que te sirva de vela … para tu entierro!*

After this sentence has been uttered by the weak one, the strong one does not go for his throat to strangle him nor does he give him a good hiding. On the contrary, it all happens, through the formulation of this wish (because it is indeed a wish in its correct subjunctive form), as if the two partners of this "exchange" had become even, even though an event has indeed happened, since a swap has occurred, since the *eraste* has become the *eromen* and the eromen the eraste. Despite the violence of the act suffered, not to mention the violence (not the same one) of the reaction to the act, the "re-act", the essential thing is that an ending takes place; after the utterance of the retort, the deal is done, each one can go back to his own business.

This would not have been the case if, as in France, the response had been the following threat: *"Tu ne l'emporteras pas au paradis!"* ("You will not take it to Heaven!"). In France and in Mexico, the elements are the same: two partners, one single object and a shift in place. However, while the French threat takes the row purely and simply to the gate of the hereafter contenting itself with suggesting that a solution could be found only there, that this hereafter would mark a limit, even without knowing why or how, the Mexican retort implies that the hereafter is the place where the problem will be effectively solved; it effectively says how, by virtue of which the problem is already solved here on earth.

What produces such a resolution? One would not yet be aware of this event if it were admitted that the weak one formulates a death wish towards the strong one, and furthermore the story does not say whether he wishes him an immediate death or after having lived for ninety years! To tell the truth, it does not matter. It only matters that the object abruptly snatched serve as a veil for the snatcher at the time when he is going to *largar las velas (to set sail, to cast off the moorings)*[8,9] in other words: to die.

Logically, the real resolution can only be obtained from an act whose content is not difficult to clarify since this content must conform to the event that occurred; it can therefore only be the act by which the weak one gives the strong one that which the strong one took from him. And it is precisely what is achieved with the declarative sentence: he relinquishes the object to him, but for his death. Death alone grants the snatched object its status of gift. Death alone transforms it into an object of sacrifice.

If the current Western culture is all about organ donation, then this present work is situated outside the current culture. Recently, on the radio, a specialist was heard declaring, when interviewed after the publicity given to the death of a child with cystic fibrosis for whom no lung donor was found:

To refuse to be a donor, declared Diafoirus[10], is like taking a treasure into the grave.

Too invested in his interests the doctor who speaks to the media forgets all the objects (nothing less than the most precious) found in the tombs of the Pharaohs, in those of ancient China and in those of many other countries and cultures, including the most remote ones. We will therefore ruffle the feathers of this modern wish to salvage the treasures that the deceased would take with him when we say: mourning is effected when the mourner, far from receiving who knows what from the dead[11], far from removing anything from the deceased, adds another loss, that of one of his treasures to his suffered loss.

Thus it is incumbent upon psychoanalysis, if it is true that it was able, with Lacan, to circumscribe the subjectifying scope of the "object little a" as radically lost object, to raise this real from a technical economy of exchange, against this very economy, to the dignity of the macabre.

> Consider what it is that hides in the nostrils, in the throat, in the belly: filth everywhere. We who are repelled to touch vomit or dung even with a finger, how then can we desire to hold in our arms the bag of excrement itself?

Odon of Cluny, in the XIth century[12], promotes the macabre to deter from sexual relations, playing necrophilia[13] against desire. However, the reverse happens, and it is well known that macabre eras were joyous, rich with the enjoyments of life for the very people who cultivated it. It is enough to read these lines in order to note that the macabre, like psychoanalysis, isolates the "object little a". Similarly, in that other text[14], where the poet takes care to indicate that the rot which takes over the corpse does not come from the ground in which it is buried, from the maggots living in it, but from the body itself which carries this rot even before its birth:

All is nothing but filth	*N'est que toute ordure*
Death, spittle and rot,	*Mor, crachats et pourriture*
Stinking and corrupt crap.	*Fiente puant et corrompue*
Beware of the works of nature ...	*Prends garde ès oeuvres naturelles*
You will see that each one conducts	*Tu verras que chascun conduit*
Stinking material products	*Puante matière produit*
Out of the body continually.	*Hors du corps continuellement.*

May this book re-establish the macabre in its function as trigger of desire in the living.

For a different mourning

Since it is a matter of putting forward a version of mourning different to the one used by the Freudian movement over the last eighty years (and now received as obvious well beyond them), as it is a question of rendering as largely obsolete this unsatisfactory version, such an endeavour seems to me to have no possible chance of working if I were to limit myself to discussing the matter theoretically. My own stakes here cannot be left aside. Moreover, even if the above comment were wrong, I still would need to go through this rebidding. In order to be convincing it is not enough to use the best and only valid argument, which is, as Freud noted, the case history. Unfurling the case history in the broadest possible manner, which is also an unfolding of the play of its seemingly most "innocuous" details, it is a modality in which the Freudian method advertises itself. Frankly speaking, it is the question of the thing itself. In fact, the version of mourning presented in this book first came to me in a nightmare. Can I avoid mentioning this when, during the three years of seminar that gave rise to this book, other dreams or nightmares intervened, orienting and displacing a proposition which decidedly was not able to remain within the bounds of what might have been preferable, at least in regard to the pleasure principle (in other words the least tension), that is: within the "discours sans parole" (discourse without speech) which Lacan favoured. This discourse remains favoured. It is, however, for me as well as for many others, able to be articulated only through speech, and only at the point where speech, in so far as it is particular, might attain, but through having given itself as such, the universal.

> The universal, if it exists, must appear everywhere, to every one, must be revealed in all its snowy, windy, insular, separate singularity.[15]

Trick of reason? Yet it is not from that that the question of mourning, as it should today be revised in analysis, occurred to me. Because I had to admit that a dead child constituted the vivid kernel of the *folie à plusieurs* in which the *folie* of Marguerite Anzieu[16], the *Aimée* of Jacques Lacan's thesis[17], was included, because I had "in my face" the fact that this madness was through and through a mourning, the inappropriate statement that she had not gone into mourning appeared to me in all its obscenity. Of course, it is through her madness that she was mourning! Manifestly, there was a misunderstanding. Psychoanalysis, in relation to mourning, contrary to its method, had veered towards the medical in the narrow sense of: what lays the norm. It is true that mourning calls for norm; nevertheless, it is not a *reason* in the true sense of this term.

Thus, my questioning about mourning found its start from this observation: there was mourning in the very place where it was said not to be, and there was a complaint that there was no mourning where it was expected to be! Some did even go as far as making some people go through mourning (but as they were conceiving it), those very people who were already going through it (but in their own way)! Manifestly, it was this expectation itself which had to be reconsidered. And with it the version (the aversion?) [*la version, l'aversion*] of mourning which vectorised it.

Hence, a simple consultation of the most classical cases in psychoanalytic literature greatly widened the gap between these two contradictory positions: the clinic is the absence of mourning, the clinic is the mourning. This second assertion is a lot less inappropriate than the one which consists in inserting something into others and then claiming that this something is not there. A fair caution asks us to consider Anna O.'s hysteria as being her mourning for her father, similarly the rat-man's obsession, or Ophelia's madness, or the imposture of Louis Althusser, mourning for an homonymous uncle, or again Pauline Lair Lamotte's delusion[18] which occurred at the very moment when she found out that her spiritual director was dying, as if to show us that her illness had the value of mourning for the one she had chosen to guide her.

This identification between mourning and the psychoanalytic clinic demanded a revisiting, as radical as needed, of the psychoanalytic version of mourning. That was in January 1992.

"Mourning and Melancholia" indeed was waiting for us: credit where credit is due.[19]

Had this canonical paper by Freud taken good care of mourning? Questioning this text, we were, together with those who took part in this examination, tossed from surprise to surprise. First surprise: Freud did not write this paper to establish a psychoanalytic version of mourning, unlike what most people after him said, or believed or wanted to believe, but taking as fulcrum a non critical version of mourning, Freud only wanted to conquer melancholia. That gross misinterpretation took hold very early and in such a way that it seems almost impossible to recover from it[20]. Mourning has been turned into…a work, whereas the term "Trauerarbeit" appears once and only once in the paper[21] and nowhere else in Freud's following papers! The ideology of work is still so predominant, that, forgetting that the word "Arbeit" appeared at the entrance of the Auschwitz extermination camp: "Arbeit macht frei"

("Work makes you free"), forgetting that the word "Work" appeared in a preeminent place in the Petainist[22] motto *"Travail, Famille, Patrie"* (Work, Family, Homeland), no one was able to see the impropriety of the reduction of mourning to a "work".

As an example of the most common position, we can quote the first lines of one of the few books dedicated to mourning in France:

> Mourning is the state in which we are after the loss of a dear one (*être en deuil*—to be bereaved), as well as the customs which accompany this event (*porter le deuil*—to wear mourning) and the psychological work that this situation implies (*faire son deuil*—to go through mourning, but also "to come to terms with something"). [Then straight after] It is the work of mourning in which we are essentially interested.[23]

For such a result to persist, a large degree of "self-blinding" was necessary. Thus the critiques of "Mourning and Melancholia" not emanating from the Freudian field had to be silenced. Not one word on Geoffrey Gorer (see note 26), not one word on Philippe Ariès, in the parochial world of psychoanalysis. But this policy of putting one's head in the sand has its limits. I was reaching them. It was indeed necessary to at last respond to Ariès' assertion according to which "Mourning and Melancholia" prolongs a romantic version of mourning, notably with this idea of a substitutive object supposed to give to the mourner at the end of his "grief work" the same enjoyment as the one obtained in the past from the lost object. It was obvious: "grief work", "substitutive object", to which one would need to add the highly problematic "reality check" and many other things, all the metapsychology of "Mourning and Melancholia" had to be reconsidered. I started this work in January 1992.

But a particular stake to which I was turning my back without knowing, was waiting for me around the corner of this necessary de-construction. It was one year later that a nightmare erupted (the nightmare of the dungeon) which I could not ignore inasmuch as it was about the very same topic of the seminar which was well under way. I took the step, unusual amongst the Lacanians, to state it publicly. But it was as if I had opened a trail and since then, at each turn of this seminar, still now as I am writing these lines, I have not ceased to be titillated by the irruption of dreams, more or less anxiety provoking but also comical, which would clarify things independently of my will.

Here I am compelled to place first the nightmare of the dungeon (and its analysis) due to its inaugural and determining character. Its occurrence was provoked by particular events which had nothing to do with the seminar. Nevertheless it happened at a turning point of the seminar when I was about to start the second year of study dedicated no longer to mourning according to Freud but to a version of mourning as it can be read in Lacan.

While practically nothing published by Lacan suggested it, it was no small surprise to discover that there was indeed in Lacan a version of mourning which had gone unnoticed. The contrary would have been indeed surprising if it is true that Lacan, by proposing his ternary—symbolic imaginary real—as a paradigm for Freudian psychoanalysis, had to reconsider from then on the whole set of clinical problems posed to the Freudian field.

Well, this version happened to confirm the one which came out of my nightmare! I am well aware that reading this last sentence one could think: "He is delirious!" or "Not surprising! He is so immersed in Lacan that even his nightmares are permeated with him!" or some other idea from the same mould (from the same "Rabelaisian dough"). Of course, I can by no means respond to this, and further more it is not up to me to decide. In the meantime, let us welcome the Wittgenstein suspicion: is it a matter of self-persuasion, or else, as I claim, an actual confirmation?

The encounter with the work of Kenzaburo Ôe[24] brought a last surprise, something akin to bliss. His short story, *Agwwîi, the Cloud Monster*, happened to confirm what came out of the previous encounter: the importance of the grief sacrifice found in my nightmare as well as in the Lacanian interpretation of Hamlet. Thus Ôe, although from a country where grace does not have the divine power granted to it in the West, allowed me, by qualifying it as gracious, to fully name this sacrifice: a gracious grief sacrifice.

My own particular experience of grief was that, having lost as a very young child, a father, I lost as a father, a child (a daughter). Most likely, the reading of Ôe triggered a succession of dreams and nightmares which put me back on that track, thus forcing me to admit that the paradigmatic case of grief is no longer today, as it was at the time of the writing of the *Traumdeutung*, the case of the death of a father, but rather the death of a child.[25]

This displacement from one generation to the other constitutes one of the major features of the version of grief developed here. Already in 1964 the sociologist Geoffrey Gorer[26] referred very explicitly to the "privileged status" now given to the death of a child in the West. However, it is once more literature which is the most illuminating. We may look into *L'Orphelin* (*The Orphan*), by Pierre Bergounioux, to read how this shifting from the death of a father to that of a child occurred, how the sons of those who slaughtered each other in 1914–1918 could only tend to reduce to nothingness the existence of their own children.

On the background of dissatisfaction towards the psychoanalytic version of mourning which was then widely accepted, several very different experiences (my own, the Lacanian reading of Hamlet and the lesson given by Ôe) converge towards another version which situates today's mourning as being essentially a gracious sacrificial act consecrating the loss by supplementing it with a little bit of self. In presenting this other version, the following pages try to highlight some of its consequences.

Grey Literature (Extract)

The nightmare (night of the 7th to the 8th of December 1992).

It happened the day after a weekend spent with my wife at her parents'. Her father, seriously ill, is declining and dying. A friend of my in-laws, almost a son to them (the son of the cleaning lady, who herself had become a family friend and as such loving and loved by the children), comes everyday to help sort out practical problems; his name is Jeannot, pet-name given to me as a child in the South of France (where my in-laws live) that I have never liked. The nightmare comprises four scenes.

Scene 1: my wife and I are visiting Jeannot in his house which I see, first image, as if it was in a small valley, on the edge of a forest, on the shore of a pond or small lake. This largish building, a kind of rather posh villa or renovated farmhouse [while transcribing those last two words[27] I thought of the photo of the farmhouse published in "*Marguerite, ou l'Aimée de Lacan*[28]] is situated close to Paris (in Fontainebleau but much closer, right on the edge of Paris). I thought to myself: "How fortunate to have such a house in such a place!" [Jeannot is unemployed].

Scene 2: we are inside the house and a discussion starts about the chimney [a problem which my in-laws had: were they going to build a chimney or not?]. I explain to Jeannot that it is good to have a chimney, that "we ourselves, in our country house, have a very large one, which goes at least from here to there, and even up to there" ("here" designates a small door on the right hand side, "there" another mark, maybe a beam or an opening, and the second "there" another mark further away).

Scene 3: the conversation peters out (like a fire!), we are starting to take our leave; looking back, I spot on the ceiling a sort of hole covered with wire mesh, a few roughly trimmed beams, all of it black with soot, in short: traces of the existence of a chimney. It surprises me a lot because Jeannot had complained that he did not have a chimney, such had been the start of our discussion and of my intervention. I have the feeling that I have been deceived, swindled. This feeling is confirmed when looking down to check what is exactly underneath this shaft [or vent], I see on the floor a blackened spot, perhaps even a few small pieces of burnt wood which unquestionably prove that a fire had been lit here. I am also surprised that it is not exactly a chimney but a fire (extinguished) right on the ground [similarly the vent is not really a range hood]; I think that such a poor installation does not suit such a posh house. All this leads to a certain uneasiness.

Scene 4: my wife and I leave through the back, I do not know why … that is the way it is…probably because someone pointed to that exit. But there is a problem. We are high on a sort of steep rampart. In addition to my previous uneasiness, I start to worry a little that we are going around in circles, that we are stuck, and I have a slight feeling of dizziness (we are high above the ground, yet in fact we are at the back of the house which leans against the foot of a hill, I suspect in my dream that this configuration is not right). On the left, there is a rather deep drop [about two or three times as high as a man] and then I see my wife jump off. For a brief moment I am worried, but she is not hurt, there she is on the ground, getting up, out of trouble. I choose not to jump and try to go to her through the other side, on the right [there is here a duplication in the two sides of the chimney which was already an issue in the second scene, the issue of the two exits]; I then find myself even higher on a kind of peak, holding on to a stone dungeon. I realise with concern that the stones are a little loose and so are the stones on which I am perched. I soon realise that I cannot move without falling. All the way down on the right, close to the place where I could crash, Jeannot looks at me totally unconcerned, smiling and waving at me, not realising in the least the situation in which I find myself. This is when, while trying to move an arm, my right arm, I notice that the stone my hand is holding onto is getting loose. It is impossible to let go of it [it is as if my hand were holding it in place], it is therefore impossible for me to move at all. I yell to Jeannot to do something but he does not hear and continues to smile at me. Full of anguish, I wake up.

Interpretation

During the day, an interpretation of this nightmare occurred to me easily. The first image is of a farm-house like the ones that are found in the centre of France. At the age of twelve, I was boarding in a similar kind of building, alone, very far away from my family; in those circumstances, that I was in some ways responsible for, I had for the first time consciously felt the enormous grief of the loss of my father. The first image is exactly that of a landscape in Chambon-sur-Lignon, the one that can be found in "La fabrique du pré" by Francis Ponge.[29]

Ponge frequently went to that particular meadow (*pré*), which has become famous as a site of resistance against the Nazis. The meadow (*pré*) in Ponge's poem ends up becoming a "près", (close to, near) which is found in the dream (i.e. "close to Paris"). This nightmare, therefore, was about my position in relation to my father's death, about the way it was still affecting me to this day. For some time certain signs had given me the inkling that the death of my father-in-law (we had a genuine affection for each other), which was imminent, resonated with the death of my father when I was five, that is almost fifty years ago! My psychoanalysis had confirmed that the way I had been kept away from my father's funeral (for my own good, of course, so that I should not be shocked, as was the belief at the time) had been detrimental to me. According to Philippe Ariès, this attitude is pathognomonic of the "feralisation" of death. Analysis had also led me to recognise the dread I had of a father not dead but...vanished. In the dream my wife managed to escape, I did not. Hence the anguish which would end up waking me.

The interpretation came to a halt there during that day; I only need to add that when I got up I had the temptation to tell this dream to my wife but I only said to her: "I had a nightmare" and nothing more, thinking that she had enough worries with her father's health without infecting her with mine. This abstention allowed things to unravel differently.

During the following night, I woke up several times and had a "flash of inspiration" (that is what I called my discovery [*trouvaille*])[30] in between sleeping and waking. The context of this flash of inspiration is related to the fact that for many years since my case study of *Marguerite*, the question of the link between mourning and sexual relation has become one of my main preoccupations, both doctrinally and personally as evidenced here. In this nocturnal wondering wandering, I thought of my dream of the night before and suddenly I saw the little dungeon on which I was nailed in the last image of the nightmare as being obviously what it was: a phallus! I immediately even thought that it was clearly a "signifier of the lack" (Lacan) since taken as a chimney shaft it was associated in the third scene with the discussion on the presence/absence of a chimney[31]. The interpretation of the day before had happily overlooked this little detail. Immediately a question, at the same time a little crazy and important, arose: what was this phallus doing in this nightmare and what was I doing hooked to it? The phallus in question, as demonstrated by its size, was in erection, and I understood then that because of its lateral position close to the summit of the dungeon the stone which was threatening to come off—and that my hand was indeed holding—was a foreskin (*prépuce*)[32]. Thinking of my wife's jump in my dream as a *saut de puce* (a flea jump!), made me burst out with laughter partly at the wit, partly at the comical situation. It was confirming in regard to the signifier (*saut de puce = faire sauter le prépuce*/ flea jump = to get rid of the foreskin) the identification, at the imaginary level, of the said stone as being my foreskin.

In Chambon-sur-Lignon one of my favourite exercises was precisely to jump from the top of a high terrace, an exercise in which I excelled whereas the other children balked at the truly impressive height from which to jump, ("two or three times higher than a man" as mentioned in scene four of the nightmare) as if one was flying. I nonetheless never hurt myself in the slightest but the exercise in question did not prevent me from having, during the first years of my analysis, an insistent Icarian nightmare: I am flying, I am flying, it is wonderful, I cover long distances, flying over hills, passing over mountains, but, without fail, it turns sour when I realise that I am not able to land. This new nightmare is a toned down version of the previous one: this time my feet are on the ground!

After this burst of laughter I fell asleep and had a brief dream: I am in bed with my wife (but she is not in the picture), maybe naked, vaguely lying on my left side with my legs bent; a man behind me puts his arm between my thighs and his hand grabs hold of my sex, more precisely of its three components [the holy trinity]. I vaguely wake up again, and start to float again between dream and sleep, surprised and embarrassed but not anxious. Since my analysis, I know that the man intervening from behind is my father That is when I burst out laughing again: I have just realised that I call my wife *"Puce"* ("Flea")! Of course, in my mind, it is a nickname for *"pucelle"* (young virgin/maiden) and also a little flea, the kind of delightful or silly (depending on one's point of view) term of endearment created by love. Up until that moment that night, however, I had never ever thought that by giving her that name I made her, metonymically, my foreskin (*prépuce*)![33]

Thinking of the nightmare of the previous night it became clear that by holding on to the stone threatening to come off, I was holding my foreskin, I was holding on to my foreskin. The only thing was, if I wanted to free myself from the death of the father with a flea jump like my wife in the dream, I had to give up holding on to that goddamned foreskin. In other words, with his death my father had taken my foreskin with him! Here we can remember Joyce identifying the god of Abraham, Isaac, and Jacob as being what he is: a "collector of foreskin".

The choice I had was of the kind "your money or your life" (*la bourse ou la vie*)[34] such as Lacan commented on: the one who is thus cornered, if he keeps the money, will lose his money as well as his life, and if he gives up his money, will keep his life but a life without money; either way the money is lost. Similarly here: I either hold on to my foreskin or lose my foreskin and my life (what kind of a life is it in which one remains up in the air holding on to a foreskin!), or I give up my foreskin and I am alive but with no foreskin. I make a note that this nightmare multiplies the alternatives; scene one: a dilapidated or renovated house, a pond or a small lake; scene two: both left-hand side and right-hand side of the chimney (in my country house the only way out is on the right-hand side of the chimney); scene four: leaving through the front door or through the back door (the "back-door" which we will find again in the next dream) and again a left-hand side or a right-hand side (the left-hand side being the way out for my wife).

In the *Traumdeutung*, Freud noted that when there is an alternative in the manifest text of a dream it is a matter of finding the unconscious one to which it relates. In this instance, better than right/left or front/back, it seems that it is particularly the topological alternative "here/there" or more exactly "near/far" which is a cipher for the unconscious alternative "the foreskin or the life". It was already present in scene one: the meadow - the small valley where at Chambon I was watching the cows by the pond where I used to catch frogs at night- with, in a textual proximity, as in Ponge's text, the *près* (near) - *cf* "near Paris";

it occurs twice in the final scene: to stay or not to stay near the foreskin but also in Jeannot's moving away. This double of myself, waving "hello" (but is it not rather a "goodbye"? It is, as we are parting) with his right hand raised like mine, thus simply reflecting my image, does not know if he needs to intervene or not, therefore to come closer or not. To stay close to the foreskin meant to lose everything, foreskin and life, while maintaining the hold of the deceased over me and not disengaging myself from the grief; to move away was to renounce my foreskin as well as to get out of mourning for the father through the act of leaving with him that which he valued so much.

Thus it became luminously clear to me that when we mourn, we mourn for someone who has, in death, taken a little bit of self. Fully awake, I realised that this was a real clinical and theoretical discovery. This impression was confirmed by the fact that it is impossible to determine the ownership of this "bit of self", that it has a transitional status (Winnicott), at least until the act of handing it over to the deceased, act which puts an end to the mourning by settling the ownership.

Translated from French by Nicole Chavannes and Françoise Muller-Robbie.

Notes

1. The very moment in which Freud wrote "Mourning and Melancholia". The publication in 1992 of a text such as the philosophical novel by Pierre Bergounioux *L'Orphelin* (Paris, Gallimard) shows that it is only today that we are beginning to fully measure the magnitude of the damage, notably the fracture that the universalisation of war brought to death and paternity.
2. Note of the translators: Kenzaburo Ôe, Japanese author born in 1935, winner of the Nobel Prize of Literature in 1994.
3. William Shakespeare, *Julius Caesar*, III, 2, 105.
4. William Shakespeare, *Hamlet*.
5. Lacan noted, very rightly in my opinion, that depression, as it is called, occurs after a subject has drawn back from an act he could not resolve not to do.
6. Here there is more than an analogy with mourning. The mourning subject is also primarily a lover [*désirant*] who does not want to be one.
7. Agalma, eraste and eromen form a battery of terms found in Plato's *Symposium*. Lacan studies them in his seminar *Le transfert dans sa disparité subjective, sa prétendue situation, ses excursions techniques* (bulletin *Stécriture*).

8. Note of the translators: in Spanish *vela* and in French *voile* translate as veil as well as sail.

9. In Spanish there is here a possible pun: "vela" also means eve (as in "on the eve of war"?) and "no darle a uno vela en un entierro" means that this one (el uno), as dead, no longer has any right to speak. Along these lines, there is also "velorio": vigil (which equivocates, since equivocation bounces back, with "velorio": taking the veil) and "velatorio": wake.

10. Note of the translators: Diafoirus is a ridiculous, ignorant and pedantic doctor in Molière's play "*Le Malade Imaginaire*".

11. This is the real issue in inheritance disputes, even in problems of transmission. The deaths of Freud and Lacan do not raise the question of what the analyst receives from Freud and from Lacan; they call upon him to determine what he will put of himself in their tombs so that they may be the dead that they are and so that the analyst may consequently be in his own place: the next one.

12. Quoted by Philippe Ariès, *L'homme devant la mort*, Paris, Seuil, 1977 p. 113.

13. There is not one word about necrophilia in "Mourning and Melancholia".

14. Also quoted by Ph.Ariès, op. cit., p. 122.

15. P. Bergounioux, *L'Orphelin*, op. cit., p. 151.

16. Jean Allouch, *Marguerite, ou l'Aimée de Lacan*, Paris, EPEL, 1st ed., 1990, 2nd ed., reviewed and augmented, 1994.

17. Jacques Lacan, *De la psychose paranoïaque dans ses rapports avec la personnalité*, Paris, Le François, 1932, 2nd éd., Paris, Seuil, 1975.

18. *cf.* Jacques Maitre, *Une inconnue célèbre, la Madeleine Lebouc de Pierre Janet*, Paris, Anthropos, 1993.

19. Note of the translators: *A tout soigneur, tout honneur.* Allouch plays with the expression *à tout seigneur, tout honneur, soigneur* being a healer/carer.

20. In a paper called "*La théorie la plus avancée du psychique*" (The most advanced theory of psychic life), in "*La Quinzaine littéraire*" No 595, 16–29 of February 1992, we can read, from the pen of an author supposedly familiar with Freud, that: "Freud reminds us constantly of the necessity to start from the pathological to understand the normal (melancholia throws light on mourning)..."; however, Freud in "Mourning and Melancholia" writes from the first line exactly the opposite: "[...] we want to try to throw light on the nature of melancholia by comparing it to the normal affect of mourning". The interest of this misinterpretation lies in the fact that it indicates that it could well be that Freud in writing his paper was not as faithful to his own method as one might think.

21. It appeared in it not as a new concept but as a compound word as German language allows them, flowing from the pen without the need to make a fuss about it.
22. Note of the translators: Marshall Pétain formed a French government collaborating with the Nazi invaders between 1940 and 1944.
23. Michel Hanus: "*La pathologie du deuil*", Paris, Masson, 1976, p. 5.
24. Here I must thank Francoise Davoine and Jean-Max Gaudillière for this encounter.
25. "For me this book has another signification, a subjective signification which I noticed only after the work was finished. I understood that it was a part of my self-analysis, my reaction to the death of my father, *the most dramatic event in a man's life*", S. Freud, "*L'interpretation des rêves*", preface to the second edition (Summer 1908) Fr. Trans.
   I. Meyerson, PUF, 1967. One could imagine that Freud wrote the untimely proposition that we underlined while still stricken by this mourning of the father and that later he did not maintain this primacy given to the death of the father. We shall see that we do not find this conjecture confirmed in his work.
26. Geoffrey Gorer *Death, Grief and Mourning in Contemporary Britain*, London, Cresset Press, 1965, translated in French by Hélène Allouch, *Ni pleurs, ni couronnes*, preceded by a preface of Michel Vovelle "*Pornographie de la mort*", Paris, EPEL, 1995.
27. From now on, the indications in square brackets will refer to thoughts that occurred to me during the act of transcribing.
28. J. Allouch, *Marguerite ou l'Aimée de Lacan*, op. cit. p. 155.
29. Francis Ponge, *La fabrique du pré*, Genève, Skira 1971. This « factory » (*fabrique*) was to inspire the heteronym "Francis Dupré" to sign the "construction" (*fabrique)* of the case of the Papin sisters (cf Jean Allouch, Erik Porge, Mayette Viltard *La "solution" du passage à l'acte, le double crime des soeurs Papin*, Toulouse, Erès, 1984).
30. Jean Allouch, "Interprétation et illumination", *Littoral* no. 31–32, « La connaissance paranoïaque », Paris, EPEL, Mars 1991, pp. 33–64.
31. In Chambon, the name of my main rival in every respect: intellectual, physical and spiritual was *Cheminée* (Chimney) and he became a volcanologist!
32. Note of the translators: *Pré-puce* can be heard as "before the flea"
33. Jean Allouch, "Interprétation et illumination", *Littoral* no. 31–32, « La connaissance paranoïaque », Paris, EPEL, Mars 1991, pp. 33–64.
34. Jean Allouch, "Interprétation et illumination", *Littoral* no. 31–32, « La connaissance paranoïaque », Paris, EPEL, Mars 1991, pp. 33–64.

CHAPTER TWENTY SIX

Psychoanalysis in the hospital

Gustavo Etkin

It could be thought that the only place for analytic practice is the private consulting room which, obviously, for this purpose must have a couch. And that outside of this psychoanalysis is impossible. In a hospital, for example.

Nonetheless, in *Studies on Hysteria*, Freud recounts that he worked as a psychoanalyst on top of a mountain. There he was sought out as a "doctor" by a young woman who presented herself as having bad "nerves". "Interested to find that neuroses could flourish in this way at over 2,000 metres of altitude, I questioned her further" he tells us. It was the era in which he oscillated between "… allowing her to relate what she wants to me", like with Emmy von N., the baroness Fanny Moser, or actively investigating by asking about memories, like this time on top of the mountain with the young Katharina, who complained of the already famous "being out of breath". Afterwards, Freud did not meet with Katharina again, although he hoped that she had "derived some benefit" from the "conversation" he had with her.

Afterwards, in 1901, in *The Psychopathology of Everyday Life*, in Chapter II, when he gives examples of the forgetting of foreign words, he recounts that during his "holiday trip" he renewed his acquaintance with "a very cultured young man" who was even familiar with some of Freud's publications, he adds. During the conversation, in which, complaining about the obstacles that his generation encountered in attempting to develop its talents and satisfy its needs, he tries to recall a line of the *Aeneid* where Dido, the unhappy priestess abandoned by Aeneas, exclaims, according to him: *"Exoriar(e) ex nostris ossibus ultor"*. But he realised that "something is missing in the verse" a word, and asks Freud to repeat it in its entirety. Freud does so. The complete line was: *"Exoriar(e)* **aliquis** *nostris ex ossibus ultor"*. He had forgotten the word *aliquis* and again he asks for Freud's help, but now in order *to know* why he forgot. Freud then asks him what occurs to him in regard to *aliquis*. He even asks him, at one moment, to "dispense with all criticism". It is free association.

And it was not a question of the meaning in Latin of *aliquis*: Someone, one ("Let someone arise from my bones, oh avenger!") but rather of its sound and resemblance—its signifying form—with other words and meanings in German, we could suppose perhaps, *liquidation* like the *end of a period* and *reliquie* like *relic*, according to the German dictionary of Slaby and Grossmann. *Aliquis*, then, which Freud's interlocutor will associate with relics, blood, "the accusation that is being brought against the Jews just now of killing a Christian at Easter in order to use his blood in their religious ceremonies". He recalls a title, "What St Augustine says about Women". After other associations he speaks of the miraculous liquefaction of the blood of Saint Januarius until, amongst the other memories and associations that appear, he speaks of a preoccupation that he has, precisely, with blood; the possibility that, during that month "a lady" would miss her period, which "would be very awkward for both of us".

This is one of the examples with which Freud shows that the formations of the unconscious, in the case of psychical overdetermination causing a circumstantial forgetting, are not specific to the neuroses, but pertain rather to psychical functioning in general in all of us in so far as we are subjects of speech. As Lacan would say, the *speaking being*. *Speaking being* or *being of speech*.

In both situations Freud operates as an analyst, and without a couch.

A couch then, which when it turns into an image, a sign that someone, by the simple fact of decorating his or her room with it, can present him or herself as an analyst, becomes comical.

It is well known that it is possible to pass a number of years reclined on the couch—to pass by/through a couch—conversing with a supposed analyst who listens to signifieds and not signifiers, who orients or suggests with greater or lesser subtlety how to behave with one's wife and with women (or one's husband and with men), who suggests which is the right psychoanalytic institution to belong to, or from whom, or not, supervision should be sought in the case that the reclined person aspires to work as an analyst (otherwise it would be a case of "divided transference"...). And for whom the truly named "patient" even carries out personal commissions, proposals of group work, puts up posters, delivers invitations, gives invitations, etc, etc. Reclining on a couch then is no guarantee of being analysed (because of this, after a certain time, different for each one, until the Moment to Conclude arrives, one has the analyst, or supposed analyst, that one merits). And, consequently, neither is sitting behind a couch a guarantee of working as an analyst, with that indifference of the surgeon with which Freud somewhere defined his practice.

Thus if it is possible to work as an analyst on a "holiday trip" or on top of a mountain to where, from all accounts, Freud did not carry a couch, it might well be thought that it is possible to work as an analyst in a hospital, with or without couch.

Even though there it is different to the consulting room, in which what is sought is an analyst where the transference, as supposition of a knowledge, is often constituted prior to the first encounter with the one it is hoped might be the knowing carrier of an ear. The transference which, as we know, is the indispensable condition for analytic practice to be effective. There it is different, not through of the inexistence of the, at times, fetishised couch, but rather by what is called, after Lacan, the "demand for analysis". On the top of the mountain Freud was sought out for a knowledge that Katharina supposed to him in relation to her "nervous" illness. On another holiday trip he, his supposed knowledge, was asked about the cause of the forgetting of a word.

But he or she who is hospitalised, for instance for cancer, does not seek the supposed knowledge of an analyst. He or she seeks, and for good reason, above all a place, the hospital, where there will be a doctor (usually it doesn't matter whom) who can save him or her, or at least prolong his or her life. He or she does not ask about a cause. What is asked for, and hoped for, are effective acts. Because, at times, it is a question of death, more or less close, at times with probable date and known name: cancer or AIDS, in the same way in which in other eras it was tuberculosis.

As we know, from 1920 onwards death is a key concept for Freud, inseparable from Eros. Death which, silent, speaks through sexuality. Death, which in Portuguese is *A morte*, can also be heard as *amorte* [love-death]. Love and death in one word. It is what in psychoanalysis is called *castration*, key concept of the Freudian discourse, which differentiates it from Jung, Adler, Reich, Rank, Melanie Klein and the American Ego Psychology, which Lacan will take up again including with logic. The logic of castration and of the phallus that represents it. The logic of jouissance and of the law. The logic of the Formulas of Sexuation. Thus it is that, although there is no explicit demand for analysis to a determined analyst, this does not eliminate the possibility of the practice of psychoanalysis with someone who knows that it is probable that he or she will die, for example, of a cancer (I say it is *probable* because, as we know, sometimes death from cancer can be avoided by an effective cut in an adequate place at a certain time). But even with such a happy end, death is close. Close to being thought about, spoken of. Listened to. So there, what is sought is life, not analysis. Something similar can be said of a psychiatric hospital, where there is not even a search or a demand. Usually the person is taken, left, hospitalised with others. And not, up until now, in order to be analysed, but rather to be "sedated", tied up—with psycho-pharmaceutics or to a bed—so that the patient does not inconvenience or scandalise the families, the neighbours and, at times, so that he or she is not violent with him or herself or with others.

The problem, for psychoanalysis, and not just in reference to the psychoses, might be what some Argentinian psychoanalysts get excited about calling the "Clinic of Borders". Borders of neurosis where, amongst other things, there would be no possibility of establishing a soothing transference according to the manual, although the question is not formulated according to the knowledge about the signifier that causes the symptom in someone who supposedly incarnates it. There is no transference. Nonetheless, also when there is transference, all of analytic practice is always a practice of borders: those that present themselves in the association called *free*; those that constitute themselves cutting sense in the enunciation of the analysand as effect of the intervention of the analyst; the scansions with which one can punctuate; the cut of the session; or, in psychosis, the circling and turning around an unnameable—foreclosed—signifier which the analyst will attempt, with care, not to interpret but to name, to offer thus as substitution in that border where the subject, though excess of paranoia or though defect in paraphrenia or in autism, attempts to situate him or herself in the Other by means of the delusion. And also the psychosomatic illnesses where the analyst will attempt to transform, to cut, a holophrase, that phrase that was squeezed together, stuck and transformed into a word, into an articulated proposition articulated in the borders of a syntax.

So that in a hospital there is no demand for analysis according to the manuals. As we said before, there one does not enter in order to demand analysis but rather life. And the reply—at times—is the necessary amputation or life as impossible.

So what could someone do there, in a hospital, someone who believes he knows the use of the psychoanalytic technique and agrees with Lacan that the purpose of his practice is the treatment as fall of the Subject Supposed of Knowledge, the traversal of the fantasm, or to go over the words of a certain proposition condition of desire and place of enjoyment, and also agrees with Freud in making possible the capacity to work and enjoy whilst living with the certainty of death, or, in another way, sustaining life in turning around the *bedrock* of castration?

Or, to put it in another way, what would be the end of analysis—the treatment—with someone who, at times, manages to know that his or her death is certain, its cause, and even its probable date? What does it matter if this person traverses the fantasm or not, and becomes convinced that knowledge is not incarnated in someone, becomes able to work and enjoy?

This anticipated non-analytic end, which at the same time is so implicated in what analysis is, this death, different for each one. The same goes for life, enjoyment, desire. It is singular, like the fantasm of each one, constituted by signifiers, which are difference. It is death that was always present in the absence of the mother, in her incompleteness, which the father represents as law, the death that the son receives from the father in his surname, death which, implicated in desire as castration, it is that which is border and enjoyment. Death then which, implicated in sexuality like it is in desire, enjoyment and castration, continued to write the letters of a history, particular and different for each one of us. Death which is written and different for each subject: symbolic. Death of absence: imaginary. Unnameable death: real.

We have, therefore, on the one hand, the possibility of analytic practice in circumstances that actualise and incarnate a key point in its theory but, on the other hand, its apparent impossibility through the lack of demand for analysis and, also, the necessity of thinking of what the treatment, or improvement, would be in these cases where death has a name and date.

In the face of this, in the first place it is a question of making known the possibility of being listened to, something which is not always of interest. At times the person just wishes for attention, care, refuge, pampering, affection, company, proofs, or that this person will not lose his or her place in the world, or the forgiveness for sins that religion can offer, whichever one it is, in exchange for the certainty of gaining a place in heaven. In such cases there is no place for the analyst.

But, at times, there is a demand to be listened to, which can be divided into two types: the necessity of speaking to anyone, to someone who can bear listening just to complaints and pain, or the demand to be listened to like someone where a text is written. Someone, in this case the analyst, who might be paper on which a history may be left written. Similar to—although fulfilling another function here—to what in another place I propose as appearance, semblant of paper or wall, that the analyst must offer to the psychotic transference where, in leaving inscribed there the certainty of a knowledge, could also return and encounter a signifier recognised as one's own, the mark of a *shifter*, as Lacan would say in taking up Jakobson's term. Different in the case of cancer, AIDS or any death with name and date. In this case it is a question of someone who seeks an ear-paper in order to leave his or her own history in writing. Different because whoever writes it in this case, at times, knows that he or she will not be able to return to read it. But it will be a text, letters for the Other.

Finally it is a question of attempting to work as an analyst solely in sustaining a listening and demonstrating that one has heard by repeating, by returning to name, according to the rhetoric offered by each discourse and according to the style of each analyst: that there were signifiers that will remain written; that there is an Other that remembers.

It is not a question then of the treatment as the final result of a demand for analysis, but rather the effect of an analytic listening offered, and, at times, accepted in such a way that makes possible the mourning of life itself, each one in his or her own way. When one can.

Translated from Spanish by Michael Plastow.

CHAPTER TWENTY SEVEN

Wallis Simpson and the three As

Gustavo Etkin

W allis Simpson, in her own way, intervened in the real/royal.[1] Historians, romantics, the elderly and the inquisitive will remember, around 1936, that a significant presence appeared in the English court, one that opened a hole in the line of succession: and Edward VIII, Duke of Windsor, who was king at that time, fell.[2] At that time it was said that between the—royal (or real)—throne and love, he renounced the throne and chose love. A noble act that gave relief to millions of whores and housemaids: love, existed. And it was so important that for love even a royal (real) throne could be spurned. Anyway, it was possible to have hope.

We might ask, nonetheless, if its phallic intrusion was in the real or in reality. Reality of the obstacles that prohibit marriage with commoners, but real of the impossible in regard to the absolute sovereignty of a king: perhaps a king could not marry just anyone? It was impossible for it to be so.

Thus it was demonstrated, once again—without the need for revolutions, conspiracies or assassinations—that for no king, no matter how great an emperor he was, could desire be law. Let's say that, as everyone knows, no king is as king as he appears.

I recalled this story because I found myself, once upon a time, in some way occupying the place of Wallis Simpson.

David, a theatre director, sought me out complaining of two inhibitions: he was unable to see, from the orchestra pit, the work he was directing, prior to the première and performed in full. His eyes would burn and fill with tears, he felt uncomfortable, uneasy. Nor was he able to risk a change to the style of the set: it was always direct, realistic, simple, unimaginative. He wanted to be able to produce his works in dreamlike spaces, unconventional, with surrealist scenery. He was a member of the Communist Party, but he was fed up with "socialist realism". He called it "mummy's Party" because his mother, like all his family, had always been Party members.

During the course of the analysis another complaint appeared: the "have to".

"Have to" work, "have to" go, "have to" do, "have to" fuck. Also, later, there was the "have to" have analysis. Because the "have to"—his fantasm—was for him the signifier of non-sense, that which is done through obligation and in the end is absurd.

It was not, nonetheless, the compulsion of the militant obsessive ritual directed towards the Øther, in search of meaning. In this case the obligation implied by the "have to" had neither objective nor addressee. It was an action that had to be carried out, something that had to be done, full stop. David did not consider the possibility of saying "no".

The sense of the absurd, nonetheless, was not limited to an act that had to be completed. There appeared moreover, in commenting on details, aspects of a situation that might imply enjoyment, and which produced a comical effect in him. For instance, the words of a woman when she fucked with him: "yes, yes, yes", which he found ridiculous and absurd and which he imitated in a grotesque manner. Or a memory, that he mentioned every so often, from when he was twelve years old: a camp with other boys, him singing *little bird, little bird, who flies over the whole world, take this letter to my love, and tell her that I am dying for her.* He would repeat the song with a distorted childish voice, mocking himself. He found it absurd that this had occurred, just like he did the applause he would receive, applause that he always hoped for, although only through his work.

"When I work well they applaud me but who applauds you when you work well?" he asked me one day. Since to applaud the enjoyment or its sign which is present in a production was like saying *yes* to him, to point him out, to indicate him as existent, but at the same time something impossible, absurd, ridiculous, meaningless. Real. Nonetheless, sublimated in work, it had some meaning: then he could hope for an applause. Even so, the possibility of saying "how gorgeous!" about something or about a woman, was absurd and meaningless.

Until the day that David lay on the couch and informed me, calmly and indifferently, that: "My name came out on a list of the Three As. If you like we can discontinue the analysis".

As Argentinians will remember, and perhaps others will know of it, in the era in which Isabel Perón was the president, the Three As (Argentinian Anticommunist Alliance), based in the Ministry of Social Welfare, directed by its minister López Rega, was a philanthropic armed group whose aim was to do good by killing communists. Because of this, those who were, or those who had been, or even those who had once had dreams in which the colour red predominated, were somewhat apprehensive. As one title of *El Caudillo* [The Leader], a magazine in which its certainties were written: *If someone is afraid of the Three As, it's for a good reason.*

Because of this it was also probable that a name in the address book of those chosen became, by metonymy, part of the original list, and the sentence was extended to include it as well. Thus I responded to his proposal by reaffirming that I intended to continue, fulfilling the agreement by which I accepted him into analysis, an agreement which I was going to sustain until it was finished (I realised afterwards that I did not clarify how or who might finish). And I also made a request of him: that he remove my name from his address book.

From then on, in other sessions, he was able to speak several times of a memory: him in the bedroom of his parents, in his bed, from which he saw them lying down in a strange position. The head of one corresponded to the feet of the other. It was not head with head, it was head with feet, and this scene—he commented—was "absurd", "ridiculous". Or, additionally, it was as if this were in a scenario, a stage on which something incomprehensible, meaningless, was being shown.

With time his two inhibitions, which where the cause of his request for analysis, disappeared. Little by little he was able to see on stage, before the première, the works that he directed, and, finally, he was able to put on a play with the setting arranged as he wished.

I told him that his analysis was finishing. The last day he left me a photograph of a moment from the staging of a work whose title referred to guests for a meal. In the photograph could be seen someone on the floor, covered with a blanket from which feet were sticking out, apparently dead. And next to his head was a man standing up, gesticulating, speaking. On the other side of the photograph, amongst other things, was written:

> ... perhaps I leave you with these dinner guests, my fantasms.
> But they are my dear fantasms.

And below, his signature.

Even though I later realised that I had not fallen as (a), since his photograph was given to the Other. Because of this his analysis, on that day in 1977, was not truly finished, which might have been the effect of traversing a fantasm in which *to fuck is to speak with the feet or walk with the mouth*, a metaphor for fellatio and cunnilingis, to say it Freudianly in Latin, his inhibitions disappearing after the aforementioned collaboration of the Three As, which allowed me to intervene reminding him of a law and demanding an act. "In the real or in reality?", I asked myself afterwards.

The act of removing my name from his address book—a list that reduplicated that of the Three As—was only in the reality of the signifiers *address book, remove, name*, and their imaginary correspondents, in other words acting upon something which, if my name continued to be in that place, would determine that his analysis *might finish*, but as Real, in other words impossible, because in such a case it would be possible that he and I might die. This, in my case, would be different to occupying the place of the dead man only as "semblant", similar to the object (a). If I had died, in this case not as semblant, but rather as a fact, I would probably not be able to listen to him.

Nonetheless this was not, I believe, intervening in the real but rather the contrary: making possible that the real did not irrupt into David's analysis. But also, and in parallel, I believe there was, yes, an intervention in the real. It was only through the fact of having said in some way (it could have been another) something that, afterwards came to ex-sist named as absurd, from the act of having designated it, which then allowed the memory of that bed where, like from the dress circle, he could see a scene that was able to be named as "absurd" but whose sexual meaning was constructed retrospectively.

I also believe I was in too much of hurry to name the address book and the act. Perhaps I should have asked: "Why?" But I was so absorbed by the real that I jumped in and came out, in that moment, designating. Giving name to the unnameable real.

Thus, like Wallis Simpson—although with the differences determined by ethics and by my sexual preferences—in addition to her intervention in the reality of the obstacles (in my case the obstacle implied by my death or by his in order to be able to continue his analysis) I found myself with the real of an impossible, naming it. She, Wallis Simpson, making herself present in an impossible. In the Royal Court/Real Cut[3] as phallic signifier of the desire of a King. And me, naming death in remembering an address book.

Intervening then in the Real in naming it. Saying. Baptising the unnameable.

Notes

1. Gustavo Etkin: "There is an equivocation, a play on words, in the word *real* in Spanish." It is translated here both as the "royal" of the monarchy or royalty and "real" for psychoanalysis as the impossiblity of being named or symbolized.

2. Added in 2004: If it had been now, perhaps Wallis Simpson might have died in an accident, like Princess Diana.

3. *Corte Real* in Spanish here can be translated both as "Royal Court" and "Real Cut". Gustavo Etkin: "I am attempting to say what is understood by 'intervening in the real'. An intervention which is to baptise something that, up until that moment, has no name. It had been impossible."

CHAPTER TWENTY EIGHT

Death and psychoanalysis[1]

Gustavo Etkin

In a paper which I presented at the Lacanoamerican Reunion of Porto Alegre in 1993,[2] I referred to the possibility of death in my clinical practice, or its consequences. Thus I referred to the possible death of my analysand, who had been included in a list of those condemned by the Three As (Argentinian Anticommunist Alliance), an armed group that, shortly prior to the military coup of 1976, kidnapped and killed those it suspected of being communists. Death, in fact, as a possibility for both of us. Could it then be said that it was death as Real?

Recalling some texts and seminars of Lacan, for example Seminar 11, *The Four Fundamental Concepts of Psychoanalysis* from1964, in it we can identify two aspects that Lacan takes from Aristotle's *Physics*: death which could then be presented as unexpected contingency, *Tuché*, and death as named, said through a signifier. The real, in the case of my analysand, could be an unexpected contingency, the traumatic for Freud, the *Tuché* that might irrupt with its absurd sound, at any moment, in the *Automaton* of the analysis as continuity. Contingency which would not necessarily be the death of my analysand and mine as a result of being his analyst: the Real can also irrupt in an acting out or in the rhetorical subtleties of the repetitions in free association.

The Real which, in that case, would obviously not be in those signifying repetitions in the speech of the analytic session—its symbolic insistence in naming it—although it would be in the repeated failure of that attempt at designation. The Real which could also be, as contingent *Tuché*, the irruption of the bark of a dog, the horn of a car, which would substitute words with a full, indifferent sound, without meaning. The Real that could in the end have been not the fact of our death, predictable contingency of the everyday reality of that era, but rather the impossibility of continuing the analysis, although, as appears to be proven up to this point for those of us who are not spiritualists, and as is said in some well known crime novel, *the dead do not speak*.

Because death, in as much as death named as death, known as final, remembered on a tomb, written about in a story, anticipated by an oracle, desired by someone who suicides, spoken as a threat, feared as an illness, justified in vengeance, sought by a hero, explained ideologically, given in euthanasia, executed in the name of the law, that death, for psychoanalysis, is not Real. It is Symbolic. And we can only get as far as not wanting to know about it, avoiding it, because there are signifiers to say it, letters with which to write it, negate it, allude to it, signify it as absence. Lack. Metaphorise it. In other words, because the human being is a speaking being, by being able to name death, to say it, he knows that in so far as Heideggerian *Dasein* (being-there-in-the-world), he is a being-for-death. Mortal.

For psychoanalysis then, given that a signifier is necessarily implied in order to say it, death is represented, said, from the perspective of life. As Freud says, Thanatos, being mute, speaks through Eros. So it is that in relation to the phallus—signifier of sexuality, of the libido, of Eros, of life—Lacan in his seminar *The Ethics of Psychoanalysis* recalls Heraclitus who says: "... Hades[3] and Bacchus are one and the same", because, we can add, Heraclitus explains bashfully:

> ... if the procession were not in honour of Bacchus and the phallic
> chant also in his honour, then such acts would be shameful.[4]

That is to say that they were not shameful because the vital phallic masquerade of the Dionysian Bacchic commemorations, those pertaining to the harvesting of the grapes and the wine, blood of Bacchus, were also a reminder of Hades, presence of death.

As we know, in Freud this implication, almost an equivalence, in the theory, appears in 1920 in "Beyond the Pleasure Principle" as the tendency of pleasure, effect of the discharge of accumulated libido, to attain total discharge. Definitive equilibrium. The peace of Nirvana, only avoided through the Principle of Constancy which maintains the minimal tension for Thanatos to be able to speak through Eros. For there to be speech, life in other words. Pleasure linked for Freud from then onwards to nearness, vicinity, with death.

Nevertheless, a little later, in "The Economic Problem of Masochism" of 1924, pleasure for Freud is no longer the effect of a simple discharge, it is also the result of an increase in tension. Alternacy. With respect to this, referring to the cause of pleasure, he says:

> Perhaps it is the rhythm, the temporal sequence of changes, rises and falls in the quantity of stimulus.[5]

A rhythm then, which oscillates between erotic tension and the discharge of Thanatos. And we can add, between the presence of the word and its absence as silence and death.

It is what the Argentinian dancer Paulina Ossona writes about in her book *Shall we dance? Let's dance!*[6] She writes: "... the human being lives swinging between two temptations: the comforting security of quietude and the danger of falling." To which she adds, referring to dance:

> All movement is a loss of that equilibrium and hence comparable to a fall. Dance then, which is action, is designated as a fall (loss of equilibrium) and recovery (return to equilibrium); both states, fall and recovery, follow each other without respite during the course of the dance.

Which in another way, reminds us of the reference we have already made to Heraclitus in that tight relation of Bacchus, a form of Dionysius, with Hades, in the *processions* in which there was so much drinking and so much dancing.

What a curious coincidence between a dancer and Freud who, eighty years previously, in 1915, in referring to *Our Attitude Towards Death*, affirms that:

> Life is impoverished, it loses in interest, when the highest stake in the game of living, life itself, may not be risked.

He later adds that:

> ... the tendency to exclude death from our calculations in life brings
> in its train many other renunciations and exclusions.[7]

Lacan, without needing recourse to the Freudian concept of energy, in
the same way as desire and the subject, defines death as an effect of the
signifier. In this, as with castration, it is always symbolic. Death that, as
lack, as the condition and place for the subject, begins in the castration
of the Øther whose *primordial representative* (although not the only one)
is the mother. Big Øther that, he tells us in the end in the most radical
way, does not exist.

There is also in Lacan, death in theory and death in one's own clinical practice, although both are implied.

Death in theory is the death of the Father as interdictor, that of
the Freudian myth of the Father of the Horde in "Totem and Taboo",
which permits him to define the Law (of the prohibition of incest) as
metaphor of the dead Father, which he also formulates logically in the
Formulae of Sexuation as death of he who, as *Exception*, says No to the
phallic jouissance of *All* the others. All but him. Death symbolised as
negation.

But death that is also twofold: the First, that of the hero, anticipated as disintegration of the specular image, that of he who knew his
fatal destiny in advance, accomplishes it in order that his name live
on, and the Second Death, that of putrefaction, the disappearance of
the body.

First death, place of the tragic hero that Lacan gives to the analyst
because he offers himself to be used as instrument/object and then
left aside for the Analytic Act that, he reminds us, is not the analyst's.
It belongs to the analysand. The absent presence of the analyst is represented in his punctuations, interventions and cuts that the analysand
may utilise in order to produce his Act, which will make possible the
emergence of a new meaning in his discourse.

A place, in short, in which the analyst intervenes as Lacan tells us, in
"The Freudian Thing"[8] by:

> ... playing dead, by cadaverising his position [...] either by his
> silence where he is the Øther [...], or by annulling his own resistance
> where he is the other with a little o. In both cases, and through

the respective effects of the symbolic and the imaginary, he makes death present.

It needs to be said, however, that this mortal silence is not necessarily always silence, mutism, but rather a being quiet in different ways, with different rhetorics, to not respond to the different styles in which appear the demands for love, those of the transference. That is, it is possible to speak without responding to the demand, or at times, paradoxically, to respond to the demand with silence. A clarification and a difference that, I believe, bring to mind those who, comically, think themselves to be "Lacanian psychoanalysts" because they never speak.

From the side of the analyst then, the death of the embodiment of knowledge that, through the transference, was attributed to him. From the side of the analysand, his encounter and possible co-existence with death as subject, given that Lacan reminds us in 1958:[9]

> The subject [...] enters the game (of signifiers) as dead [*mort*], but will only play as alive.

In other words, in the case of his analysis, we could say that he begins it as a suffering—and synthesised—Ego, that great symptom, and finishes it perhaps as analysed, divided as a subject, even though he will nonetheless not stop having an Ego (let us recall, in this regard, the Borromean Knot). It is not by having been psychoanalysed, having passed through an analysis, that he will no longer have an Ego and an Unconscious. Even if some symptoms might disappear, or even if one might manage to live with them. One still dreams.

An end to an analysis then, is in no way an integration, synthesis or "suture", but rather a specific and different means—for each one—of an encounter with the certainty of one's own death, passing through, as a condition for this, the conviction that the Øther does not exist and then to have the possibility of mourning—symbolising—the fall of the knowledge that was supposed in the analyst. Which perhaps afterwards, sometimes, will perhaps allow him to remember, or even to write a history without crying. Encounter with his condition of subject represented through signifiers which will never be him, and which some day perhaps, will also be his name on a tomb. An encounter with a bearable sadness that nonetheless is not death but rather a means of remembering it.

Translated from Spanish by Nati Sangiau and Michael Plastow.

Notes

1. Paper presented at the seminar, "Dialogue about death", organised by the Faculty of Philosophy and Human Sciences of The Federal University of Bahia, in 1998.
2. "Wallis Simpson and the Three As".
3. Hades, the king of the dead, always lives in hell.
4. Heraclitus. *Fragmentos Filosóficos* 15. Los Presocráticos, Vol. II. Mexico City, El Colegio de México, 1944.
5. Freud, S. "The Economic Problem of Masochism." (1924) *The Standard Edition of the Complete Psychological Works of Sigmund Freud*, Volume XIX, p. 159.
6. Ossona, Paulina. ¿*Bailamos?* ¡*Bailemos!* Argentina, Ed. Tekné, 1995.
7. Freud, S. "Thoughts for the times on war and death." (1915) *The Standard Edition of the Complete Psychological Works of Sigmund Freud*, Volume XIV, pp. 289–290.
8. Lacan, J. "The Freudian Thing." *Écrits*.
9. Lacan, J. "On a question preliminary to any possible treatment of psychosis." *Écrits*.